The Resilient Church

The Resilient Church

THE NECESSITY AND
LIMITS OF ADAPTATION

•

Avery Dulles, S.J.

1977
DOUBLEDAY & COMPANY, INC.
GARDEN CITY, NEW YORK

Library of Congress Cataloging in Publication Data

Dulles, Avery Robert, 1918–
The Resilient Church.

Includes bibliographical references and index.
1. Church. 2. Catholic Church—Doctrinal and
controversial works—Catholic authors. I. Title.
BX1746.D82   261.8
ISBN: 0-385-11610-1
Library of Congress Catalog Card Number 76-29790

To
YVES CONGAR, O.P.,
whose scholarly labors
over more than four decades
have enriched the Church
and made it more resilient

Contents

The Resilient Church

Introduction

...ts in church history so decisive that they set the
...historical era. For Catholic ecclesiology the Sec-
...seems to have been such an event. More than a
...ncil the Catholic ecclesiologist has no choice ex-
...estions in the light of what the Council initi-

...ouncil had two foci: the inner renewal of the
Roman Catholic Church, and the fostering of more positive and
fruitful relationships between the Church and other human communities—the other Christian churches, the other religions, and the
secular culture of our age. These two foci are not wholly separable
from each other. In fact, it was expected that a more receptive attitude toward external groups and agencies would greatly assist the
Catholic Church in its own self-renewal, and that that renewal, in
turn, would enable the Church to relate itself more effectively to the
rest of the human family.

In the present book I am not trying to explain again what Vatican
II said and meant. This has already been sufficiently done by others.
Rather, I am seeking to appraise and carry forward the theological
work of Catholic ecclesiology in the decade since the Council.

The chapters of this book deal with nine crucial issues that have
commanded attention since Vatican II. The first is mission: What is
the Church supposed to bring about as a result of its presence in the
world? Many have sought to prove that the Church exists not for its
own sake but for the sake of the world. Although these authors have
some valid points to make, I prefer to assert, as at least equally true,
that the Church's mission is, first of all, to become the Church. Its
chief task, in other words, is to make itself an authentic symbolic
presence of Christ in the world. Since Christ is actively at work
renewing all things, including the Church, this first chapter leads
directly to the second, dealing with church reform. Reform must, I
contend, be accepted more radically than in the past. It must be al-

lowed to call into question the basic structures of the Church. Yet reform must not be allowed to introduce ideas and practices foreign to the true spirit of Catholicism. Whatever is taken in from outside must be assessed by this criterion: Does it make the Church more than previously a society of faith, of hope, and of love? In other words, does it make the Church more the Church?

The application of these principles to doctrinal renewal provides the theme for my third chapter. As a guiding principle I accept, with some necessary reservations, the formula of "historical situationism." New doctrinal statements, I maintain, must respond to new demands with a view to preserving the full impact of the gospel. In Chapter IV I follow up this general principle with some more specific considerations of those pervasive themes of modern culture which seem to call for vigilance in order that the Church be not undermined. With an eye on the Hartford Appeal, I call attention to the danger that the Church might become so politicized or psychologized as to lose sight of the transcendent or divine dimension of its own mission. Once again, the test would be, "Let the Church become the Church!" Let it not become a therapeutic society, a political party, or even a public interest group.

Chapters V and VI turn to more typically inner-Catholic problems. The first deals with doctrinal authority, with particular reference to the pastoral magisterium of the bishops. After noting the desirability of closer collaboration between bishops and theologians in their respective teaching functions, I examine the delicate problem of dissent within the Church. Freedom of discussion, I contend, is crucially important for creative interaction in the Church and consequently for authentic renewal. The problem of the papacy, discussed in Chapter VI, is primarily an inner-Catholic issue but not exclusively so, for other Christian communities have been distressed by the apparent absolutism and juridicism of the First Vatican Council. Increasingly in our day, non–Roman Catholic Christians call attention to the value they would find in a papacy "renewed under the gospel." Some such renewal, I point out, would be welcomed by Catholics themselves, who are not entirely satisfied to let the language of Vatican I stand as the last word. But care must be taken to avoid reducing the papacy to a merely ornamental role.

The question of church membership, the theme of Chapter VII, is acute both for Roman Catholicism and for ecumenism. I attempt to sketch the contours of a theory of membership as "communion" (in the biblical and patristic sense of "koinonia"), and in this connection I express some thoughts on the significance of the membership in the body of Christ shared in common by Christians of different ecclesiastical allegiances. In my next chapter I pass on to a discussion of the conditions under which eucharistic sharing is permissible and desirable, both for the spiritual progress of the individual and for fostering the unity of the Church. In this chapter I seek not to minimize the difficulties caused by unresolved disputes about the nature of the Eucharist and the requirements for sacramental ordination. Finally, in the closing chapter, I examine the changing faces of ecumenism and seek to set forth some ideas on the proper objectives for the ecumenical movement in the circumstances of today's world. In this connection I speak of the value of building up "a heterogeneous community of witnessing dialogue."

In all these chapters I seek to pick my way among the current theological opinions, indicating my choices in favor of some opinions and in opposition to others. I have tried to indicate the authors on whom I rely and to give references likewise to valuable literature expressing views at variance with my own. I trust that I do not give any impression of setting myself above those theologians from whom I seem to differ. Indeed, some of them are among the most creative and learned writers in the field. The fact that a theologian happens to be in agreement with me on a given issue does not make him—or me—necessarily a better theologian than one who thinks otherwise. Further, as the attentive reader will observe, certain theologians who are my allies on some points appear to fall into the category of opponents on other issues. I should explain, also, that in my efforts to pursue the orderly progress of my own argument, I have not always found it possible to explain the context in which other authors were speaking. In the complexities of today's theological scene, the positions one takes inevitably depend, in part, on the particular audience one is addressing. Thus I do not intend to suggest that authors from whom I appear to differ were saying the wrong thing in the concrete situations which they were seeking to address.

This book takes its origin from talks or articles that were originally separate units, but it is not, properly speaking, a collection. I have chosen pieces that bear on a few very central ecclesiological issues confronting the Catholic Church amid the present winds of change. I have thoroughly reworked nearly all these pieces for inclusion in the present volume. The following notes on the earlier versions may be of interest to some readers.

Chapter I, originally a lecture given on April 22, 1975, at Loyola College, Baltimore, includes, in its present form, some materials from my testimony of February 3, 1975, at the Bicentennial Hearings on Liberty and Justice for All, held at the Theological College, Washington, D.C. That testimony appears in the volume on the First Preparatory Hearing for the Bicentennial (Washington, D.C.: NCCB, 1975).

Chapter II grows out of an unpublished lecture given for the Continuing Religious Education Lecture series at Georgetown University, Washington, D.C., May 13, 1975.

Chapter III includes some materials from two unpublished lectures on the Development of Doctrine given at Mount Angel Abbey, St. Benedict, Oregon, on April 11, 1975.

Chapter IV, the major portion of which was newly written for this volume, includes some paragraphs from my article on the Hartford Appeal and Ecumenism for the volume *Against the World for the World*, edited by Peter L. Berger and Richard J. Neuhaus (New York: Seabury, 1976).

Chapter V is taken in part from an unpublished lecture given at the Bishops' Theological Institute at the Catholic University of America, Washington, D.C., on June 25, 1975. It includes also some material from my presidential address at the Thirty-first Annual Convention of the Catholic Theological Society of America in Washington, D.C., on June 12, 1976. That address appears in the C.T.S.A. Proceedings (vol. 31 [Bronx, N.Y.: Manhattan College, 1976], 235–46) and in *Origins*, 6, no. 6 (July 1, 1976), 81–88.

Chapter VI reproduces with a number of adaptations my article "Papal Authority in Roman Catholicism," in P. J. McCord, ed., *A Pope for All Christians?* (New York: Paulist Press, 1976).

Chapter VII follows the general lines of an unpublished paper given at Marquette University, Milwaukee, Wisconsin, on March 31, 1974. As indicated in the footnotes, it also incorporates in more concise form, the basic argument of my published Père Marquette

Theology Lecture for that year (Milwaukee: Marquette University Theology Department, 1974).

Chapter VIII, newly written for this volume, incorporates some materials from my article "Intercommunion Between Lutherans and Roman Catholics?" for the *Journal of Ecumenical Studies*, 13, no. 2 (Spring 1976), 250–55.

Chapter IX reproduces in large part a previously unpublished address given to the North American Academy of Ecumenists in Cincinnati on September 26, 1975.

It is evident that these nine chapters by no means exhaust the list of themes in which contemporary Roman Catholic ecclesiology is developing through vital theological exchanges with other groups, Christian and non-Christian. But these chapters, I hope, give a sufficiently wide sampling to indicate the general style in which Catholic theology, while retaining fidelity to its own sources, can appropriate valuable new insights gained from contemporary experience. Dialogue with other groups can bring about a mutual purification and rapprochement through forthright witness and respectful listening.

Although this book draws upon a variety of talks and articles, it has, I believe, a genuine unity of concern and outlook. It seeks to establish whether and how the Church can be fully adaptive without losing its distinctive message and mission. The title, *The Resilient Church*, is intended to indicate my conviction that the Church has the power not simply to accommodate itself to the pressures placed upon it but to respond creatively and to exert counterpressures upon its environment. Unlike many ecclesiastical conservatives, I hold that adaptation need not be a form of capitulation to the world, but that an adapting Church should be able to herald the Christian message with greater power and impact. Unlike certain liberals, I am deeply concerned that the Church, in its efforts at adaptation, should avoid imitating the fashions of the nonbelieving world and should have the courage to be different. Difference is not to be cultivated for its own sake but is to be fearlessly accepted when Christ and the gospel so require.

A twofold critique runs through the following pages—the first, directed against those conservatives who through fear or complacency balk at adapting the doctrines and institutions of the Church to the times in which we live; the second, against those liberals whose programs of adaptation are based on an uncritical acceptance of the norms and slogans of Western secularist ideologies. My positions cannot easily be labeled as either conservative or liberal, though on some points I am in sympathy with each of these tendencies. My aim is to combine, as far as possible, the daring of the liberal with the caution of the conservative, the openness of the liberal with the fidelity of the conservative. The effect of this book, I hope, will be to strengthen the position of those Christians of every tradition who cannot situate themselves easily within either the liberal or the conservative camp.

I am deeply indebted to John J. Delaney, the recently retired Catholic editor of Doubleday & Company, for having stimulated and assisted me in the conception and planning of this book. My thanks are also due to the Reverend Richard N. Berube, S.S.E., to Louise M. Des Marais, and to the Reverend Robert A. Mitchell, S.J., for reading this work in manuscript and for providing many helpful comments. Finally, I should like to thank the Reverend Joseph A. Panuska, S.J., Provincial of the Maryland Province, for granting me permission to have this work published.

Avery Dulles, S.J.

To those under the law I became as one under the law—
though not being myself under the law—that I might win
those under the law. To those outside the law I became as
one outside the law—not being without law toward God
but under the law of Christ—that I might win those outside the law. To the weak I became weak, that I might win
the weak. I have become all things to all men, that I might
by all means save some. I do it all for the sake of the gospel,
that I may share in its blessings.

1 Corinthians 9:20–23

Every renewal of the Church essentially consists in an increase of fidelity to her own calling. Undoubtedly, this explains the dynamism of the movement toward unity.

Decree on Ecumenism, § 6

I. Rethinking the Mission of the Church

Not long ago, a young Protestant came to my office to consult me about some theological questions. About the time of his graduation from high school, he told me, he experienced a personal conversion to Jesus as his Savior. Since then he has made it his chief business to give witness and preach. He is now attending a Bible college and working as an evangelist in the streets of Washington. That young man clearly radiates a sense of mission. His faith is so important to him that he feels almost a compulsion to share it with others. In his own way he could say of himself what the apostles Peter and John said to the officers of the Sanhedrin: "We cannot but speak of what we have seen and heard" (Acts 4:20). As he left I was struck by the thought that many thousands of young people like him are at work spreading their religious faith very successfully in the world of our day. And yet I could not help but wonder how many Catholics have such an overwhelming sense of mission. How do they conceive of mission?

Catholics generally seem to think of mission as the task of the Church rather than of the individual. In a sense this is correct, for Church and mission are essentially related to each other. But all too often, I fear, this persuasion means that the individual feels no personal obligation to take any initiative. Catholics tend to wait passively for some directive to come down from on high, and when it does they are all too likely to receive it without enthusiasm. For this passivity there are historical roots.

My own recollections of Catholicism go back to the late 1930s. At that time American Catholics were a model of docility and obedience. While performing their personal religious duties with scrupulous care, they were not very vocal or active in spreading the faith. Lay Catholics, in their reverence for the ordained, felt unequal to the task of explaining what the Church believes or why. To understand such complicated matters, they felt, was the task of the clergy. But the majority of the clergy were almost totally taken up in caring for the Catholic faithful. Hence the average priest and lay person were likely to feel that missionary activity was not their responsibility.

Although missionary activity was not seen as incumbent upon every Catholic, it was intensely pursued as a special vocation. Catholics saw it as imperative for salvation that others should be brought to share the faith and sacramental life of the true Church. Hence they were eager to support the missions. A relatively large number of Catholics joined missionary orders and congregations, whose members were revered figures, for it was the task of missionaries, as Benedict XV had said in *Maximum illud* (1919), "to open the way of life to those hurrying to destruction."

During the 1940s and 1950s increasing numbers of young lay persons, usually graduates of Catholic colleges, became involved in what was called the lay apostolate—the participation of the laity in the mission of the hierarchy. These lay people were for the most part content to play a secondary role, under the direction of the clergy, although many of them were in fact more brilliant thinkers, speakers, writers, and witnesses to the faith than most of the hierarchy in whose service they worked. Under the leadership of lay intellectuals who had come to this country from Europe, such as Etienne Gilson, Jacques Maritain, Frank Sheed, and Dietrich von Hildebrand, converts streamed into the Church in increasing numbers—and many of them had a strong desire to pass on to others the vision that they had embraced.

Then in the 1960s, Vatican II sought to take advantage of the growing dynamism in the Church. Never has a council insisted so much on the missionary responsibility of the entire People of God. As Pope Paul VI has observed, the objectives of Vatican II "are definitely summed up in this single one: to make the Church of the twentieth century even better fitted for proclaiming the Gospel to the people of the twentieth century."[1] The fundamental thrust of the Council is well conveyed by the opening lines of the Constitution on the Church: "Christ is the light of all nations. Hence this most sacred Synod, which has been gathered in the Holy Spirit, eagerly desires to shed on all men that radiance of His which brightens the countenance of the Church. This it will do by proclaiming the gospel to every creature (cf. Mk 16:15)."[2]

The nature of the Church's mission is further specified in article 5 of the same Constitution—namely, "to proclaim and to establish among all peoples the kingdom of Christ and of God." In its Decree on the Missionary Activity of the Church, the Council sought to give more precise guidance for the extension of the Church to the unevangelized regions of the earth. In its Decree on the Apostolate of the Laity it sought to overcome any undue clericalism and to clarify the call to witness that flows from the very nature of faith itself and from the sacraments of baptism and confirmation.

It might have been hoped that the Council would lead to a great intensification of missionary endeavor. This hope, however, has not been realized. In most countries the decade since the Council has been one of internal conflict, confusion, and disarray. The Church seems, for the first time in centuries, to be an uncertain trumpet. Catholics are no longer clear about what they should believe and do. Very many younger members of the Church are no longer proud of their Catholic identity, much less on fire with enthusiasm to spread it to others. How did it happen that a council so intent upon increasing the missionary dynamism of the Church actually led to a decade of disorientation, polarization, and apathy?

In part, the reasons lie beyond the control of the Church itself. As a result of the new mass media, people are so preoccupied with immediate secular issues that their attention is distracted from the Church and its traditional concerns for eternal truth and everlasting life. Further, there is a growing awareness of the culturally conditioned aspects of religious belief and expression, giving rise to hesitations about seeking to transmit one's beliefs to persons of another culture. The so-called "foreign missions" have undoubtedly been affected by the end of the colonial era. The rising nations of Africa, Asia, and Oceania are understandably suspicious that Western missionaries may be, consciously or unconsciously, tools of cultural and economic imperialism.

In spite of these difficulties, however, militant churches and sects continue to expand rapidly all over the world. Groups such as the Adventists, the Mormons, the Jehovah's Witnesses, and the Unification Church are greatly increasing their membership on many continents; and in the United States the more evangelical and conservative churches continue to grow rapidly. Why does not the Roman

Catholic Church, with its traditional emphasis on mission and with the added impetus given by Vatican II, exhibit a similar expansive power?

Much of the difficulty, in my opinion, is connected with the teaching of Vatican II. According to the expressed desires of Pope John XXIII, Vatican II was a council of renewal and reform (Pope John spoke of "updating"—*aggiornamento*). This invitation to change, following upon many centuries of relative stability, unleashed a sudden surge of questioning, turmoil, and internal criticism. This criticism, in turn, gave rise to a measure of self-doubt and to a certain crisis of identity. A time of critical self-scrutiny surely has its value; it may indeed be necessary; but it is not the most auspicious moment for confident missionary expansion.

Several leading ideas of Vatican II made for particular difficulties. For instance, the Council promoted the idea that the Church is under judgment. In place of a triumphal Church it spoke of a Church called to humble service toward the world. It accepted the idea that revelation and grace are not the exclusive property of Catholicism or even of Christianity, and that the possibility of salvation lies open to the unevangelized. Further, the Council sought to inculcate greater esteem for freedom of conscience and for cultural pluralism. It called for respectful dialogue with other Christian communities, with other religions, and with secular ideologies. It impressed upon Catholics their duty to assist in the solution of the great secular problems facing humanity in our time. A council dominated by themes such as these was bound to have a disorienting effect upon the Church's missionary thrust.

On a balanced view, which may be more accessible to future historians than to contemporary observers, it may become evident that the apparent losses of the past decade ought rather to be seen as a redirection of energies. The Church, as I have elsewhere sought to show, is a many-faceted reality: It is institution, community, servant, herald, and sacrament.[3] The recent years have seen what may be called a loss of institutional strength and self-esteem and a corresponding waning of enthusiasm for the institutional aspects of mission. There is less desire than in the generation before the Council to bring new members under the institutional umbrella of the Church, thus assuring the perfect orthodoxy of their belief and their juridically correct relationship to the hierarchical leadership. Since the institutional aspects of the Church are the most easily measured, the sociological picture of the current period of church history tends to be particularly discouraging.

Although the concepts of mission and institutional aggrandizement have been closely linked in the recent past, it is well to remember that the two are not synonymous. In the past few years the most successful forms of Christian mission have been directed to aims other than church extension. The two most conspicuous movements have been the effort to create warm, neighborly communities and the struggle to promote justice in the larger secular society. Given certain safeguards, both of these thrusts are potentially fruitful. They should therefore be considered in our present reflections.

Reacting against the strong institutionalism of the Counter Reformation, many Catholics in the 1960s began to feel that the Church ought to be conceived primarily in terms of community rather than institution. The community, in this sense, is the people themselves joined to one another by informal, interpersonal relationships. The institutional aspect of the Church was felt to be alienating; it provoked apathy and even hostility. Oppressed by the bureaucracies of secular society, many looked to the Church to provide the community values of spontaneity, freedom, and love. The gospel, it was argued, had power to break down all the barriers that divided people into separate and opposed classes—master and slave, rich and poor, Jew and Gentile. Jesus' message had power to create loving concern and charity, so that people could be truly concerned for the good of others. Thanks to this mutual love, authentic community could be born.

This movement of the 1960s has by no means spent its force. In Latin America today new vitality is being given to the Church by the so-called "base communities" (*comunidades eclesiales de base*), which are defined in the Medellín documents of 1968 as "a community, local or environmental, which corresponds to the reality of a homogeneous group and whose size allows for personal fraternal contact among its members."[4] Not only in Latin America but also in many parts of North America, Europe, and Africa there are groups who "see their experience of Church in small communities as an alternative or a complement to parish life within the Roman Catholic tradition as it presently exists."[5] The ecclesial experience in such communities tends to be "primary" or interpersonal rather than administratively structured. In the United States such "base communities" frequently grow up in connection with student associations, Marriage Encounter groups, and prayer groups, especially charismatic. Often the members not only worship and pray together but also live and work together.

Even where it does not lead to "base communities," the search for community has notably affected the lives of Catholics since the Council. The new liturgy, as provided by the Council, made ample provision for personal interaction, with home Masses, dialogue homilies, the spontaneous prayer of the faithful, the greeting of peace, and congregational singing. Seeking to achieve maximum benefits from this less formal type of common worship, small homogeneous groups have arisen in which the members worship together with a maximum of freedom and participation. In some cases this has led to "floating parishes" (with or without episcopal approval) and liturgical practices contrary to the official rubrics.

There is something thoroughly right in this search for interpersonal community—something that ought to, and probably will, continue. Karl Rahner asserts: "The Church of the future will be one built from below by basic communities as a result of free initiative and association. We should make every effort not to hold up, but to promote this development and direct it on to the right lines."[6] Such groups are consonant with the recent emphasis upon the freedom of the act of faith and of membership in the Church and with the recognition that faith demands commitment to an apostolic life in community. Mutual charity, moreover, is not just a luxury in the Church. It is an essential token of the Church's existence. "By this all men will know that you are my disciples . . ." (Jn 13:35). In recent centuries Christians have not been conspicuous for their mutual love and intimate sharing. Catholicism, in particular, promoted a rather individualistic piety combined with a deep sense of loyalty to the ecclesiastical institution, especially as centered on Rome. Except in certain communities of vowed religious, the interpersonal dimension of the Christian life has been rather neglected.

On the other hand, the communitarian vision of the Church, when played off against the institutional, easily falls into excesses.

"Communal Catholics," in the sense described above,[7] sometimes found themselves drawn into antipathy to the institutional Church. The more people prize their spontaneous, local community, the more likely they are to detach themselves from the parish, the diocese, and the universal structures of the Church. The more value they set on creative liturgies and spontaneous prayer, the more impatient they will probably grow at the restrictions of canon law and rubrical prescriptions. The more they cherish the immediate experience of life together, the less interested are they likely to become in maintaining communion with the Church Catholic of all ages and places. For some Catholics, therefore, enthusiastic commitment to interpersonal community led to a true crisis of identity. They lost interest in the transcendent dimension of the Church's life, and grew impatient with the strong authority structures that are intended to safeguard that transcendent dimension from being eroded by the limited vision of particular times and localities.

Not surprisingly, therefore, some of the more experimental forms of Christian community fell apart. Many of the priests and nuns in the movement left to get married. Some joined the "underground Church." In a few cases small communities and floating parishes carried their opposition to the point of schism. Instead of being agents of reconciliation, therefore, certain progressive communities became sources of discord and division. Others, like the hippie colonies of the same period, fell apart of their own weight. By experience they discovered for themselves that communes of love cannot be sustained without tradition, discipline, and personal conversion. Characteristic is the following testimony given by the editors of a periodical emanating from a small community-building group in Chicago:

The experience of our own small community in Chicago, however, is probably far too typical of what has happened with many. We watched helplessly with bewilderment and disillusionment as all our highest dreams and noblest efforts to build community crumbled around us. There were many reasons for this: our lack of wisdom in handling interpersonal friction, a fear of authority, a pride that often kept us from learning from others. As we look back, perhaps the biggest reason is that we simply did not understand the centrality of the Spirit to building community; now our greatest hopes in rebuilding stem from the beginnings of an "unclogging" of the Spirit among us.[8]

The most basic lesson to be learned is perhaps the impossibility of separating Christian community from Christian faith, or of separating Christian faith from the total teaching and experience of the Church. A romantic vision of spontaneous community leads inevitably to conflict and disappointment. Right order, according to the gospel, demands that our love should be focused first of all on God, who alone is absolutely to be loved. The love of neighbor is secondary to the love of God, and must reckon with human defects. Essentially, Christianity is kept alive by the tremendous and unsurpassable love of God shown forth in Jesus Christ—a very stringent, demanding kind of love, expelling naïve illusions. Only if we concentrate on that love, and cultivate it through study, prayer, and sacramental life, can Christ fully dwell in our hearts by faith, so that we become filled to overflowing with the plenitude of God's own love. It is this unselfish love of God and neighbor, made known to us in the Scriptures and in the perennial teaching of the Church, that gives to Catholic Christians their religious identity and mission. Granted this sense of identity and mission, informal communities such as the family, the circle of friends, and the neighborhood can be a tremendous support to Christian living.

Scarcely had the community concept of mission gained a foothold when it was overtaken by a second priority. The great social encyclicals of Pope John XXIII, followed by Vatican II's Pastoral Constitution on the Church in the Modern World, awakened the larger Catholic community to a keener sense of its responsibility to contribute not simply to the development of the Church but to the general progress of human society. In the less optimistic years of the late sixties and early seventies, this meant the effort to help stem the effects of environmental pollution and the growing economic disparities between rich and poor nations. Paul VI's 1967 encyclical *On the Development of Peoples* and the document "Justice in the World," issued by the International Synod of Bishops in 1971, both successfully highlighted the social dimensions of the Church's mission, as currently perceived. Many found compelling force in the key sentence of the Synod document: "Action on behalf of justice and participation in the transformation of the world fully appear to us as a constitutive dimension of the preaching of the Gospel, or, in other words, of the Church's mission for the redemption of the human race and its liberation from every oppressive situation."[9] The same document made it ineluctably clear that the Church's obligation to struggle against every form of sin included a mandate to combat social injustice and institutionalized violence, as manifestations and occasions of personal sin. Inspired by the recent social teaching of the Church, many began to speak of "social sin."[10]

This social-action movement, like the movement for community-building, has suffered from the exaggerations of some of its more ardent apostles. Certain theologians, reading the official social teaching in the light of secular theologians such as Dietrich Bonhoeffer, John A. T. Robinson, and Harvey Cox, contended that the principal task of the Church was neither to bring its own members to eternal life (as in the institutional vision) nor to form a cozy community of friends (as in the vision just considered), but to reshape secular society.

Several American Catholic theologians, in the years immediately following the Council, popularized the idea that the Church had hitherto been too introverted and narcissistic.[11] From Bonhoeffer such theologians quoted the aphorism "The church is the church only when it exists for others."[12] The biblical term "diakonia" was appropriated for the purposes of this secular theology—though with little respect for the original meaning. Whereas in the New Testament "diakonia" usually means either the service of God or service rendered to Christians, it became, in the vocabulary of these secular theologians, a designation of the Church's service to the world. Such service, moreover, was seen in secular and social categories. The Church, according to this theology, fulfills its mission to the extent that it succeeds in transforming the world into a place of peace, justice, freedom, and brotherhood. In this way, it was thought, the Church could be instrumental in ushering in the Kingdom of God.

Secularization theology had a very special analysis of the relationship of the Church to the Kingdom of God. In the first place, the Church was seen as totally subordinate to the Kingdom. The Kingdom, it was maintained, exists for its own sake, and the Church for the sake of the Kingdom. Besides the Church, there were said to be many other agencies that also serve the Kingdom—social and humanitarian organizations as well as political entities such as the United Nations and the civil state. The Church, then, is one of a number of organizations that contribute to the establishment of the Kingdom. From this followed another thesis: Not all are called to the Church, but all are called to the Kingdom. The call to join the Church was viewed as a special vocation directed to some few, analogous to the call to become a Jesuit or a Trappistine, except that no one took permanent vows to remain in the Church. Thus departures from the Church, it was suggested, need not be taken too tragically, provided that the persons in question still remained devoted to the Kingdom.

Finally, these secular theologians depicted the Church as a merely provisional organization. The Church, they hold, exists within history, but when the final Kingdom comes, it will vanish without a trace. Thus no one ought to absolutize the Church.

In the anti-institutionalism of the postconciliar years, secular theologians were convinced that they had rediscovered the true mission of the Church. I would argue, on the contrary, that their view of the Church was not only practically suicidal—since it seriously undermined devotion to the Church—but theologically false. The ecclesiology I have just summarized is at odds with Scripture, with the great Catholic tradition, and with the explicit teaching of Vatican II, all of which consider the Church to be the very body of Christ and the temple of the Holy Spirit. The Church on earth, according to these sources, is an anticipation or sacrament of the Church that is to be. When Christ returns in glory, therefore, the Church will not merely survive but will fully come into its own. Since the Kingdom of God itself exists on earth, as does the Church, in provisional and uncompleted form, the Church is no more subordinate to the Kingdom than the Kingdom to the Church. The glorified Church—the *ecclesia triumphans,* as it was called by the medieval theologians—will stand at the very heart of the new creation.

As regards the question of vocation, neither Scripture nor tradition, so far as I am aware, teaches that anyone is called to, or enters, the Kingdom of God unless he is also called to, or enters, the Church. The idea that the Kingdom of God is a kind of penumbra surrounding the Church is as theologically awkward as the old theories that made the "soul" of the Church something more extended than its body.

More fundamentally, I would object that in this secular vision, as in the community vision previously outlined, the centrality of Christ is overlooked. In the Christian view it makes no sense to speak—as did the secular theologians of the past decade—of a perfect human community or of the Kingdom of God without any conscious relationship to Christ. Where people fail to recognize the lordship of Christ, their human community is defective and they are not properly related to the Kingdom of God. For it is in Christ, and only in him, that God is establishing his Kingdom. In seeking to avoid ecclesiocentrism, these new theologies ceased to be Christocentric or even theocentric; they became simply anthropocentric.

A progressive Dutch theologian, a decade ago, wrote a book entitled *The Grave of God.*[13] His thesis was that the institutional Church, by its self-defensiveness, was largely responsible for the so-called "death of God." In my view the title of this book could appropriately be transferred to the masochistic Church of secularization theology. In that Church God never really lived. Secularistic theology was a product of the same movement as the "God is dead" theology, and is now as dead as the atheistic Christianity by which it was accompanied.

Did secularization theology, then, contribute nothing to the rediscovery of Christian mission? It did serve, in some ways, to direct attention to the Christian responsibility to labor for peace, prosperity, freedom, and justice in the world. If we are truly devoted to these aspects of the Kingdom of God, we must seek to realize these values on earth. "Thy will be done on earth as it is in heaven." The Gospels make it clear that we may not stand by indifferently while our brothers and sisters are hungry, naked, sick, and imprisoned. Today this implies not only that we should administer to individuals in need—a very concrete and personal form of charity specifically mandated by Jesus—but also, it would seem, that we should, to the extent of our competence, contribute to the reform of social and political institutions that are the causes of hunger and injustice in the world. The secularization theologians rightly maintained that this is a serious obligation for Christians and for the Church. We cannot be content to pray and sing hymns while the world is being made practically uninhabitable for millions of human beings. This recognition, of course, is not entirely new. It has been inculcated, in one way or another, by the social encyclicals since the time of Leo XIII.

Secularization theology, however, was not always very helpful in showing how to deal with the very obvious limitations to the Church's competence in the sociopolitical area. To decide whether a given military intervention is necessary, or whether a particular tax bill will be beneficial, or whether a certain housing project should be sponsored, one has to know a great deal more than what is written in the Bible or handed down in Christian tradition. Nor is it enough to be prayerful and to receive the sacraments devoutly. One has to know something about military affairs, economics, or sociology. Unquestionably individual Christians, and groups of Christians, may take strong positions on such matters, but the value of their positions will depend in large measure upon their expertise in secular disciplines that have no particular relationship to Christian revelation and piety. Even when certain Christians—whether laity, religious, or clergy—are well informed about these matters, they cannot confidently speak out on such questions precisely as leaders in the Christian community. They owe their qualifications, at least partly, to their competence in the relevant secular disciplines.

In recent years there has been a great deal of pressure on the Church, as a major force in the formation of public opinion, to take specific stands on all kinds of social and political issues, even to the extent of endorsing particular bills in Congress or favoring one labor union against a rival union. Given the dynamics of the political process in modern society, it is inevitable that such pressures should arise. Some people take the view that it is timid for the Church to "avoid taking a stand." That may sometimes be the case. Very often, however, it will take more courage and determination to resist the pressures than to give in. By yielding to the pressures, the Church will please some of its constituency but will alienate others. Special-interest groups are always glad to use the Church when it is pliant to their demands, but they do not respect the Church for being their tool. When the Church yields to opposed pressure groups, they become enraged.

At various times and places the Church has become heavily involved in politics, even to the extent of being allied to a so-called

"Christian" or "Catholic" party. Sometimes the Church has even invoked ecclesiastical penalties to prevent its members from voting for rival parties. In the United States, thus far, our experience has been more fortunate. The Church has generally avoided taking positions on political or social questions except where there was a clear issue of a moral or religious character. I would personally hope that this healthy tradition will be maintained.

The official statements of church leaders have consistently recognized a clear distinction between the gospel message, which is binding on all Christians, and specific sociopolitical solutions, which are matters of opinion within the Church. Vatican II, for instance, declared in its Pastoral Constitution:

> Often enough the Christian view of things will itself suggest some rather specific solution in certain circumstances. Yet it happens rather frequently, and legitimately so, that with equal sincerity some of the faithful will disagree with others on a given matter. Even against the intention of their proponents, however, solutions proposed on one side or another may easily be confused with the gospel message. Hence it is necessary for people to remember that no one is allowed in the aforementioned situations to appropriate the Church's authority for his opinion. They should always try to enlighten one another through honest discussion, preserving mutual charity and caring above all for the common good.[14]

The 1971 Synod of Bishops likewise recognized the complexity of applying the values of the gospel in the social arena: "It does not belong to the Church, insofar as she is a religious or hierarchical community, to offer concrete solutions in the social, economic, and political sphere for justice in the world."[15] The same caution is reflected in the perceptive statement of the Administrative Board of the U. S. Catholic Conference, issued on February 15, 1976. "A proper understanding of the role of the Church," it declared, "will not confuse its mission with that of government, but rather see its ministry as advocating the critical values of human rights and human justice." It went on to say:

> The application of gospel values to real situations is an essential work of the Christian community. Christians believe the gospel is

the measure of human realities. However, specific political proposals do not in themselves constitute the gospel. Christians and Christian organizations must certainly participate in public debate over alternative policies and legislative proposals, yet it is critical that the nature of their participation not be misunderstood.

We specifically do not seek the formation of a religious voting bloc; nor do we wish to instruct persons on how they should vote by endorsing candidates.[16]

I myself have on various occasions attempted to suggest some principles whereby the official leadership of the Church can effectively support measures that seem to them to embody Christian values, and oppose programs that seem to them contrary to the gospel, while avoiding the kind of authoritarianism that would infringe on the responsible freedom of members of the Church. On one occasion I recommended five such principles: that before speaking, the authorities should get the best advice from truly competent experts; that they allow it to become known how they have gone about reaching their decisions; that they speak in a manner that invites thoughtful agreement rather than one that seems to threaten those who dissent; that it be clearly stated that church members may disagree if they have found contrary authorities or reasons that seem to them of greater weight; and, finally, that the official leaders should not merely speak but should follow up their words with appropriate actions. This last caution would preclude mouthing high principles about human rights, while denying these very rights in the Church itself.[17]

It is above all necessary that the Church, in its concern for social justice, should not overlook the full dimensions of the good news given to us in Christ. Justice in the biblical sense of the term far transcends the structured relationships of human society. The justice of the Kingdom of God is a grace to be implored in prayer. It is an all-embracing gift, interior as well as exterior, individual as well as communal. Total justice, in fact, is an eschatological blessing to be conferred at the end of time by the coming of God himself.

Because we live in an imperfect world, it is inevitable that many deserving people will never receive an abundance of worldly riches, good health, friends, or security. Many will be crushed by unfavorable circumstances, whether by natural catastrophes, innocent miscalculation, human malice, or unjust social systems. So far as the bodily eye can see, the lives of such unfortunates have been failures. Christianity, however, has a message of hope even for these victims. It assures them that God, as a loving Father, opens up to all the possibility of eternal happiness. The blessings of eternal life are so great that, in comparison with them, all this earthly suffering is as nothing. This, I think, is basic to the doctrine of the gospel, and this the Church must always preach.

The Church, therefore, must never speak of social benefits in such a way as to make it appear that those who receive them are already saved in this life, or that those who lack such benefits have already failed to achieve the goal for which they were created. It must constantly preach that human salvation consists principally in a life beyond our earthly experience. The Church must be careful never to give the impression that the rich can save the poor or that the poor, by militant action, can save themselves. There is much that they can and should do, but salvation in the full and proper sense of the word remains the gift of God alone. Men and women can at best be occasions or instruments in preparing one another to receive this divine blessing.

I doubt that people will come to the Church or will remain loyal to it simply because of the Church's effective social ministry. They do not expect or demand that the Church should settle the grave social, economic, or political problems vexing the world. People do not generally turn to the Church to do for them what might also be done by a political party or by a public-interest group such as Common Cause.

So far as I am aware, people generally turn to the Church, if they do turn to it, for quite different reasons. They look to it to communicate a sense of the presence of God and of loving communion with him. In their daily lives they feel overwhelmed by worldly problems and by the realization that these problems will remain long after they have died. They need strength to continue to live in a world in which there is so much misery and injustice. They need assurance that in spite of the very modest results of all their efforts, their struggles to be honest and helpful to others are ultimately worthwhile.

These considerations bring us back to our theme of the Church's mission. The primary responsibility of the Church, in my opinion, is neither to aggrandize itself as an institution nor to sponsor snug little communities of friendly individuals nor to reform the social and economic structures of secular society. Its first and foremost task is to call people to a new life in God—a life mediated especially by faith and worship.

By faith I here mean, most basically, the conviction that God's redemptive love surrounds and sustains us. The Church can help us to live in trust and hope because it assures us that we are loved, redeemed, and called to eternal life in Christ. The visible success that we achieve here on earth is only a fraction of our total existence. According to revelation, success or failure is ultimately measured not by what we achieve by way of visible results but by how we stand in God's sight. This simple message of faith, so familiar to us all, is not easy to accept or live by. To accept it from the heart requires a deep personal conversion similar to that of the young man mentioned at the beginning of this chapter.

A living personal faith inevitably comes to expression in testimony, both by word and by personal example. The Church, because it is a community of faith, is by that very fact a witnessing community. As Paul VI says in his recent Apostolic Exhortation, "Evangelizing is in fact the grace and vocation proper to the Church, her deepest identity."[18]

This brings me to the second essential aspect of the Church's mission: worship. Worship is what happens when the Christian community gathers to be shaped by the word of God and to respond with praise and prayer. In circumstances of worship the message of the gospel is heard with maximum power, and Jesus makes himself personally present with his faithful people.

As suggested earlier in this chapter, certain distortions can arise in liturgy when primary emphasis comes to be placed on the horizontal or human dimension. Many people do not want a noisy, talkative, demonstrative liturgy. The important thing is not the presence or absence of physical sound but the mysterious presence and self-manifestation of God, whether in audible word or in silence. For the authentic spirit of worship we could not do better than seek inspiration from the Apocalypse, which contains so many echoes of the primitive Christian liturgy. We are invited to imitate the twenty-four elders who cast down their crowns before the throne, singing, "Worthy art thou, our Lord and God, to receive glory and honor and power, for thou didst create all things, and by thy will they existed and were created" (Apoc 4:11).

A Church centered on God and on God's gift in Jesus Christ should not obstruct the praiseworthy endeavors of building human community and of transforming social structures. It should powerfully assist its members to do both. Faith in a God who is love spontaneously issues into charity, and charity impels us to seek to benefit all who are in need. Revelation tells us that we live always in the presence of God, that he sees into our hearts, and will reward every deed performed out of love, even if unsuccessful, as if it were done directly to himself. Faith and worship help to overcome the selfishness in our hearts that is the foremost obstacle to human community and social reform.

The important thing is not so much what the Church says and teaches as what it is and does. Through proclamation and worship Christ himself becomes present in the midst of his people, reshaping their attitudes and remaking their lives. By its sacramental action, the Church can give its members a thrilling experience of encounter with the living God. By making them partakers of the Paschal mystery it can release untapped energies in their lives and thus give a transcendent, undying significance to all their efforts, including their struggle to achieve human community and social justice. By making its members open and responsive to the Holy Spirit, it allows them to receive guidance from God himself, even in areas where the Church does not have the answers.

In the 1930s, after some years of being distracted by the exaggerations of the "social gospel," the Protestant churches fell to a very low ebb. About that time a cry was raised, "Let the Church be the Church." As this cry was heeded, the churches began to concern themselves again with faith and worship. There was a great renewal stretching through the 1940s and 1950s.

Since the 1960s, Catholicism has been passing through a similar crisis. Secularization theology has eaten away at the doctrine and tradition of the Church. At present, if I am not mistaken, many are asking the Catholic Church to be the Church again. They do not want it to be just a club of gregarious believers, although church members may, if they choose, form clubs. They don't want the Church to become a pressure group, a lobby, or a public-interest group, although they are quite happy to see church members join voluntary associations of this type. They look to the Church as such to do what it alone can do—that which, without the Church, simply would not be done. They want the Church to herald the good news that God loves his human creatures with a saving love, and that through faith in Christ we can have assurance of eternal life. They want the Church to give adoration, thanks, praise, and worship, and in this way to put its members in living contact with the living God. Without prayer and worship the gospel will remain a dead letter; it will not actually penetrate and transfigure the lives of the faithful, so that God may be continually praised in them.

If the Church is to be the Church, it must have a clear sense of its own identity and mission. How is the Church to be defined or described? According to Vatican II the Church is "the universal sacrament of salvation."[19] After some years of work in ecclesiology, I am inclined to think that there is no better definition. A sacrament is a sign—not an empty sign but a full sign, a sign that indicates the presence of the thing signified. The Church as sacrament must signify and embody the presence of God's saving love in Christ, renewing the face of the earth. We may never take it for granted that the Church is already fully Church. In every generation it must labor to make the redemptive love of Christ, directed toward the whole human family, a tangible and palpable reality. It must draw men and women of every kind and condition into a dynamic union dominated by faith, hope, and charity.

Why should the Church strive to become an effective sign or symbol of Christ's presence in the world? I know of no better answer than that which St. Paul gave to a similar question: the love of Christ, he said, compels us (2 Cor 5:14). The Church feels a divine compulsion to praise and glorify Christ the Lord and to spread the glory of his grace all over the face of the earth.

Our problem in this chapter has been to identify the mission of the Church. According to my understanding, the Church's mission is to become the Church. It must constitute itself in the world as an efficacious sign of Christ, much as Christ, the most basic sacrament of salvation, is the paramount sign of the love of God. By becoming an efficacious sign, the Church will progressively draw its members into the saving movement of faith, hope, and charity, so that they too will be transformed into living and potent symbols of Christ's presence in the world.

The mission of the Church, quite evidently, is borne not by the clergy alone but by all Christians. By spreading faith and love wherever they go, they bear witness to the wonderful deeds of God and attract others to share in the peace and freedom that Christ alone can give.

II. Church Reform Through Creative Interaction

The Church, as we have seen in our first chapter, exists "to proclaim and to establish among all peoples the kingdom of Christ and of God."[1] Although this goal was clearly set forth by Vatican II, Catholics since the Council have experienced hesitations and disagreements as to its implementation. They have been afraid that in their missionary activity they might be proclaiming and extending something other than the reign of God—something attributable rather to human initiative or even sin. For the Council, as I have mentioned, initiated a process of updating the Church's doctrinal and institutional heritage. Vatican II's call for purification and renewal has tended to undermine the efficacy of its call to mission and witness. After considering the missionary mandate, therefore, we must now turn our attention to the question of inner-church reform. This will be the subject of the next two chapters. First I shall discuss the problem of church reform in general; then, in Chapter III, I shall turn to the more specialized problem of renewal in the area of doctrine.

Prior to the Council, it might have seemed that church reform could only be a Protestant program. In point of fact, Luther's aim had been not to found a new Church but to purify the existing one. Calvin likewise considered it his life work to bring about "a reasonable and Christian reformation," restoring the Church to its original purity on the basis of the word of God.[2] By the time of John Milton, some Protestants were beginning to recognize that the process must be extended "even to the reforming of Reformation itself."[3] In the present century the slogan "ecclesia semper reformanda" ("the Church always in need of reform") has become widely accepted among Protestants and Catholics alike.

In the Catholic tradition, the idea of church reform has a long and complicated history. In the patristic era, the idea was present, but it was generally taken to signify personal amendment rather than institutional renewal. Only in the Middle Ages did it become apparent that in some cases moral and spiritual reform could not be achieved without doctrinal and structural changes. The Gregorian Reform in the eleventh century effected sweeping institutional changes under the leadership of a renewed papacy. In the later Middle Ages, the emphasis shifted again. For the conciliarists, the papacy became not the chief agent but rather the chief target of reform.

After the Protestant Reformation, the idea of reform was treated more cautiously in the Catholic Church. Reform of morals and discipline offered no difficulty, and was in fact vigorously pursued by the Council of Trent. But from the sixteenth century to the twentieth, doctrinal and structural reform were suspect. The Church was on guard against innovations that might weaken its links with its own past.

This defensiveness, however, was abandoned under John XXIII. Vatican II cordially welcomed the idea of reform, even in the areas of structure and doctrinal formulation. The classic text is from the Decree on Ecumenism:

> Christ summons the Church, as she goes her pilgrim way, to that continual reformation of which she always has need, insofar as she is an institution of men here on earth. Therefore, if the influence of events or of the times has led to deficiencies in conduct, in Church discipline, or even in the formulation of doctrine (which must be carefully distinguished from the deposit itself of faith), these should be properly rectified at the proper moment.[4]

The idea of reforming the Church is a problematical one. A Catholic reformer of the early sixteenth century, Giles of Viterbo, put the difficulty well when he said to the Fathers at the Fifth Lateran Council, "Men must be changed by religion and not religion by men."[5] Does reform of the Church mean that sinful creatures like ourselves presume to reshape the Church of God? How can fallible believers have the audacity to tamper with the doctrines, structures, and rites of holy Church? If this were permissible, what interest would the Church continue to hold for any reasonable person? If the Church has any use or relevance, this is because its teaching and ministrations are something more than human.

This difficulty is answered in part by a closer analysis of the meaning of the term "reform." Unlike transformation, which implies a radical change by which one thing is converted into another, reform means a change that keeps intact the original nature and identity of that which is being changed. Reformers, therefore, are not revolutionaries; they do not intend to destroy and recreate; they are moderates who respect the integrity of that which they are seeking to refashion. Reform in the Church takes its norm and inspiration from what has already been given in Christ. For this reason, church reform may also be called "renewal."

It is indisputable that Christians are continually in need of reforming themselves according to the teaching and example of Christ. Vatican II points out that this need of reform extends to the Church itself insofar as it is a community of sinners:

> While Christ, "holy, innocent, undefiled" (Heb 7:27), knew nothing of sin (2 Cor 5:21), but came to expiate only the sins of the people (cf. Heb 2:17), the Church, embracing sinners in her bosom, is at the same time holy and always in need of being purified, and incessantly pursues the path of penance and renewal.[6]

The need for reform in the Church touches not only the laity but also priests and religious, bishops and popes. If we understand by the Church the people who compose it, we may say that the whole Church is sinful and in need of a conversion of heart.

Taking for granted the need and importance of interior or personal reform on the part of all Christians, I should like to address myself at present to a more problematical area: the corporate reform of the Church as an institution. Historically such reform has been conceived in various ways, which may, with some simplification, be reduced to three.

1. Not uncommonly it has been assumed that the Church was perfect at its inception but that it gradually became corrupt with the passage of time. On this theory, reform would be a restoration of the original state of perfection or, in a word, repristination. Many reform movements of patristic and medieval times proceeded on the assumption that Church reform meant the elimination of accretions or corruptions and a return to the purity of the beginnings. In the sixteenth century, Luther and Calvin vehemently insisted that they had

no intention of introducing any innovation, but simply of restoring the doctrine and structures of the apostolic Church. The polemical exchanges between Protestants and Catholics of the Reformation period clearly show that each confession claimed to be faithful to the apostolic heritage and accused the other of profane novelties.[7]

The restorationist doctrine of reform has some value insofar as it provides powerful motivation to correct abuses and corruption that plainly conflict with the gospel. On the other hand, this theory is generally criticized in our day for unduly idealizing the period of Christian origins and for exaggerating the value of the remote past as the norm of faith and practice for today.

2. In nineteenth-century Catholicism a very different concept of reform was popularized. Newman and others held that the Church must constantly develop. Organic metaphors, depicting the Church as a vine or as a growing body, were sometimes invoked.[8] Against the objection that development would be a departure from what God and irregular character of historical change. Furthermore, by canon-Christ had bestowed his own Spirit upon the Church as its soul. Growth, they contended, does not involve an adulteration of the Church's nature, for the Church by its own vital principle assimilates all that it takes into itself from secular culture. By growing, therefore, the Church simply actualizes its own potentialities.

The developmental concept of reform rests upon a somewhat optimistic estimate of the powers of human nature aided by grace. Protestants have held that the theory neglects the pervasiveness of sin. Recently the organic theory has come under criticism from another quarter. Some object that it relies too much on biological metaphors and is too ecclesiocentric; that it tends to neglect the discontinuous and irregular character of historical change. Futhermore, by canonizing past developments, the theory tends to hamper interest in corrective reforms. Consequently we have seen the emergence of a third theory, which takes amendment more seriously than the second and takes history more seriously than the first.

3. The most striking feature of twentieth-century theories of reform, both Protestant and Catholic, is their attention to the interplay between the Church and its environment. Pope John XXIII and Vatican Council II recognized that reform may be required because of what is going on not simply within the Church but on the

larger stage of world history. Institutions perfectly legitimate in themselves might become obsolete by reason of developments in secular knowledge and society. The Church is therefore under constant obligation to keep abreast of the times. Reform is not simply a matter of internal evolution but of dialogue between the Church and other human communities.

This third concept of reform might be designated as one of creative interaction or response.[9] Unlike the previous two theories, it acknowledges that the Church can properly accept innovations that do not simply grow out of its own previous ways of speaking and acting, not because they were wrong in themselves, but because they have ceased to be appropriate. Reform by way of development and assimilation may have seemed an adequate model when the Church was the controlling influence in Western culture. But today a proper respect for the autonomy of secular life demands a less possessive and more dialogic relationship. The Church must resourcefully respond to the initiatives of others, not necessarily by taking over the slogans of secular culture, but by sifting and reshaping them to fit the Christian message.

Implicit in the new concept of reform, as I understand it, is a radically changed concept of the Church. The Church comes to be understood no longer substantialistically but rather relationally. On the older monologic view, it seemed possible to delineate in an exact way the essentials of the Church. On the new dialogic view the forms and structures of the Church must be constantly revised in view of the shifting human environment in which the Church lives and carries out its mission.

As a matter of fact the Church has always adapted itself, but in earlier times, when change was still very gradual, one could still look on adaptation as a superficial accommodation not touching the very essence of the Church. A distinction was made between the divinely given structures of the Church and the minor adjustments by which these were made operational in particular times and places. Today it is recognized that the forms of Church life and organization, and even the propositions expressing Christian faith, vary with the historical and cultural situation. The Church constantly changes to maintain a fruitful dynamic relationship between a people immersed in history and the God who has revealed himself in Jesus Christ.

On all three theories there are limits to reform. The Church is forever bound to maintain continuity with its origins and with Christ its Lord. But each of the three theories gives a different answer to the question, what in the Church is irreformable? On the first theory, the Church would be perpetually obliged to retain intact the original deposit of faith, sacraments and ministry; it would have no power to alter what the Lord had instituted. On the second theory, the authentic developments that occurred in postapostolic times would likewise be irreformable, in the sense of irreversible, since they had been inspired by the Holy Spirit. On this ground many Catholic theologians argue that certain doctrines and institutions that arose after the time of the apostles, must be forever retained in the Church.[10]

On the third theory, to which I am personally attracted, it is difficult, and perhaps even impossible, to specify irreformable elements either in structure or belief that could under no conceivable circumstances be relinquished. For the concrete form of any development is admitted to be historically and culturally conditioned. Fidelity, then, is not a matter of simply holding on to certain objective constituents that were present at an earlier time. Rather it is a matter of doing what is required in order that the gospel may remain living and effective. Continuity comes to be seen not as a material but as a formal notion. When the situation changes, new objective forms may be required to maintain that dynamic relationship of the faithful community to God that was established through the Paschal event. The Church does not have arbitrary power to change its teachings, its structures, and its practices at will; it stands under the gospel, and only the demands of the gospel can determine what must be retained and what must be altered for the sake of continued faithfulness.

Although this new understanding of reform is not explicitly stated, to my knowledge, in the council documents, it harmonizes excellently with the teachings of Vatican II on adaptation and renewal. According to the Constitution on the Church in the Modern World, the Church must react creatively to the personalization and socialization characteristic of our times. It must allow its "visible and social structure" to be enriched by "the development of human social life." Thanks to the acquisition of new skills and the advancement of human knowledge, it is possible and necessary for the Church to find new ways of conceiving and expressing the Christian message and to engage in a "living exchange" with the diverse cultures of people.[11] In the light of these principles, the various statements of the Council about dialogue between the Church and contemporary culture, about positive relationships with other churches and religions, and about collegiality, dialogue, and participation within the Church itself take on deeper significance. These statements may be seen as a creative response to the will of God as discerned in the signs of the times in which we live, and thus as reform according to our third model.

In the past decade the creative interaction initiated by Vatican II has brought forth a number of wholesome fruits. Thanks to the spirit of openness and dialogue introduced by the Council, Catholics have gained a deeper appreciation for the authentic values in other Christian traditions, in the non-Christian religions, and in various secular faiths and ideologies. As a result, the Church has largely overcome its previous estrangement from contemporary thought and culture. Catholics, moreover, have achieved a much sharper awareness of their responsibilities toward the larger human community and of the need to perceive the demands of the gospel in the vicissitudes of secular history. In all these respects Vatican II effected major reforms in the Church's relationship to its external environment.

In the first few years after the Council, significant internal reforms were achieved. There was a great proliferation of new agencies, such as parish councils, pastoral councils, priests' senates, national and regional bishops' conferences. The International Theological Commission and the International Synod of Bishops were launched. The permanent diaconate for married men was restored. The liturgy was thoroughly revised and translated into the vernacular. The process of revising the Code of Canon Law was broached with vigor.

In nations accustomed to the liberal democratic tradition, there has been a movement to introduce into the Church the principles of constitutional government and something corresponding to a bill of rights. The Canon Law Society of America proposed to the bishops in this country a set of due process procedures which have in fact been recommended by the National Conference of Catholic Bishops and approved in Rome. In the United States and in several European countries, there is a strong movement to introduce principles such as the following:

Separation of powers in church government (executive, legislative, and judiciary);

Election of popes and bishops by clergy and laity;

Pastoral councils with a deliberative (i.e., decisive) vote;

Accountability of bishops and pastors to the whole people of God;

Universal declaration of Christian rights;

Due process legislation protecting even those who dissent from official church doctrines;

Admission of divorced and remarried Catholics to the sacraments;

Ordination of women;

Optional celibacy for priests;

The right of the ordained to resign at will from the ministry.

For several years, the reform movement seemed to be going well. It was assumed that, while a few older pastors might continue to resist, the vast majority of Christians, including especially the laity and the younger clergy, would be enthusiastic for reform. The event proved otherwise. In nearly every country there occurred a painful and costly split between liberals and conservatives. The Church became divided between right-wing and left-wing Catholics, each trying to counter the moves of the opposite party. A harassed band of moderates found itself hooted at from both sides.

The period of the late sixties, especially, was dominated by a phenomenon known as polarization—a state of inflammation in which practically all conflicts of opinion are taken up into a struggle between opposed parties, each seeking to refashion the Church according to its own ideals. In such a polarized situation, according to Karl Rahner,

. . . the individual has to face the dilemma either of belonging to a particular group or of being regarded as its enemy, or at least suspected in principle of being hostile; he is forced in each and every question to ally himself with a particular group; only those supporters are promoted who have devoted themselves heart and soul to this particular group; when something new is proposed, the first

question is always whether it suits the group or is likely to damage its prestige. We are certainly in danger of this sort of polarization today.[12]

As a result of polarization, the reform movement launched by the Council slowed almost to a standstill. The leadership of the Church was placed in a position where it could not go either backward or forward without losing the support of a major portion of the constituency. Each party effectively checked the programs of the other, and expressed its own acute dissatisfaction with the status quo.

Polarization, in my opinion, is more deleterious to the Church than any external opposition. When the Church suffers persecution from hostile powers, it often reacts with heroism and energy. Polarization, however, produces lethargy and disgust. In the late sixties (continuing on into the early seventies), polarization brought about a serious reduction both in numbers and commitment on the part of clergy, religious, and lay leaders, as well as a dramatic fall-off in conversions. A polarized Church simply cannot attract new members and new leaders of high caliber.

During the acute phase of polarization, about the time of the major university riots and the antiwar demonstrations, a significant segment of church reformers moved from moderation to radicalism. They hoped that where persuasion had failed, threats and force might succeed. Some turned to the secular media in order to bring the glare of publicity to bear on what they regarded as ecclesiastical abuses. Others threatened to campaign against church collections. Strikes, picket lines, and noisy demonstrations became the order of the day. At several major assemblies of bishops radical groups seized the occasion to stage disruptions. It seemed as though we were about to witness the appearance of a class of ecclesiastical weathermen (or weatherpersons)!

Fortunately these tactics were met with the contempt that they deserved. Like universities, churches simply cannot allow their policies to be formed by confrontation. Such procedures simply invite rival groups to bring pressure in the opposite direction, thus producing a stalemate. While they accomplish no good, these tactics do accomplish harm. They make it almost impossible for the leadership to exercise wise initiatives. By spreading disaffection and contempt, the protesters cause others, less committed than themselves, to abandon the Church entirely. Indeed, they give the impression that the Church, far from spreading love and reconciliation, is a scene of mutual recrimination and backbiting.

Why has the reform movement fallen into its present impasse? The causes are deeply rooted in history. By accusing the Protestants of innovation, the Catholic Church in the sixteenth century became committed to conservatism. This attitude was fortified by the polemics against the eighteenth-century freethinkers and against the materialistic socialism of the nineteenth century. The Catholic revival of the nineteenth century was closely linked to a romantic nostalgia for the Middle Ages and to political restorationism. Having been trained for several centuries to resist the spirit of the times, Catholics were ill prepared for Pope John's program of *aggiornamento*. The bishops themselves, though they voted for the documents of Vatican II, never overcame their anxious fears that dialogue and participation might lead to confusion, anarchy, and a dissolution of the Catholic heritage. The same may be said, with even greater emphasis, of the Roman curia, which has never been cordial to the principles of collegiality, subsidiarity, adaptation, and pluralism.

A further difficulty is that the progressives, in their attempts to implement the reforms of Vatican II, failed to develop a truly theological rationale for their program. For many of them adaptation apparently meant a reconstruction of the Church according to the principles of contemporary liberal democracies. In reading their work one has the impression that they begin by accepting the dogmas of contemporary secular social theory—in its "left of center" representatives—and then go to the Bible or tradition with a view to finding support. Their theological probings are selective and slanted. They go to the sources not to be instructed but to find arguments for the views to which they are antecedently committed.

Some of the reformers are fond of quoting John Stuart Mill's statement "My love for an institution is in proportion to my desire to reform it."[13] On the lips of a committed churchman these words may be an authentic expression of love. But the phrasing is unfortunate. It sounds as if a wife were to say to her husband, or a husband to his wife: I love you only to the extent that I wish to see you different than you are. The liberals' love for the Church, at times, seems to be almost conditional. They ask whether we really need the Church, and reply only in a hypothetical way. We need the Church, some tell us, only if it gets out of the "salvation business" and becomes an effective agency for the promotion of a better social order.

Progressives of this kind, in my opinion, have often done a disservice to the Church. Having been mistaken for two thousand years about its essential nature and mission—they seem to be saying—the Church can recover itself only by going to school with the disciples of John Locke and Jean Jacques Rousseau. For my part, I would maintain that the world has no need for a church that simply echoes the popular slogans of the day and reduplicates the work of secular organizations. The Catholic Church, I submit, has a rightful place in the modern world if—or rather because—it continues to bear witness to its own tradition of faith and builds upon its own sacramental, priestly, and hierarchical heritage.

What is at stake here is the fundamental concept of the Church. The Church, as I have already contended, is essentially a mystery of grace, a wonderful encounter between the divine and the human. Even in its visible structures, the Church is not a mere organization to be judged on grounds of efficiency, but a sacrament of God's saving deed in Jesus Christ. From this it follows, in my judgment, that the Church's forms of speech and life, and indeed its entire corporate existence, must be such as to mediate a vital communion with Christ the Lord. The Church must be a place of prayer and worship, praise and witness. Any institutional change in the Church must be carefully assessed for its effect on the spiritual life of the members. Does it intensify their faith, their hope, their charity? Does it help them to center their lives on Christ and to ground their existence in the God who raised him from the dead?

The religious consciousness, which lies at the heart of the Church's existence, is nourished by symbolism. Christ, the Church, and the sacraments are powerful symbols expressing, communicating, arousing, and intensifying the life of faith. The manifold institutions and ceremonies of the Church speak to levels of consciousness that seem to have eluded the liberal reformers. Hastily taking over the principles of the Enlightenment, they seek only to rationalize, to demystify, and to desacralize. Neglecting the secret wellsprings of

religious fidelity, they heedlessly sweep away the symbols of the past,
leaving the faithful in a barren desert without familiar landmarks or
even an oasis where one may pause and rest. A learned commentator
on the theological scene has perceptively summed up the situation:

> One of the problems in the present-day Church, as in human so-
> ciety in general, has been that we have undertaken to change
> things without really knowing why they were the way they were.
> But the success of planning for change depends largely on our un-
> derstanding of why the things we wish to change are the way they
> are. When we have approached the liturgy, for example, we have
> often done so ingenuously, without an understanding of, or even a
> decent empathy for, the deep unconscious structures that the lit-
> urgy registers. All human institutions are the product of conscious
> and unconscious forces and it would seem obvious that in anything
> so deep and so imbedded in history as is the liturgy the uncon-
> scious component would be far greater than in most other institu-
> tions. . . .
>
> Other institutions within the church, the practice of devotion to
> Mary, clerical celibacy, the vows of religion, attitudes toward mar-
> riage, are also the result of very, very deep unconscious drives as
> well as of conscious rationalizations. They are not to be explained
> by any conspiratorial theories of history, if only because conspir-
> atorial theories always tell you more about those who propound
> the theories than about what the theories are supposed to account
> for.[14]

In their commitment to rapid and radical change, the most impet-
uous reformers have tended to speak as though everything before
Vatican II had been darkness and oppression. Pastorally this has
been a disaster. Why should anyone turn today to a Church that has
so consistently been wrong in the past? What faithful member of
the Church can overnight cast off the beliefs and devotions on which
his faith has been nurtured and substitute a whole new system of
supports? How can anyone who is forced to call into question the
whole basis of his spiritual life become an effective witness for the
tradition within which he stands? As an elitist group, the reformers
have shown little respect for the problems of the ordinary faithful.
Some of them seem to take positive delight in spreading horror and
amazement—an action in which they are gladly abetted by venal

publishers and sensational journalists. It is not surprising, therefore, that the reformers are neither loved nor trusted in the Church as a whole.

The reformist program for constitutionalism in the Church and a Christian bill of rights needs to be critically reviewed in the light of the principles just enunciated. Let me raise a few questions about freedom and equality in the Church. According to the reformers, "The Christian, who lives in the Spirit, cannot allow his life to be governed by the purely external restraint of law."[15] Statements such as these, interpreted without regard for the qualifications doubtless intended by their authors, can be seriously misleading. We seem to be in dire need of a deeper theology of both freedom and law. Such an analysis, I suggest, might show that the freedom with which Christ has made us free is very different from the civil freedom so ably defended by the heirs of the Enlightenment. Academic freedom, as conceived by the American Association of University Professors, does not necessarily coincide with the freedom of the preacher in the pulpit or the freedom of the seminary professor. To me, at least, it seems obvious that the Church, as a community of faith and witness, cannot allow its members, its organizations, and its official spokesmen to undermine its corporate mission and message. Certainly there is a place for freedom of inquiry and speech in the Church, but one cannot establish that place by taking over, without revision, the principles of the ACLU.[16]

For the reform theologian, operating in the current liberal tradition, it seems almost axiomatic that Christian freedom implies the right of priests to get married or to leave the ministry as well. A strong case can indeed be made for optional celibacy and for great leniency toward those who find themselves ill-suited to the present discipline for the ordained ministry. But the arguments are not all on one side. The liberals make it too easy for themselves because they neglect the sacramental aspect of the priesthood. In my own view, the permanent commitment of the priest and his undivided consecration to the work of the Lord is a powerful sign of God's active transcendence and of the surpassing value of what Jesus calls the "pearl of great price." To do away with priesthood in the traditional sense and to substitute a ministry conceived in purely functional terms is scarcely an advance. I do not believe that a priest who looks upon his vocation as just another job—perhaps even as a temporary

or part-time occupation—can personally symbolize the total commitment of the Church to Christ its Lord.

So too with the problem of divorced and remarried Catholics.
There is more involved here than the physical or psychological satisfaction of individuals. Any solution that the Church finally adopts to
this vexing problem must in my opinion respect the special value of
permanent and monogamous marriage as a symbol of the union between Christ and his Church—a symbolism already set forth in the
New Testament (Eph 5:22–33). In the midst of an ad hoc, throwa-
way civilization, in which sexual partners are traded in as casually as
last year's Buicks, the Church must use its influence on behalf of
fidelity. Compassion must of course be exercised in difficult cases,
but if pastoral exceptions are made, they should not be hailed as the
first fruits of a new and happier dispensation in which married people are liberated from their vows.

The liberal program of equality in the Church should be subjected
to a similar critique. The dogmatic egalitarianism of the Jacobins can
scarcely be our guide. All members of the Church, to be sure, share
the same basic dignity and are called to the same eternal destiny.
But this does not require, in my opinion, that church government
should be based on representation from below or that the leaders
should serve at the pleasure of the people. I am not at all sure that
we would have better bishops if they were elected by diocesan pastoral councils, and I very much doubt that the Church would be im-
proved if the bishops were bound to comply with a majority vote of
their pastoral councils. The authority of pastors, as representatives of
the Lord, should be limited by the gospel but not by the passing
desires of the community. A relatively independent hierarchy is
much needed as a check on the instability of public opinion.

Mesmerized by certain populist political slogans, some naïve progressives have imagined that rank and file Christians are inflamed
with passion for reform. In point of fact the average lay Christian is
quite uninterested in the reforms most cherished by the liberal
clergy. The majority of the faithful are probably unaware of the
reasons for protecting the right of speculative theologians to hold
new and untried theories; and they would probably oppose the admission of women to holy orders. If the liberals are serious about
reforms such as these, they would probably be better advised to pin
their hopes on dialogue with the hierarchy than on taking their case

to the people. After all, it was the pope, the bishops, and theologians, not the general will of the faithful, that put through the reforms of Vatican II.

For my part, I believe that it is important for the Church to have a hierarchy somewhat shielded from the pressures of public opinion, though not unaware of what the people are thinking. Bishops endowed with common sense, a moderate competence in theology, and a real sensitivity to pastoral needs can inestimably help to mediate the painful conflicts in which the Church is presently involved. Bishops are rarely avant-garde reformers and for the most part, in my opinion, should not be. Nor, on the other hand, are they generally blind to the need for reform and modernization. With a certain awareness of the complexities of the situation, they can understand what the progressive intellectuals are trying to do and can protect them against fanatical traditionalists who can brook no opposition. On the other hand, the bishops can moderate the impetuosity of the radical elite and help them to see the need for proceeding less abrasively. Time must be given for the Church as a whole to absorb the shock of Vatican II. Time will be needed, also, for the reformers to develop a strategy that is based not simply on the axioms of the Enlightenment but on the full resources of the biblical and Catholic tradition.

As a conclusion, it seems desirable to distinguish the respective tasks of the theologians, the pastoral leadership, and the ordinary faithful. Each group, I believe, has a twofold responsibility for helping to overcome the present polarization.

Let me speak first of the theologians. They should, in the first place, recognize the necessity of ongoing reform. The mission of the Church cannot effectively be carried out if the doctrinal standards, the forms of worship, and the governmental structures of the Christian community are obsolete. Vatican II clearly set forth the need for updating in all of these areas, so that the Church would no longer be tied to past cultural forms. On the other hand, theologians should not uncritically take over whatever the secular world seems to find appealing. They should propose only changes that have been carefully checked for their consonance with God's revelation in Christ. It will be their task to show as clearly as possible that whatever reforms they urge do not denature the Church but on the contrary restore it to itself.

As for the pastors, they must be alert to educate the people to the need for change. Too often in the popular mind the role of the bishops is seen in terms of defending what is old. As good shepherds, they should try to be ahead of the flock, leading them forward into the new age. It is not fitting that the leadership of the Church should be dragged reluctantly into the modern world. On the other hand, pastors have a responsibility to be cautious. They should not too easily trust the judgment of progressive intellectuals. They should not impose even good reforms without at the same time making it clear why the earlier practice is being abandoned. The episcopate in the past decade probably failed to explain sufficiently what they had done at the Second Vatican Council and why.

Finally, two recommendations must be directed to the faithful—that is to say, to the great majority of Christians who are neither theologians nor pastors. On the one hand, they must exert themselves not to look upon change in itself as evil. They must not cling irrationally to outdated forms and structures, as though every modification of language and procedure were an assault on the deposit of faith. They must remind themselves that God lies beyond all that can be captured in human speech and ritual, and hence that the accustomed forms of speech and worship should not be absolutized. They must not be so set in their ways that they close their ears to everything new.

On the other hand, it would be a mistake to pursue change for its own sake. Everything depends on what is being discarded and what is being adopted in its place. The faithful must learn to be prudent and discerning—to accept only those changes which, after being tested, are found to intensify Christian life and commitment. Some of the supposed reforms introduced since the Council, usually on private authority, appear to have led in the opposite direction.

If theologians, bishops, and faithful would seriously strive to follow the very simple principles here outlined, the present stalemate between liberals and conservatives could, I believe, be quickly overcome. The Church could once again take up that continual reformation of which it always stands in need—especially today, when so much of its ecclesiastical style and procedure is out of phase with the times.

III. Doctrinal Renewal:
A Situationist View

The concept of reform, discussed in the preceding chapter, is applicable to all aspects of the Church's life: morality, governmental structures, discipline, liturgy, and doctrine. The last area, that of doctrine, is the most sensitive of all, at least for Catholics. The Catholic Church is deeply conscious of its responsibility to proclaim, without dissimulation or attenuation, God's revelation in Christ. Like other Christian bodies, the Catholic Church is irrevocably committed to the teaching of the Bible and to the articles of the creed—especially those basic articles dealing with the triune God, the Incarnation, the death and resurrection of Jesus, and our hope of unending life. Like most other Christian bodies, too, the Catholic Church cherishes in its own tradition certain specific teachings which it regards as non-negotiable. They are badges of the Church's identity.

Since the nineteenth century, the term "dogma" has functioned as a code word to signify certain specific and precisely formulated teachings so important and so evidently contained in revelation that the Church can never cease to teach them confidently in the name of the revealing God. Dogma, understood in this sense, provides a kind of limiting case or negative instance of reform. It has been claimed to be irreformable. But in an age of rapid and radical change, marked by burgeoning pluralism, the received concept of dogma, with its note of irreformability, has become problematic. A distinguished Roman Catholic theologian recently published a book with the title *The Case Against Dogma*.[1] The present chapter, in its discussion of doctrinal renewal, may throw some added light upon the question whether dogma can and should survive.[2]

In order to set the problem in the proper historical perspective, it will be necessary to summarize some theological theories from previous centuries. This background, although it might appear tedious, will serve to clarify the distinctive characteristics of our own era, so that we may better speak to current problems.

Prior to the nineteenth century, theologians had practically no awareness of real doctrinal change. Popes and councils did not look upon themselves as innovating but simply as reasserting the faith that had been given once for all to the saints of old (cf. Jude 3). This generalization may be illustrated with reference to Thomas Aquinas. He recognizes that the articles of faith underwent an increase from the time of the patriarchs to that of the apostles.[3] In the apostolic age, however, the revelation reached completion. Everything essential for Christian belief is contained in the creed[4]—either the Apostles' Creed, which Thomas takes to be primitive, or the Nicene-Constantinopolitan Creed, which he regards as a fuller statement of what is in the Apostles' Creed.[5]

Thomas is aware that from time to time ecumenical councils have authoritatively settled controversies among Christians. Chalcedon's decisions regarding Christology afford a classic paradigm. Such conciliar decisions ("determinationes," Aquinas calls them) do not really amplify the creeds; they simply declare, in opposition to heretical distortions, the real meaning of the previously known articles.[6] The verbal additions are not viewed by St. Thomas as positive extensions. On the contrary, he insists, they simply preserve what was previously believed. Their purpose is negative and defensive.

In accordance with these principles, Aquinas tries to show that the Western addition to the creed of the statement that the Holy Spirit proceeds "from the Son" (*Filioque*) as well as from the Father asserts nothing that was not implicitly asserted by the original form of the creed.[7] St. Thomas would not ascribe to the pope any power to impose as matters of faith any beliefs not already included in the creed itself, properly understood.[8]

The theologians of the Reformation and Counter Reformation were captivated by what Robert Wilken, in the book already referred to, calls "the myth of Christian beginnings," and thus became openly hostile to dogmatic development.[9] Protestants and Catholics alike appealed to the criterion that had been used by Vincent of Lérins against the disciples of Augustine: true Christianity is "what has been believed always, everywhere, and by all" ("quod semper, quod ubique, quod ab omnibus creditum est").[10] The Protestants generally held that Scripture alone is the touchstone of the pure, apostolic faith.[11] The Catholic position, made official at the Council of Trent, was that the apostolic deposit of faith was accessible through two equally dependable channels, Scripture and tradition.[12] Neither communion would admit that it was innovating, but each accused the other of having done so. Even in twentieth-century Roman Catholic treatises one finds the Protestant reformers labelled "Novatores" (innovators).

Catholic theologians of the seventeenth century continued to insist that the modern teachings of the Church went back to apostolic times. In the words of the Jansenist Antoine Arnauld, "All the dogmas of the faith are as old as the Church; all of them were individually (*distinctement*) believed by the Apostles and have been preserved by an uninterrupted succession of tradition in the consciousness of at least a part of the pastors and the faithful."[13] Bishop Jacques-Bénigne Bossuet, Arnauld's contemporary, was of the same opinion. "All false doctrine," he wrote, "will betray itself at once, beyond all doubt and discussion, wherever it appears, by its novelty, inasmuch as it will always be something that was not perpetually known."[14]

According to theologians prior to the nineteenth century, therefore, doctrinal reform could not take the form of true progress or development. Improvement could mean only a return to the pure and integral teaching of the apostolic Church.

In the nineteenth century, evolutionary thinking began to assert itself in many disciplines. G. W. F. Hegel, in particular, excogitated an all-embracing dialectical philosophy in which the Church and its doctrines were viewed as inextricably enmeshed in the universal process whereby the Absolute Spirit emerges. Charles Darwin, a little later, was to apply evolutionary thinking with startling success to the biological problem of the origin of species. Under the circumstances it was inevitable that theologians should devise evolutionary theories of their own. In Germany, Johann Adam Möhler of the Catholic Tübingen school proclaimed that Christianity, as a living faith, is subject to development and progress under the guidance of the Holy Spirit.[15] In England John Henry Newman became the first great theorist of our subject. Development he saw as a continuous organic process whereby the Christian idea, under the irradiation of the Holy Spirit, opens into full flower in the consciousness of the believing community.[16]

Bossuet had objected to the Protestants: "You change, therefore you are not in the truth." Newman's objection to the Protestants of his day was almost the opposite: "You are not in the truth because you remain static."[17] In Newman's estimation the Church of England failed to show the same signs of vitality as the Catholic Church, which had developed as far beyond the Fathers as the Fathers themselves had beyond the New Testament. The same arguments that enabled Newman, in his Anglican days, to defend the Church of England against the Lutherans later compelled him, in his own judgment, to relinquish Anglicanism in favor of Roman Catholicism.

When Newman came to Rome in 1846 to prepare for ordination as a Catholic priest, he discussed his theories of development with the Roman College Jesuits Giovanni Perrone and Carlo Passaglia, both of whom were close students of Möhler and the Tübingen school. In 1847 Perrone wrote a short book on the definability of the Immaculate Conception of the Blessed Virgin. Pius IX, then in temporary exile with his curia at Gaeta, read Perrone's brochure and perceived the immense possibilities it offered for a revitalized papacy. After several years of consultation with theologians and bishops, Pius IX in 1854 defined the dogma of the Immaculate Conception on his own authority. By this bold authoritative action "Pio Nono" helped to pave the way for the dogma of papal infallibility, which was to be defined in 1870 by Vatican Council I. For the century following 1854 the Catholic Church dramatically cast off the static mentality that had governed its response to the Protestant reformers. The new mobilism reached its high-water mark in 1950, when Pius XII, following the same procedures previously used by Pius IX, defined the bodily Assumption of the Blessed Virgin. In the papal and Marian dogmas of this hundred-year period, development was seen not negatively, as defining a specific truth that had been attacked, but positively, as extending the body of necessary beliefs.

The new attitude of the magisterium toward development posed difficult problems for theology. The Church remained committed to the view that the deposit of faith had become complete with the apostles—a view evident in the decrees of Vatican I and emphatically restated in the Roman condemnations of Modernism. And yet the new dogmas were proclaimed as truths revealed by God. How could these two assertions be reconciled? According to the only possible theory that did not deny the very terms of the problem, the new dogmas must have been at least implicitly contained in the apostolic deposit of faith. Yet in defining these dogmas, the magisterium felt no obligation to prove by historical research that these dogmas were primitive. It seemed sufficient to establish that they were believed as revealed by the Church of today. For the Church claimed infallibility for its assertion that these truths were in fact revealed. To show how the new dogmas were contained in the original deposit was, according to the popes, the task of theologians.[18]

Theologians, taking this assignment very seriously, produced theories of development that fall into two general categories—the logical and the organic.[19] The logical approach,[20] which sees the new truths as the result of syllogistic reasoning, draws heavily on the work of Counter Reformation Jesuit theologians such as Luis de Molina and Gabriel Vásquez; it was perfected early in the twentieth century in the rival theories represented respectively by two Dominicans, Reginald Schultes and Francisco Marín-Sola. In general the logical approach was well suited to explain certain developments—such as the progression from the doctrine of the two natures in Christ to that of the two wills—but was unsuccessful in showing that certain modern dogmas, such as the Immaculate Conception, had been precontained in any propositional truths known in apostolic times. The logical approach was forced to admit something very like new revelation or else to disguise the real novelty of the modern dogmas. Thus the logical theories of development, for all their ingenuity, ended in an impasse.

The fundamental flaw in the logical theories was their assumption that revelation essentially consists of propositional truths. This assumption was rightly contested by the other main school, which I call the organic. Drawing on the work of Möhler and Newman, the modern proponents of the organic theory—notably Karl Rahner and Edward Schillebeeckx, writing in the 1950s—held that divine revelation was originally communicated not in the form of propositions but as an indistinct whole, known through a kind of global intuition.[21] Revelation, as a self-communication of the divine, inevitably exceeds the limits of what the human mind can comprehend in discursive thought or formulate in propositional terms. The development of dogma is thus a vital process in which faith unfolds under the interior guidance of the Holy Spirit, who implants in the hearts of the faithful an instinctive sense of what is, and what is not, a valid expression of revealed truth.

The Marian dogmas, on this theory, did not have to be derived from statements about Mary in the Bible or in apostolic tradition. They could be explained as fruits of the Church's meditation on what was implied in the vital relationships between Jesus and his mother as concretely described and suggested in the Bible—the Bible itself being read and interpreted by the Church in an atmosphere of prayer and worship, under the guidance of the Holy Spirit.

The logical and organic theories, for all their differences, have much in common. Both look upon revelation as a body of supernatural knowledge that reached completion with Christ and the apostles. They agreed that dogma is an authoritative statement by the Church of a truth implicitly contained in the deposit of revelation, and that for a truth to become dogma it is necessary and sufficient that it be infallibly known as divinely revealed. Once the Church knows with certitude that a given truth is revealed by God, it can never again be ignorant. The growth of dogma, therefore, is cumulative and irreversible. The Fathers knew more dogmas than the apostles, we know more than the Fathers, and our descendants will know more than we. The definition of a dogma, on both these theories, is a very solemn act, for by its very nature it commits all future generations to conform to something not previously seen as essential. From the time of its definition the dogma becomes binding under pain of heresy upon all Christians. It is not surprising, therefore, that as the burdens of belief became more apparent, the production of new definitions slowed down. In the century following Vatican I only a single dogma was defined—that of the Assumption of the Blessed Virgin Mary.

Since about 1950 the theories of homogeneous development so subtly elaborated in the course of the previous century have begun to wane in popularity. There seems to be a widespread feeling that there is no need for further multiplication of dogmas. The knowledge explosion, among other things, may have changed our attitudes. We suffer not from a paucity of certified statements about God and the other world but from an inability to grasp the meaning, relevance, and credibility of the statements already made. With the rapid cultural changes and growing pluralism of recent decades and the more stringent criteria currently being applied to linguistic formulations, many older formularies appear problematical. Because unassimilable formulas are a burden to the spirit, it is not surprising that certain Christians feel the urge to put part of their dogmatic heritage in brackets. They want to express the basic Christian message in the simplest possible terms, in language that strikes home to ordinary people, and in a manner that has an evident impact on lived experience and concrete behavior.

For all these reasons, current thinking about development tends to fall into a pattern aptly described by George A. Lindbeck's term, "historical situationism." According to this view, "the Church's doctrines are thought of as the products of the dialogue in history between God and his people and as the historically conditioned and relative responses, interpretations and testimonies to the Word addressing man through the scriptural witness."[22] Doctrine, therefore, does not evolve by a process of "continuous and cumulative growth,"[23] nor does it remain fixed at some primitive stage. New formulations are needed to maintain old truths and give them relevance and credibility in new circumstances. In the process of development, the Church does not allow its teaching to be passively shaped by the forces of secular history, but it creatively interacts with its sociocultural environment—as I have already maintained in speaking of church reform in the last chapter. New doctrines, therefore, should grow out of a "living exchange" in which the message of the gospel is restated so that it has meaning for, and impact upon, the people of a given time and culture.[24]

The situationist theory of dogma, I would hold, responds to three pressing demands currently felt in Roman Catholicism (and, in varying degrees, in some Protestant churches): to lighten the burden of assenting to doctrines handed down from the past, to find apt ways of expressing the heart of Christian faith, and to speak more appositely to presently pervasive errors. The situationist theory may be discussed in relation to each of these three guiding principles.

For many centuries Roman Catholicism has been concerned with preserving continuity in its tradition. As previously stated, the development of dogma has been understood to be cumulative and irreversible. There comes a point, however, when the weight of the tradition is felt to be oppressive; when formulations forged in radically different situations than one's own fail to be a source of enlightenment and guidance. More and more Christians suspect that it may not be necessary for every Christian to affirm personally all that is "on the books" as a dogma or defined truth of faith. Can a failure to accept some canonized formulation of faith—some ask—be compatible with the acceptance of faith itself?

The situationist theory permits a positive answer to this question. For one thing, it takes over from the organic theory of development the idea that revelation itself is not a matter of propositions. The truth of the gospel is the saving truth of God, made personally present to us in Jesus Christ. The mystery to which the Christian stands committed is something that cannot be fully specified in explicit propositional language. It was therefore possible for the first Christians to be fully dedicated to the faith without personal awareness or acceptance of what have subsequently been defined as dogmas. It is impossible to say how St. Peter or St. Paul would have reacted if they had been asked what they believed about, for example, the Immaculate Conception or the Assumption of the Blessed Virgin.

Vatican I, in its Constitution on the Catholic Faith, affirmed that the hidden mysteries of God "by their nature so far transcend the human intellect that even after they are revealed to us and accepted by faith, they remain concealed by the veil of faith itself and are as it were wrapped in darkness."[25] In a similar vein, Vatican II pointed out that the pilgrim Church is able to show forth the mystery of the Lord "in a faithful though shadowed way, until at last it will be revealed in total splendor."[26] The formulations of faith will always fall short of expressing the full richness of the divine mystery to which they refer.

In view of the transcendence of the content of faith, one may properly hesitate to speak of "revealed doctrines," although such expressions occasionally appear in church documents. It must be recognized that the categories used in ecclesiastical definitions are human and that the definitions therefore fall short of adequately expressing the content of revelation itself. Dogmas must be seen as human formulations of the word of God, not undialectically identified with the revelation they transmit. Thus it is possible for one and the same faith to be expressed in formulas that stand in tension with one another. The believer who has difficulties with one or another of the canonized formulas may be more keenly conscious than some others of the elusiveness of the revealed mystery.

To this first point, which would be admitted by organic developmentalists, a second may now be added, more specific to historical situationism. Dogmas are *culturally conditioned* expressions of revelation. In an important Declaration issued in 1973 (*Mysterium ecclesiae*), the Congregation for the Doctrine of the Faith acknowledged a fourfold historical conditioning.[27] Statements of the faith are influenced by the presuppositions (i.e., the "context of faith and human knowledge"), the concerns (i.e., "the intention of solving certain questions"), the thought categories (i.e., "the changeable conceptions of the given epoch"), and the available vocabulary (i.e., "the expressive power of the language used at a certain point of time") of the culture in which they were composed.

It would be possible to show, in a longer treatment, that almost any dogmatic formulation bears the signature of the time and culture from which it emanates. The difficulty that a contemporary Christian has in accepting some ancient dogmas may come not simply from the fact that faith itself is a challenge to our human minds, but also, in part, from the fact that the formulations of faith are somewhat outdated. Historical situationism calls attention to this culturally conditioned character of the statements of faith, and therefore makes room for a somewhat critical posture on the part of believers. An unreadiness to assent to certain venerable doctrines may stem from the dated character of the formulation.

Many historical situationists reject infallibility, understanding this as binding the Church always and everywhere to doctrines that may have a rather limited pertinence and comprehensibility. They would say, perhaps, that the dogma of papal infallibility, as defined by Vatican I, was a time-conditioned response to the situation of Roman Catholicism in Europe in the second half of the nineteenth century, and consequently that it is inappropriate to the present situation.

In my own view, historical situationism does not preclude an acceptance of infallibility, provided that the latter be moderately understood. Infallibility does not demand that a given formulation of the truth be always and everywhere imposed, but only that it be not directly contradicted. It means that when the Church, through its highest teaching organs, defines a truth pertaining to revelation, divine providence, working through a multiplicity of channels, will preserve the Church from error. But it may well be necessary, as the generations pass, to reinterpret the defined dogma in accordance with the presuppositions, thought categories, concerns, and vocabulary of a later age.

By acknowledging the need for constant reinterpretation of the Church's dogmatic heritage, the situationist theory of dogma, in my judgment, liberates the present generation from undue servitude to the past. It allows the past formulations to function as guidelines, while leaving ample room for creativity in the proposal of the Christian message for today.

The second guiding principle for doctrinal reform in our time, I have suggested, is that of simplification. This demand is particularly pressing because of the long dominance of the logical and organic theories which, with their insistence on irreversibility, had an inbuilt tendency toward increasing complexity. As the centuries passed, the development of dogma was constantly being forced outward from the center to the periphery. From the great Trinitarian and Christological controversies, settled by the early councils, attention shifted to grace, eschatology, sacraments, and ecclesiology, and at length, in the nineteenth century, to Mary and the saints. Within each of these major areas there was a constant movement from central and basic questions to those that were more subtle and refined. Thus the later patristic councils got into learned speculations about the supposed relationships between the "two wills" in Christ; the later medieval councils tried to settle intricate disputes about subsistent relations in the Trinity and about the nature of the fire in hell and purgatory; the seventeenth-century popes became involved in erudite controversies about the relationship between grace and free will; and the twentieth-century Mariologists wanted the Church to define technical questions such as Mary's supposed mediation of all graces. At the time when Pope John XXIII announced his intention to call an ecumenical council, many assumed that this would mean an infallible definition of some new Marian privilege or of some other question that had thus far been freely disputed in the Church.

Pope John, however, with his uncanny sensitivity to the demands of the times, made it clear that he did not favor any new definitions under anathema. He perceived, perhaps, that many Catholics were beginning to feel that the process of cumulative development had reached a kind of saturation point.

In an essay published shortly before Vatican II, Karl Rahner called for a radical shift in the direction of doctrinal development. It would be a mistake, he declared, to assume that development must always be a movement from the one to the many, from the simple to the complex. Progress, he explained, does not inevitably entail the multiplying of individual assertions. "Just as important," he contended, "indeed, strictly speaking, still more important, is the development in the line of simplification, towards the single mystery, an intensification of the experience in faith of what is infinitely simple and in a very essential way obvious."[28]

In many ways, Vatican II facilitated the movement here recommended toward simplification, intensification, concentration. The Council carefully refrained from defining any new dogmas or imposing any new anathemas. It aimed to exhibit the unity of the faith by linking together dogmas that had previously been seen in isolation. Thus it sought to advance Mariology not by according Mary new titles, but by integrating Marian doctrine more successfully with Christology and ecclesiology. So, likewise, it strove to establish positive links between the doctrine of the papacy and that of the episcopate as a whole.

In a text altogether crucial for our present question, the Decree on Ecumenism asserted that there exists a certain "order or hierarchy of truths, since they vary in their relationship to the foundation of the Christian faith."[29] In this sentence the Council called attention to the variety of importance among the defined dogmas, and invited the faithful to concentrate upon those most intimately connected with the fundamental mystery of our salvation.

Since Vatican II, there has been a great deal of speculation as to the norms for determining which doctrines are primary or central and which secondary or peripheral, but there does not seem to be any consensus.[30] From the literature familiar to me I would judge that at least seven views have been proposed.

1. The primary truths are those contained in the primitive kerygma (that is to say, the original proclamation of the Christ event by the apostles); all others are secondary.

2. The primary truths are clearly attested in Scripture; all non-Scriptural teachings are secondary.

3. The primary truths are those that must be believed as means of salvation; secondary truths are not necessary except as a matter of obedience (*ex necessitate praecepti*).

4. The primary truths are those set forth in the creed; all others are secondary.

5. The primary truths are those predicated of divine persons; all truths about created persons and things are secondary.

6. The primary truths are those upon which others rest as conditions of their intelligibility, and hence are logically prior to truths that are secondary.

7. The primary truths are those that pertain to our last end, whereas secondary truths refer to means that lead us to that end.

Synthesizing points made in several of these views, we might perhaps say that the primary or central truths are those that express the central mystery of God's saving work in Jesus Christ—the work that forms the principal theme of the Christian kerygma as set forth in the New Testament and in the historic creeds. Other truths of faith are somehow derivative from this central message; very frequently they are not explicitly set forth either in the Bible or in the creeds. Secondary truths, of course, are not to be discarded. They are truly illuminative of the mystery of Christ and the Church and thus are helpful for a life that is in conformity with the gospel.

Recognition of the secondary character of certain doctrines permits a more relaxed attitude toward them. The Church can of course demand that a given doctrine, even though secondary, be positively and distinctly professed. But it is also possible for the Church not to insist upon this. If in fact one were to require the faithful of our day to understand and profess distinctly each proposition ever defined under anathema since the Council of Nicaea, the Church would be faced with an impossible educational task. In practice many ancient anathemas have been allowed to fall into oblivion.

Historical situationism, as I have already pointed out, recognizes that dogmas are responses to particular sets of circumstances. Anathemas have generally been drawn up against particular movements which have been perceived as clear and present dangers to the integrity of the gospel. When the threat ceased to be actual, the anathemas have been forgotten. Who pays any attention today to the strange theories attributed to the disciples of Origen in the condemnations drawn up by the Emperor Justinian? Or who remembers the ideas of Peter John Olieu rejected by the Council of Vienne? I doubt that anyone today would be penalized for questioning that the human soul is the substantial form of the body—even though this has several times been defined, even under pain of heresy![31]

Bearing in mind all the historical relativities to which allusion has already been made, I believe that it may not always be advisable or necessary to require direct assent to ancient formulations of faith, composed in contexts alien to our own. I would think it proper for the Church to teach secondary doctrines without anathemas or other ecclesiastical censures except in particular historical junctures where their denial poses a serious threat to Christian faith and life.[32] The Church's doctrinal policy might suitably be governed by two ancient principles—those of parsimony and economy. The principle of parsimony would forbid imposing more than the necessary minimum to avoid harmful deviations from the gospel. In matters of doctrine, I suggest, freedom should be allowed insofar as possible and curtailed only insofar as necessary—a general maxim applied to secular society in Vatican II's Declaration on Religious Freedom.[33] The principle of economy would require us to be slow to insist upon secondary points which our hearers are not yet prepared to accept. Respecting the free and personal character of the assent of faith, we ought not to insist that individual believers should see everything from the beginning or that they should assent to doctrines in which they can as yet find no meaning, relevance, or credibility. Patience is demanded to give people time to grow into the fullness of the truth.

In pursuing the kind of concentration or simplification recommended by Karl Rahner and endorsed by Vatican II, it might seem sufficient to focus attention on the early creeds, which are generally thought to be a sufficient declaration of the central articles of Christian belief. Tempting though this course might seem, there are two compelling reasons for denying that a return to the patristic creeds would be an adequate response. In the first place, these creeds make

a series of disconnected affirmations without any clear indication of
the thematic unity that binds together the various articles. A traditional creed does not bring out the inner meaning or intelligibility of
the Trinitarian processions and the economy of salvation history. It
simply states the realities or facts to which Christians, as members of
the Church, subscribe. We cannot expect these creeds to provide the
kind of unified intelligibility demanded for an intense and concen-
trated act of faith.

Second, as Rahner has pointed out,[34] the early creeds impress our
contemporaries as being far removed in thought patterns and language from the idiom of our time. For the average secularized
believer of today, a short formula can scarcely bring faith to a sharp
focus unless it takes its departure from the point at which we experience our own existence. It cannot simply begin, as do the ancient
creeds, with the biblical concept of God as Father.

Not surprisingly, therefore, there has been in recent decades a remarkable proliferation of newly composed short formulas of faith.[35]
Some of these, such as the Presbyterian Confession of 1967,[36] have
been efforts to supplement older confessional standards, such as the
Westminster Confession or the Heidelberg Confession. Some have
functioned as a quasi-credal basis for union churches, such as the
statement of faith of the United Church of Christ in this country[37]
and the revised statement of faith of the United Church of Canada.[38] Some have been ecumenical in intention—for example, many
of the "statements of the hope that is in us" prepared or collected
for the Accra meeting of the World Council of Churches' Commission on Faith and Order in 1974.[39] Some of these short formulas are
attempts by theologians to summarize what they regard as the core
of the Christian message for people of our time. In this class one
could place the brief confessions composed by Karl Rahner,[40] Walter
Kasper,[41] René Marlé,[42] Hans Küng,[43] and Monika Hellwig.[44] And
finally, there are many anonymous statements of faith by individuals
and student groups, some of which have been gathered up in periodi-
cals or anthologies. To compare and analyze all these developments
would be a rewarding task.

Relying upon analyses that have already been made, we may haz-
ard certain generalizations.[45] On the whole the new creeds and confessions reflect a pastoral rather than a speculative concern. Many

take as their point of departure the problematical and painful experiences of life today. In speaking of God the Father they accent his paternal goodness as a motive for trust. They look to Jesus as a loving servant and as a model for ourselves. Going beyond Chalcedon, the new Canadian creed designates Jesus not simply as true man but as *the* true man.[46] Often enough, the divinity of Jesus is depicted almost as a corollary of his perfection as a man. The work of God in our time—sometimes attributed to the Holy Spirit, receives no less emphasis than his great deeds in bygone ages. Several of these confessions stress the obligation of Christians to co-operate in the promotion of God's Kingdom here on earth. The eschatological future is treated with notable reserve. Some kind of future order of justice, peace, and glory is occasionally alluded to, but nothing definite is stated about the resurrection of the body or about heaven, purgatory, and hell.

The privately authored confessions, as distinct from those that are intended to serve the official needs of churches, are often reticent with regard to traditional Trinitarian language. They dwell by preference on the person of Jesus and on his meaning for life in our world. Characteristically, these confessions seek to communicate the Christian message in familiar, colloquial language, although they regularly strike a certain note of reverence. Whether of set purpose or not, they seem well adapted to an age in which public opinion is largely shaped by journalism and the mass media.

Appealing as many of these statements are, they cannot serve, nor are they intended to serve, as substitutes for the creeds and dogmas handed down from the past. Their aim, for the most part, is mediational: They intend to highlight aspects of the Christian message that can readily be related to the experience of people today. They do not have a normative character in establishing boundaries not to be crossed. They do not fully integrate the believer into the universal and abiding faith of the Church. Rather, they arouse a certain interest in the faith and point the way toward the fullness of the Christian message. To this extent they have an undeniable, though limited, utility.

This brings me to what I have earlier referred to as the third guiding principle for doctrinal reform in our day: that the Christian message should be proclaimed in a manner that challenges the pervasive errors in contemporary culture. Short formulas of faith, according to Gregory Baum, must "protect the faithful against the errors that pervade the culture in which they live." A creed, in Baum's estimation, must guard the faith "from the corroding influence of the worldly environment."[47] Since the authors who frame the creed inevitably live in the world of their own day, it is not easy for them to fulfill this task. Especially when their aim is to update the Church's heritage and to achieve relevance to the contemporary situation, they are likely to be trapped into a more or less unwitting acceptance of the point of view of the world to which they speak.

It is in this connection that the most serious questions arise with regard to the value of the confessions of the past two decades. As we have noted, they seek to mediate between the traditional faith of the Church and the experience of persons immersed in contemporary secular culture. For this reason they do not begin with the idea of God, as gleaned from the documents of revelation, but rather from the world as experienced by our contemporaries. They accent what Christianity has to bring to the needs and cravings of the present day. Some are anthropocentric, even ethnocentric, rather than Christocentric or theocentric. Reading certain of these modern confessions, a traditionally minded Christian could easily get the feeling that they subordinate the Father to the Son, neglect the distinct personality of the Holy Spirit, concentrate only on the humanity of Jesus. The task of believers in the secular world is strongly emphasized to the neglect, perhaps, of grace, of worship, and of hope for eternal union with God.

The polemical function of confessions of faith has a long and honorable history. In certain New Testament passages the expression "Jesus is Lord" appears to have been a rallying cry of Christians in opposition to the Caesar cult of the Hellenistic world. In other contexts this and similar confessional expressions seem to have been consciously directed against the reigning polytheism. To proclaim that Jesus is the Christ could also be, and frequently was, an assertion of faith against the Jews who denied the messiahship of Jesus.[48]

The need for a polemical confession of faith was acutely felt during the church struggle in Nazi Germany. Some Christians, friendly to the Hitler regime, reinterpreted the Christian message in such a way as to support the Führer's claims. Against these "German Chris-

tians," as they were called, a number of evangelical pastors came together in 1934 under the leadership of Karl Barth and issued at Barmen a proclamation to the effect that it was idolatrous to link the unique lordship of Jesus with the ascendancy of Adolf Hitler. The Barmen Declaration was a new confession of faith in opposition to a clear and present threat to the Church's integrity. In effect it was dogma. It anathematized the positions of the German Christians.[49]

With their eye on the Barmen Declaration a number of German Lutheran theologians, such as Ernst Kinder, Bernhard Lohse, and Heinrich Vogel, writing in the aftermath of World War II, clearly espoused what we have here called the "historical situationist" theory of dogma. The Church, they said, periodically finds itself in crisis situations in which it is called upon to confess the faith in a new way, directly repudiating the evils then threatening to corrupt the Christian witness. The fresh articulation of the Christian faith that arises out of such situations has authentic binding force for the Church and may in this sense be designated by the term "dogma."

From within the Roman Catholic tradition, Gregory Baum, reflecting upon what transpired at Vatican II, sketched a similar theory of dogma. For the traditional notion of development, with its overtones of continuity and homogeneity, Baum proposed to substitute the idea of "refocusing the gospel." But he sees this not as a simple acceptance of, but rather as a challenge to, the prevalent secular culture:

> By re-reading scripture and creeds, and, above all, by listening to the world of men and discerning God's voice in it, the Church is able to express the divine reply, revealed in Christ, to the crucial question. Through this process, in which the Spirit is creatively involved, the Church re-focuses the Gospel as the Good News for its own age. Because of God's presence in her life, the Church is able to find the central message and thrust of divine revelation which makes it the salvational reply to the present question that threatens to undo human life.[50]

The assumptions of secular humanism, which today underlie so much of the culture of the Western world, have very little in common with the perversions of Nazi ideology. Nevertheless, the Christian should not complacently assume that the dominant secular culture is congenial to the gospel. There is need, even today, for groups of Christians to ferret out and denounce the prevalent forms of idolatry. One effort to do so, the Hartford Appeal for Theological Affirmation, will be studied in our next chapter. It represents an effort by a private and unofficial group of theologians to rouse the Christian churches to oppose the reigning secular mentality.

From the historical and theological reflections in this chapter, it has become apparent that doctrinal change and renewal have always occurred in the Church, though the pace and style of modification have greatly varied. In the early modern period, when the fact of doctrinal change became evident, the Church was somewhat isolated from the modern world, and tended to spin out new dogmas by continual reflection upon its own patrimony. This process was accounted for by theories of "dogmatic development." In the past generation, when the Church has been seeking out fresh contact with the modern world, doctrinal renewal has included three guiding principles. First, the Church has sought to liberate itself from undue domination by its own past by taking greater cognizance of the historical conditioning of the ancient formularies of faith. Second, efforts are being made to restate the central Christian message in a manner that comes home to persons who are steeped in the secular culture of our day—and thus with new foci, new categories, and new language. Third, the Church has become more conscious of its responsibility to expose the potentially unchristian presuppositions of the dominant culture. In our next chapter we shall further examine some recent efforts by Christian theologians to identify seductive themes that tend to undermine the power of the Christian message and thus to weaken the Church's ability to address the tasks to which God calls it.

IV. The Critique of Modernity and the Hartford Appeal

As previously pointed out, one of the fundamental aims of Vatican II, according to the intentions of Pope John XXIII, was modernization—a modernization not simply of the Church's law and administrative machinery but also of its manner of understanding and presenting the faith. The Council, especially in its Pastoral Constitution, attempted to identify the distinctive traits of our times and to indicate how an updating of the Church could be accomplished without detriment to the Church's God-given constitution and mission. In this way Vatican II supported the efforts of those theologians who were attempting to reinterpret the message and tasks of the Church in relation to the times in which we live. Since the Council, forward-looking theologians have sought not only to press for reforms specifically authorized by Vatican II, but even to go beyond the letter of the Council in the updating of the Church.

As mentioned in our earlier discussion of polarization, conservative and reactionary Catholics have feared that *aggiornamento*, carried out according to the program of the progressives, will lead to a loss of Christian and Catholic identity. Beginning with Cardinal Ottaviani, who in 1966 wrote to the chairmen of the Bishops' Conferences concerning abuses in the interpretation of the Council's teaching,[1] Roman curial officials have sought to monitor departures from approved doctrine, but their efforts have often been met with ridicule from the liberally oriented press and with defiance on the part of doctrinal innovators. At the present juncture it seems imperative for Catholic theologians who fully endorse renewal as urged by Vatican II to manifest a sincere concern that the implementation of the Council's aims shall not lead to a dissolution of Catholic Christianity. In this effort they may expect significant help from thinkers of other Christian traditions—Protestant, Anglican, and Orthodox—who are similarly concerned that the Christian message in all its distinctiveness be kept alive in our day as a challenge to the new paganism that is threatening to engulf society.

To Roman Catholics, even those with a short historical memory, the perils of modernization are already familiar. The term itself suggests "Modernism," an ill-fated venture in updating at the turn of the twentieth century. The more radical Modernists operated on the premise that Christianity could not be defined in terms of any definite message or stable structure; that it was a protean religious movement with an indefinite capacity to accommodate itself to the trends of the times. In the face of this threat Rome felt compelled to react in what can only be called a heavy-handed manner. Failing to give recognition to what was legitimate in the Modernist program, official Catholicism seemed to endorse what Blondel labeled "Veterism"—the canonization of the authoritarian and extrinsicist theology that had prevailed in Catholic circles since the mid-nineteenth century. Blondel and others, seeking to find a middle path, came under suspicion from both sides and soon found themselves almost without a constituency.

The problem of our day, then, is to achieve authentic modernization without a new Modernism and without destructive polarization. As a first step I would suggest that it is necessary to take a long, hard look at the ambiguities in the very concept of modernization. As J. G. Herder observed nearly two centuries ago, the spirit of the times is a powerful demon that casts us all under its spell. Every age has its blind spots. Since history exhibits precipitous declines as well as remarkable resurgences, there is no guarantee that what is most recent is necessarily most authentically Christian or most worthy of adoption. The history of the West in the past several centuries has not been controlled by predominantly Christian influences, and still less by Catholic convictions, and thus one may expect to find that many of the prevalent ideas and institutions will be difficult to harmonize with the Church's mission and message.

The modernization of the Church, therefore, can hardly mean an uncritical adoption of the latest fruits of Western civilization. Rather it must mean a more serious effort to address the modern world in language that will be understood and to speak to the concerns of people involved in contemporary secular life, with all its accompanying temptations, anxieties, hopes, and opportunities. While the Church must make the effort to render the Christian message intelligible to the inhabitants of today's world (including the Church's own members), there is no guarantee that it will be easy or even possible to set forth the content of Christian revelation in concepts and categories that are readily available in our secular culture. If many centuries were required to make Platonism or Aristotelianism into apt vehicles for orthodox Christian thought, we need not expect that the philosophical systems of modern Europe and America can be used without modification as the media of Christian theology.

What, then, are the predominant characteristics of the modern world? According to nearly all observers the modern climate of opinion has been greatly affected by secularity. Langdon Gilkey speaks for many when he writes that the secular spirit "represents the cultural *Geist* of our time."[2] While the authors do not fully agree on the nature of secularization, many would be willing to accept Peter Berger's description: "Both social institutions and individual lives are increasingly explained as well as justified in terms devoid of transcendent referents. Put differently: The reality of ordinary life is increasingly posited as the *only* reality. Or, if you will: The common-sense world becomes a world without windows."[3] While admitting that the causes of secularization are still a matter of dispute among competent scholars, Berger himself believes, with Max Weber, that the causes are primarily to be sought not in movements of ideas—not in the abstract rationality of science or philosophy—but in the "functional rationality" of modern capitalism, bureaucracy, and industrial production. These social formations of modernity, says Berger, "encourage activism, problem-solving, this-worldliness, and by the same token discourage contemplation, surrender, and concern for what may lie beyond the world. Put simply, modernity produces an awful lot of noise, which makes it difficult to listen for the gods."[4]

Christian theologians generally distinguish between secularization and secularism. By the latter they mean secularity in acute form—a philosophy of life that is naturalistic and implicitly atheistic. Some theologians, while repudiating secularism, feel that Christian or biblical faith is entirely compatible with secularization. Langdon Gilkey, however, rightly warns that the process of secularization brings with it a new attitude that tends to undermine the traditional Christian affirmations. The "secular spirit" postulates the kind of universe in which the central realities of Christian belief—creation, grace, redemption, revelation, incarnation, miracle, etc.—either have no place or must be so radically reinterpreted that one might seem to be preserving only the name. Hence the problem, as Gilkey remarks:

> When the process of *aggiornamento* "opened the windows of the church" to the fresh breezes of modernity, those open windows also let in the chill blasts of naturalistic atheism and indifference, of a form of secularistic thought and life antithetical to religion of any sort and so to any interpretation of the Christian faith, ancient or modern.[5]

Almost no Christian is opposed to modernization as such—as though the past were by nature sacred and the new essentially profane. The problem arises only when one gives specific content to the term "modernization." If the modern spirit, as many claim, is the secular spirit, and if the secular spirit contains at least a tendency toward secularism, modernization in our day is at best problematical. In the mid-sixties a number of theologians, underestimating these problems, pressed for a radically revised, secular Christianity. Since that time liberal and progressive theologians have continued to press for modernization, but more soberly and cautiously than their predecessors. They have been seeking to work out some kind of accommodation with the modern mind while avoiding secularity in extreme and virulent form. Langdon Gilkey and David Tracy may be taken as representatives of this more recent trend.

No Catholic can fail to read with interest Gilkey's vision of what a modernized Church would be. On the one hand Gilkey calls upon the Catholic Church to reject "supernaturalism"—a system that Gilkey describes so pejoratively that it could scarcely be found even in the cruder textbooks of Neo-Scholasticism. On the other hand, Gilkey bids the Church to come to terms with "the worldly or naturalistic forms of modern experience,"[6] which would seem to include affirmations such as the following:

> While in faith we may believe that the divine reality transcends nature, still, for us the divine is not conceivable as another realm but solely as the source of created life here and now; and for us, even Christians, *this* life is our sole context and its perfection our

sole goal. . . . We all tacitly believe we are called as Christians to fulfill our *humanity*, not to transcend it; and further, as ministers, our task is not so much to lead people to another sphere but to help them to fulfill their natural life here, to increase their human well-being, personal depth, communal love, and material and emotional security. The relevant evils to be overcome are those issues around us here and now, of social injustice and justice, of war and peace, and not a hell threatening thereafter. Consequently even our religious goals and the relevant heavenly Kingdom are here and now.[7]

The Church today as servant—Gilkey goes on to say—"really knows no function except that of ministering in this life to redeem the ills of men."[8] The hierarchy has no special competence to set forth the true interpretation of the gospel. All dogmas are fallible. The autonomy of reason demands that personal judgment and conscience take priority over every form of authority. The sacraments must be interpreted not as links with the churchly realm of existence but as relating the divine presence to human life generally. As one finishes reading this series of recommendations, one wonders whether Gilkey's program for the future of Catholicism does not amount to its replacement by something else—perhaps by a liberal form of Protestantism that has forgotten the useful lessons contained in Barthian neo-orthodoxy.

Heavily influenced by Langdon Gilkey and Schubert Ogden, the Catholic theologian David Tracy believes it possible to do Christian theology without abandoning secularity. In his *Blessed Rage for Order* he proposes a "revisionist" program predicated on the supposition that Christian faith can be fully reconciled with the faith of secularity. By the latter he understands "that fundamental attitude which affirms the ultimate significance and final worth of our lives, our thought, and actions, here and now, in nature and in history."[9] Christian faith, as Tracy portrays it, provides "an existentially appropriate symbolic representation of the fundamental faith of secularity."[10] Thus Tracy's "modern Christian" "believes that the Christian faith is at heart none other than the most adequate articulation of the basic faith of secularity itself."[11] Nowhere does Tracy suggest that Christian revelation might challenge or correct the basic secular faith or transvalue its implicit values. Wherever a conflict appears between Christian commitment and the faith of secularity, it is the former rather than the latter which must be revised.

From the authors we have mentioned, it is apparent that secularity is not simply a descriptive but rather a normative term. To quote Berger again, "a secular definition of reality is posited as normative and the religious tradition is translated in such a way as to conform to this norm."[12] A Christian who has found light and strength in the biblical and traditional forms of Christian proclamation will have questions as to whether this is the best procedure. Is it not bound in the long run to produce an anemic form of Christianity?

During the middle and late 1960s, the challenge to secularization theology came principally from conservatives who had little sympathy with the objectives of Vatican II. But in the seventies an increasing number of moderates have come to feel that the Church, in taking over the self-understanding, the programs, and the priorities of various secular groups not committed to the gospel, was espousing a generalized humanism and diluting its own power to make a distinctive contribution. To be sure, the Church needs to assimilate new information and adopt new techniques that secular developments have provided, but it must not allow itself to accept the secular outlook as normative.

One of the most vigorous proponents of modernization, Gregory Baum, has shown a keen awareness of the need for discrimination. We have already quoted him to the effect that the Church in every age must "find the central message and thrust of divine revelation which makes it the salvational reply to the present question that threatens to undo human life."[13] Creeds and dogmas, he asserts, must "protect the faithful against the errors that pervade the culture in which they live" and guard them "from the corroding influence of the worldly environment."[14]

Since the Syllabus of Errors (1864) the various churches have from time to time attempted to diagnose the prevalent errors of the day. The anti-Modernist documents, especially the encyclical *Pascendi dominici gregis* (1907) attempted to point out the insidious character of a pervasive movement of the day. In a more limited framework, the various statements of church leaders against Nazism, such as Pius XI's encyclical *Mit brennender Sorge* (1937) and the Barmen Declaration considered above in Chapter III, attempted to expose the demonic character of what was, for many Christians of the time, a seductive program.

In our contemporary culture, with its intellectual bureaucracies and knowledge industries, this kind of critical scrutiny becomes both more urgent and more difficult than ever before. As Karl Rahner points out, heresy in our time is assuming a new and more elusive form.[15] In former ages, he says, the mental world of the individual was determined for the most part by things he could explicitly know. Hence heresy took the form of propositions that could be shown to be in logical contradiction to the formulas of faith. Today we live in an age when our mental universe is largely determined by a tissue of assumptions that make up the "public mind" of the society. We are immersed in, and dependent upon, a mental world that lies largely beyond our comprehension or control. Many of the unspoken assumptions of our culture are out of harmony with Christian faith and attuned rather to secularism or to some neopagan religiosity. Thus we imbibe from our environment a kind of "latent" or "implicit" heresy. If we were to give objective conceptual expression to everything present in our minds—including our prejudices, attitudes, preferences, and inclinations—we would find ourselves uttering many propositions at variance with the expressed faith of the Church. This is true even of the Christian whose explicit beliefs are, by ecclesiastical standards, entirely orthodox.

Because this latent heresy has a tendency to remain implicit, Rahner points out, it is all the more dangerous. Such heresy is very difficult to distinguish from legitimate trends and from authentic contemporaneity in one's understanding of faith. At times, Rahner observes, latent heresy is to be found simply in "the false proportions, the wrong dose"—in an undue emphasis that can scarcely be verified by objective criteria.[16]

A number of writers of the mid-twentieth century have attempted to identify through brief aphorisms those prevalent assumptions of our culture that express, communicate, and reinforce the latent heresies of the time. In one of the preliminary meetings before the Amsterdam Assembly of the World Council of Churches, the Swiss theologian Emil Brunner submitted a list of eleven axioms of contemporary proverbial wisdom that were in his judgment contrary to biblical and Christian conviction. Inspired by Brunner's list, groups in several countries prepared their own lists of axioms, which are printed along with Brunner's in one of the volumes of the Amsterdam series.[17] The ten axioms from America include items such as the following:

(1) Truth is established only by proof, and ultimate truth is unknowable.

(3) Human nature is fundamentally sound, but needs guidance and correction to achieve its fulfilment. "Sin" is just another name for ignorance or correctible imperfection, or biological lag.

(6) "God" is really a projection of man's ideals.

(8) Other-worldliness is dangerous because it distracts attention from the effort to gain freedom, security, and justice in this life; and anyway we know nothing about what happens after death.[18]

This line of investigation, which could have led to something like a "Hartford Appeal," seems not to have been further pursued in the World Council.

Private theologians, however, have occasionally followed this direction. Particularly striking is the list of twenty-six heretical attitudes characterizing radical Catholicism drawn up by James Hitchcock.[19] Several of these are worth quoting to give the flavor of this list and to provide a point of comparison with the Hartford Appeal, soon to be analyzed:

(4) Men of the emerging future will be possessed of total freedom and spontaneity and will have no need for laws, customs, traditions, and institutions.

(6) Part of this evolution is the convergence to a universal consciousness on the part of all sorts and conditions of men. Special identities such as race, nation, and religion will disappear. Those who affirm special identities are therefore acting against history and against the Spirit. An exception are those

separatist movements which appear to be progressive, such as Black Power.

(11) To be fully "human" is equivalently moral perfection; sin is inhuman and resides chiefly in institutions and social customs.

(18) Religious beliefs have meaning insofar as they can be translated into wholly human terms; otherwise they are meaningless and distracting.

(19) The Church is primarily a political reality, whose value is determined to the degree that it promotes social change and progress.

Hitchcock's list is a telling exposé of what might be called the mentality of the progressive Catholics of the late sixties, especially in circles heavily influenced by Teilhard de Chardin.

In 1974 W. A. Visser't Hooft, former General Secretary of the World Council of Churches, published a brief sketch of contemporary neopaganism.[20] The spiritual climate, he contended, is no longer secularistic but pervaded by a religiosity more akin to ancient nature-worship than to a robust biblical faith.

Among these efforts to diagnose the pervasive religious errors of the day, a special place, in my opinion, belongs to the "Appeal for Theological Affirmation" issued in late January 1975 by an ecumenical group of theologians meeting in Hartford, Connecticut.[21] The conveners of the group were two astute Lutheran thinkers, Peter L. Berger and Richard John Neuhaus. Concerned by the growing loss of the sense of the transcendent in American Christianity they composed in the early spring of 1974 a list of twelve "themes" which they characterized as deleterious to the work of the Church. After an extended process of discussion and revision through correspondence, and ultimately through a weekend meeting of interested theologians, the Berger-Neuhaus draft became the Hartford Appeal. In published form, this statement comprises thirteen themes, to each of which is added a brief explanatory paragraph. The appeal was initially signed by a group of eighteen scholars including six Lutherans, five Roman Catholics, two Orthodox, two Christian Reformed, and one each from the Methodists, the United Church of Christ, and the Presbyterians. The denominational affiliations, however, are not of great importance, because the signers were invited, and accepted, simply as individuals, not as representatives of their denominations. After the conference, six other persons, who had been involved in the preliminary consultations but who could not attend the weekend at Hartford, asked that their names be added to the list of signers.

The aim of the Hartford Appeal was not to issue a new Christian creed. Although it presupposes a body of shared convictions among the signers, it makes no effort to summarize what they believe in common. No mention is made of the basic dogmas of the Trinity and Incarnation. The authors, all of whom presumably accepted the great creeds of Nicaea and Constantinople, felt no need to draw up a new statement of faith—though they did not deny the desirability of composing new creeds and confessions especially suited to the times in which we live.

It would have been entirely possible for the Hartford Conference to draw up a list of recent theological opinions seen as dangerous or heretical—for example, certain new interpretations of the divinity of Christ or of the meaning of his resurrection. Some reporters, in fact, wrote up the Hartford Appeal as though it had been a summons to orthodoxy. In view of the present polarization between liberals and conservatives in nearly all the churches, it is easy to understand how the impression arose that Hartford was a conservative manifesto directed against certain unnamed liberal theologians. Hartford, however, was not directly concerned with orthodox or heterodox doctrines as held within the community of faith. It does not descend into detailed theological debate; still less does it condemn particular theologians. Even when it touches on themes such as the resurrection and the mission of the Church, the intention is not to endorse some specific theological option but rather to safeguard the very possibility of genuine theological discourse. As George Lindbeck has said:

> The Hartford Appeal is *sui generis* because it battles for the possibility of theology rather than itself proposing a theology. It does not affirm, but rather asks for affirmation; it does not theologize, but rather calls for theology; it does not confess the faith, but rather pleads that it be confessed; it does not present any particular

version of the Christian Gospel, but simply points to some features which any version should have.[22]

The intent of the Hartford Appeal is clearly negative and admonitory. It may be described as a common attempt by Christians of various traditions to identify certain widely pervasive assumptions that are in fact undermining the vigor and integrity of Christian faith, witness, life, and action. It makes an effort to grapple directly with what Rahner has described as "latent heresy." Because its aim is to focus attention on what is latent or implicit, the Appeal signalizes not theses but themes. The distinction is important, for, as George Tavard points out, "Theses are clear-cut positions that are believed, taught, professed. Themes are assumptions that are harbored, lived with, lived by."[23]

Among recent ecumenical efforts, Hartford is practically unique in confronting the dominant cultural patterns. Whereas other ecumenical statements tend to be as accommodating as possible in their search for a wide consensus, the Hartford Appeal stands out as a self-consciously controversial document. In setting out to unmask the secret infidelity at work in both our popular and our academic culture, the statement almost invites contradiction. It seeks to expose the massive problems presented to all the churches by the rampant immanentism, secularism, psychologism, and sociologism of our age—a convergent movement that leaves no room for the transcendent except as a kind of myth or as a way of describing some inner private psychological "peak experience" that might as well be induced by drugs or by techniques of "transcendental meditation."

The unifying element in the thirteen Hartford themes is the apparent loss of the sense of the transcendent. This lack of awareness is closely connected with the phenomenon of secularization, analyzed above. Many people today have the impression of living in a "world without windows," in which anything that even seems to point to the beyond is somehow reducible to the immanent. The transcendent is regarded as an illusion, comparable to the impression of unlimited distance that can be created by setting up two mirrors opposite one another, so that each reflects the images in the other. If it is assumed, in an implicit and unexamined way, that the world is totally self-contained, one can easily explain away everything formerly taken as a sign of the transcendent. For example, the secularized psychologist traces to some kind of infantile "father complex" any moral sense of accountability to a transcendent Creator and Judge.

Once it is conceded that all our ideas about God and eternal life are psychological projections or figments of social ideology, the meaning and value of faith statements are radically transformed. Their function is no longer to communicate any genuine knowledge concerning the transcendent, nor to enable us to be "justified" before God, but rather to help people live gratifying and useful lives here and now, within history. In such a situation it is almost inevitable, as Berger observes, that "church programs then become experiments in self-discovery, psychotherapy, or political activity, as the case may be."[24]

No one at Hartford would deny that scientific and technological progress is a reality, and that it has brought with it important clarifications even regarding the transcendent. Our awareness of cultural pluralism and historical conditioning has sharpened our sense of relativity, and has brought home to us in new ways the remoteness or "absence" of God. For the medieval religious imagination, Dante could suitably depict hell, purgatory, and heaven as if they were in continuity with earthly space and time, but for us this imagery is more difficult. We are more acutely aware that God lies immeasurably beyond all that we can imagine or directly conceive—a fact theoretically known to sophisticated theologians of every age, but not always clear to popular piety. Profiting from this new situation, secularity invites us to dismiss the transcendent as totally irrelevant to our present life and thought, even as unreal. Recent secular theology, while disavowing dogmatic secularism, has failed to challenge sufficiently the secular tendency to make an implicit metaphysics out of positivism and agnosticism, to absolutize the relative, and thus to destroy any possible cognitive bridge between this world and the transcendent.

The dominant secular intelligentsia, caught up in the bureaucracies of the universities and the "knowledge industries," can easily become autocratic in their attempts to dominate the future of religion. In many admired works of theology an unhealthy narcissism of the present generation is promoted. Since Dietrich Bonhoeffer, innumerable authors have repeated, without Bonhoeffer's reservations, the slogan that we are the first generation of a world "come of age." All previous ages are serenely dismissed as infantile. Leslie Dewart, for instance, asserts:

> . . . Christian theism should first become conscious that its traditional form has necessarily and logically been childish and infantile to the very degree that it has corresponded to an earlier, relatively childish, infantile stage of human evolution. Theism in a world come of age must itself be a theism come of age.[25]

About the same time, others, with equal plausibility, were concluding that theism itself is infantile and that adulthood requires us to forego any sense of having what Christians call a "Father in heaven." And thus we came to have brave heralds of a new "Gospel of Christian atheism."

Concerned with distortions such as these, Hartford's first theme repudiates the exaltation of modern thought to the point where it becomes the standard to which every thinker, speaker, and writer must conform. In questioning the triumphant superiority of "modern thought," however, Hartford carefully avoids any reactionary archaism. It warns against the dangers of canonizing the thought forms of any particular era, whether that of the thirteenth-century Scholastics or of the sixteenth-century Protestant reformers. Hartford asserts that all world views, including those of the greatest theological geniuses, are affected by their own historical situation, and hence are "necessarily provisional." To assert transcendence is to protest against captivity to the "prevailing thought structures not only of the twentieth century but of any historical period." By implication this first theme condemns a fundamentalistic interpretation of both biblical statements and magisterial pronouncements.

Hartford's second theme addresses the problem of religious language. In the immanentist or secularist view, all genuine knowledge is said to be subject to the norms of mathematical demonstration and empirical verification. Religious statements are therefore relegated to the sphere of the noncognitive, as the influential British analysts R. M. Hare and R. B. Braithwaite vigorously argue.[26] Paul van Buren, in *The Secular Meaning of the Gospel*, speaks of a consensus among certain linguistic philosophers to the effect "that 'simple literal theism' is wrong and that 'qualified literal theism' is meaningless." The language of faith, consequently, tells us nothing about God, but still it may have meaning when taken to refer to the Christian way of life. By means of it the believer may be able "to enlighten his listener concerning his 'blik'" or communicate something about his attitudes and commitments.[27]

In opposition to these very widespread views (still defended in substance in van Buren's more recent books),[28] the Hartford signers confidently affirm that God language has cognitive content. They repudiate the subjectivism that would remove faith statements from the realm of reasonable discourse or reduce them to statements, at best, about the believer himself.

Even within Catholic thought, which comes out of a tradition strongly favoring natural theology, one encounters an increasing tendency to diminish the cognitive import of God talk and to concentrate on the anthropological implications. Thus Gregory Baum advocates a symbolic approach which understands "the Christian religion as a set of symbols . . . [by which] people . . . define their lives and create their world."[29] Summarizing one of his major works, Baum advocates a humanistic and this-worldly reduction of statements previously taken to refer to the beyond:

> In my own book, *Man Becoming*, I have tried to develop a theology that is empirically based throughout. Without denying the possibility of dealing with the God problem in purely philosophical terms, I have spoken of God in terms drawn from man's secular consciousness, criticized and enlightened by the Christian message. In *Man Becoming* I try to translate every sentence about God, contained in the traditional creeds, into a sentence dealing with human possibilities promised to man and changes of consciousness offered to him.[30]

In the essay here quoted, Baum brackets himself with Leslie Dewart, Eugene Fontinell, and Eulalio Balthazar as a representative of the "new Catholic theism." This new system, it would appear, is primarily a response to the *Zeitgeist* which, Baum informs us, makes it "impossible to think of God as a being over against and above human history. . . . God cannot become an object of man's mind, of which he can acquire some knowledge, however analogous, and about which he is able to make true statements."[31] If this is the case, statements about God, it appears, could refer only to a concept or symbol; we could not truly say, as the Hartford signers do, that God made us. Rather it would seem that, in the language of Hartford's third theme, "religious language refers to human experience and nothing else, God being humanity's noblest creation."

Wolfhart Pannenberg, in his perceptive comments on the Hartford Appeal, rightly remarks that it is a two-edged sword, directed both against a fundamentalistic conservatism and a shallow modernism.[32] In opposition to both, it insists that theological statements intend to be statements of truth and are therefore subject to rational discourse. The new conservatism and the new radicalism alike prefer a religion of pure subjectivity and nonrationality.

The same curious alliance between the reactionary and the radical which we have just noted in connection with the doctrine of God exhibits itself again in the realm of Christology, the subject of Hartford's fourth theme. Here the Christ of faith is cut loose from the Jesus of history, thus giving unlimited scope to the accommodationists to concoct a Christ according to their own positions on the ideological spectrum. As George Forell incisively puts it:

> The effort to make Jesus into a political agitator of the left, like the *Comrade Jesus* of the late Sarah Cleghorn and all the succeeding attempts to see him as an early version of Ernesto "Che" Guevara, so popular in certain circles, are equaled in intensity by the even more bizarre attempts to make him the prototype of the successful businessman and the inspiration for the victorious defense of capitalism against socialism and communism. Here Bruce Barton's book *The Man Nobody Knows* must stand as the classical example of Jesus' alleged capitalist relevance.[33]

To anyone not satisfied with this range of options one might recommend the strange and haunting book of Malachi Martin, *Jesus Now*, in which the author takes the reader on a journey through the quagmire of some thirty "distortions, deformations, and illusions piled around our view of Jesus,"[34] thus leading the reader toward a final encounter with the Jesus Self who is present here and now.

The new theology, when it tires of imaging Jesus in political categories, turns quickly to psychology. Just as anti-Christian polemics has exploited the literature on paranoia to establish that Jesus was a deluded fanatic,[35] so humanistic Christology reinterprets Jesus as the paragon of the well-adjusted personality. Piet Schoonenberg, following Bernard Bro, describes him as "the only existence that has ever been psychoanalytically pure," having in relation to his Father "no trace of an Oedipus complex."[36]

It is difficult either to prove or to deny such statements, because the New Testament, our fundamental source, is not particularly interested in the human perfections of Jesus. It does not tell us whether he was healthy or handsome or well informed, though it does imply that he was not well educated by the standards of the time. What interests the biblical authors is not that Jesus is the finest flowering of human development—if indeed he was this—but that he is God's word and deed on our behalf. As George Tavard puts it in reply to Gregory Baum, "The locus of God's self-communication was not and is not humanization. It was, and is, the subhumanization of the man Jesus in the tortures of the Crucifixion."[37] Christian theology must keep the spotlight on the utter uniqueness and transcendence of what happened in the career of Jesus Christ. If this is obscured, the Christ event will not elicit the kind of worship and thanksgiving needed to sustain the Christian community in its vibrant relationship to God.[38]

Hartford's Christological affirmation takes the form of a warning against the persistent human temptation to project an image of Jesus reflecting our own cultural or countercultural ideals of human excellence. This would indeed be, as Hartford puts it, a reversal of the "imitation of Christ." It needs to be emphasized that Jesus, as known through the historical and theological statements in the Christian sources, is a real figure in the light of whom we can bring judgment on the popular folk heroes of our time.

Just as certain writers look upon God as a symbolic projection of human ideals and aspirations, so others speak of the "Christian story" as a fiction—for David Tracy, the "supreme fiction"—which has meaning to the extent that it represents authentic human possibilities. Tracy criticizes Pannenberg for insisting that the "fact of Jesus" is the *actualization* of a possibility rather than the re-presentation of a possibility.[39] To all appearances Tracy is content to say that the early Christians were inspired to invent a good story about Jesus.

It is not apparent why, if a similar story were to be told about Martin Luther King, Jr., Dr. King would not be as much the Christ as Jesus was.[40] Tracy's Christology, if I have correctly understood it, would seem to fit the widespread tendency to ignore the reality of God's redemptive action in the flesh-and-blood Jesus, and to substitute for this an interest in the power of the Christian story to provide appropriate symbols for expressing a basic human experience. To my mind this involves a disastrous weakening of the Christian message and a radical departure from everything that since biblical times has been reckoned as genuine Christianity. I think it not too strong to apply to this expedient the charge in the Hartford Appeal that some "attempt to exploit the tradition without taking the tradition seriously."

In the new immanentist perspective all religion is simply a human effort to express symbolically an inner-worldly experience. Hence the question of truth and falsity in religious claims becomes practically devoid of meaning. This may be illustrated with reference to Hartford's fifth theme, dealing with the relationship between Christianity and other faiths. Responding to Hartford's denial that all religions are equally valid, and that the choice between them is a mere matter of personal preference, Gabriel Moran asserts that the theme is simply a straw man.[41] Yet in the same issue of *Worldview* with Moran's comments, the Protestant ethician John C. Bennett declares: "I have long been troubled by the tendency—flowing from a desire to avoid a false Christian triumphalism and to listen with openness to the adherents of other faiths—to assume that all religions are equally valid."[42] Moran himself might be reckoned a contributor to the unfortunate tendency deplored by Bennett, for in *The Present Revelation* he writes:

> The question, "Is Christianity the true religion?" is not only unanswerable; it is a question that should not be asked. The question only arises because of false presuppositions brought to the first religious question. It would be more to the point to ask: Does this religious question make sense to me? Does any religious tradition throw light upon my life? Is one religious tradition the best one for me? To the person who asks this kind of question it is unthinkable that he could judge his own religion right and other religions wrong.[43]

One's assessment of the other religions will be closely connected with one's understanding of salvation. Is salvation an eschatological and imperishable gift of which we have assurance only through Jesus Christ, the risen Lord? This traditional Christian affirmation is embarrassing to secular theology. George Johnston, Dean of Religious Studies at McGill University in Montreal, presents for consideration Gustave Todrank's secular redefinition of salvation as "profound satisfaction and transforming fulfilment."[44] He concludes, however, that even when so reinterpreted the notion of salvation remains too remote from the society in which we live, and should be rejected.

> It is with no intention to be discourteous or to "knock" the faith by which another man lives that I have now to say that saving my soul does not interest me as a man in 1972. . . . Deliverance from sin brings up the problematic of God; eternal bliss conveys almost no meaning. Atonement by Jesus on our behalf is just as implausible since he is so distant in history and is unlike most of us. The Church will have to reckon with the probability that the salvation of his soul is no urgent issue for contemporary man.[45]

Dr. Johnston, at the end of his article, settles for the "assurance that a meaningful life is possible provided people become truly human, truly men as God intends."[46]

It is questionably true that in a "windowless world" terms such as "salvation" must either be totally discarded or be radically reinterpreted so that they no longer signify a transcendent gift from a transcendent Giver but a human achievement accomplished within history by inner-worldly powers. Hartford, having rejected this immanentistic world view, can in its sixth theme reject the idea that "to realize one's potential and to be true to ourselves is the whole meaning of salvation."

Theme 13, which may be considered in this connection, asserts that the Christian understanding of human fulfillment includes most centrally the hope for life beyond death. From the statements already quoted by authors such as Gilkey, Tracy, and Baum, it should be clear that for Christian secular theology the hope for everlasting life is marginal if not illusory. The essential is, in Tracy's phrase, "the ultimate significance and final worth of our lives, our thoughts and actions, here and now, in nature and in history."[47] Whether or not Tracy here means to deny life beyond death, Schubert Ogden, whom Tracy follows on many points, does not leave the matter in doubt. He says that he is not convinced by the evidence in favor of continued subjective survival after death, and that the question is, from the standpoint of Christian faith, an open one.[48]

The seventh and eighth themes deal with fulfillment and self-realization as norms for morality and worship. The repudiated position regarding sin (Theme 7) simply calls attention to an inevitable corollary of an immanentistic world view. The rejected definition of evil is approximately that of Gregory Baum, who defines sin as "man's pathological resistance to growing up."[49] I say "approximately" because Baum, as a very sophisticated theologian, knows how to say new things while maintaining continuity with the Catholic theological tradition. But he so shifts the emphasis to human growth and maturity that many of his readers, less reverent toward the tradition, will easily let the theistic dimension of sin drop into oblivion. The Hartford Appeal, as Pannenberg has noted, calls for "a more realistic evaluation of the human situation than secular humanism has been able to offer. . . . The assumption that everything human is good is illusory and leads only to greater chaos and disaster."[50]

For Christians who believe that it is possible to relate oneself by knowledge and love to the transcendent God, worship is of vital importance for fostering this personal relationship. Through acts of adoration, repentance, thanksgiving, and petition the believing community grows in familiar intimacy with God. In the perspectives of secular humanism, however, worship is of doubtful value. To John Wren-Lewis, a British Anglican lay theologian, the centering of one's life on ritual and sacrament is evidence of "paranoid fantasy-obsession."[51] To be abreast of our nonreligious culture, he maintains, churchmen "must break away radically from almost all, if not all, of their traditional religious pursuits." In this they can be guided by Jesus, who, according to the same writer, "used the word 'God' to refer to the vital energy of personal life itself, the energy of love." So understood, religion can become a mode of enrichment for the individual worshiper and the community. Worship is thus diverted from its original focus on God and is made a means for personal and communal self-realization, as stated in Theme 8 of the Hartford Appeal.

The clergy become the administrators of an avowedly therapeutic institution, on the supposed ground that Jesus himself was the supreme therapist.

A perceptive Freudian writer, Philip Rieff, in his *The Triumph of the Therapeutic*, brilliantly illustrates how our contemporary culture is pervaded by a permissive ethic of self-realization, in which mental health is raised to the highest value. Without necessarily endorsing Rieff's total position, one can find in his book ample confirmation of Themes 6, 7, and 8. According to Rieff, the role of the churches and the clergy, in the emergent culture, is no longer to preach or mediate salvation but simply to help people fulfill their human potential in community. His description of the new theology—though not his evaluation of it—coincides almost precisely with that of Langdon Gilkey, who has already been quoted to the effect that ministers now have no other task than to help people "fulfill their natural life here" and achieve "material and emotional security."[52] The present ferment in Roman Catholicism, Rieff remarks, does not seem to be so much a renewal of spiritual perception as a move toward sophisticated accommodation to the new permissive therapeutic attitude.[53] Anyone who has been in touch with seminarians over the past decade can verify the extent to which concern for counseling has taken the place of a serious interest in biblical studies or systematics. The withdrawal from the social activism of the 1960s does not represent a revival of interest in the truth of revelation, and could hardly do so, for the theological community, under the impact of the trends denounced by Hartford, shows little confidence in the possibility of authentic knowledge concerning the transcendent.

The anti-institutionalism commented on in Hartford's ninth theme is more a mood than a theory. The mood is understandable enough, for we have suffered from an excess of institutionalism in religion as in many other fields. Yet the reaction against institutionalism can be just as excessive and even more dangerous. It leads to the kind of "Free Church movement" advocated by Rosemary Ruether, who rejects the very idea of the Church as an identifiable organization or, in her own phrase, "sacred organism."[54] The "radical Christianity" which she commends is "not interested in ideas about Christ or the Kingdom . . . [or] in the church, community or eucharist except as an expression of man."[55] The reduction of the Church to the "merely human" could not be more complete.

Themes 10 through 12 are primarily concerned with the Church's involvement in social action. No complaint has been so persistently directed at the Hartford Appeal as that it sounds the call for retrenchment in this area. A distinguished theologian, in a letter to *The New York Times* (unpublished, to the best of my knowledge), accused the Appeal of fostering "a mixture of gnostic dualism and private piety" and of pushing the churches toward "retreat from concerns about bigotry, greed, and war." These charges arise from the fact that Hartford was indeed critical of certain kinds of social involvement, and was widely reported in the press as though it were the voice of a new individualistic pietism. A careful reading of the Appeal itself, however, shows that this interpretation is mistaken. At many points the importance of social action is underscored. For example, Theme 7 calls for

serious and sustained attacks on particular social or individual evils.

Theme 9 recognizes that

institutions and traditions are often oppressive. For this reason they must be subjected to relentless criticism.

Theme 10 affirms:

The Church must denounce oppressors, help liberate the oppressed and seek to heal human misery.

Theme 11 states:

Christians must participate fully in the struggle against oppressive and dehumanizing structures and their manifestations in racism, war, and economic exploitation.

Theme 12 declares:

The struggle for a better humanity is essential to Christian faith and can be informed and inspired by the biblical promise of the kingdom of God.

In view of these reiterated expressions of social concern, it seems irresponsible to accuse Hartford of promoting "gnostic dualism and private piety" and of encouraging a "retreat from concerns about bigotry, greed and war." The emphasis on a lively sense of the transcendent, which dominates the Hartford Appeal, is in no way contrary to social concern. Theme 11 points out that it would be a false idea of transcendence that would induce one to "withdraw into religious privatism or individualism and neglect the personal and communal responsibility of Christians for the earthly city." According to the traditional understanding accepted at Hartford, transcendence implies the presence of God to "all aspects of life" (Theme 11). To banish God from his own creation, exiling him to some ethereal realm, would be in effect to deny his transcendence.[56]

Once this has been clearly recognized, it is correct to add that the Hartford Appeal cannot easily be fitted into the patterns of "secular ecumenism" according to certain models recently proposed in the World Council of Churches. The difference is indicated in the enunciation of Theme 10, beginning with the words "The world must set the agenda for the church." In denouncing this theme, the Hartford Appeal deliberately set itself in opposition to a trend that was popular in some World Council agencies in the late sixties. For example, a 1967 report of the Department on Studies in Evangelism, drawn up in preparation for the Uppsala Assembly, contained the statement "The message and structures of the churches can only be formulated with respect to the immense variety of actual realities amidst which we live. *Hence it is the world that must be allowed to provide the agenda for the churches.*"[57]

This report makes reference to a prior article by Walter Hollenweger, Executive Secretary of the WCC Department on Studies in Evangelism, the concluding paragraph of which reads as follows:

Find out the agenda of the world! Ask the people outside the Church: What are the issues of today? Where does it hurt? Do you expect something from us, and what? In the communities of the churches we always talk amongst producers without ever taking into account our customers. We produce—not unlike those manufacturers in Russia—goods which nobody asks for: stuffed animals, bears, giraffes, elephants. Sometimes we change sizes and colors, but basically it remains the same. They get stored in the *thesaurus ecclesiae.* How could we know what the people need? How can we find out the agenda of the world if we deliberately throw the experts of the world out of our committees?[58]

The idea that the Church ought to receive its agenda from the world, although not explicitly repeated by the Uppsala Assembly, was allowed to color Section II of the *Uppsala Report,* entitled "Renewal in Mission," as may be seen from the quotations already given. This section emphasized that the Church exists for the sake of "others" and that missionary priorities must be continually revised because the world is always changing. As one of the criteria for determining priorities it suggested that mission should encourage Christians to "enter the concerns of others to accept their issues."[59]

When the slogan "the world provides the agenda" was originally coined, it served to bring out a neglected truth: namely that the Church, while adhering to the gospel, has to keep its eye fixed on the mutations in secular culture in order to address appropriately the people of a given age and condition. This the Hartford theologians would gladly affirm. It must also be acknowledged that the Church, as a human organization, has much to learn from the world in which it carries on its mission. God speaks to us not simply through the Bible, ecclesiastical documents, and pastoral leaders but also through the "signs of the times," as Jesus pointed out to his adversaries.

Speaking for myself as a signer of the Hartford Appeal, I would agree with John C. Bennett that there is a "grain of truth" in the discarded slogan. As he says, "It is often interaction with the world that has enabled the churches to gain new understanding of the meaning of their own faith."[60] His illustration of the principle of religious liberty is a case in point.

On the other hand, as Professor Bennett himself says, the slogan is rightly rejected. Etymologically, and according to the first dictionary definition, "agenda" means "things to be done." The slogan therefore seems to mean that the "world" should tell the Church what the Church is to do. This would be a serious violation of right order. In fidelity to its mission, and in service to Christ, its sole Lord, the Church cannot allow itself to become a tool of groups that do not share the Church's goals. If it simply carries out the bidding of non-Christian coalitions, the Church ceases to perform that distinctive service for which it is uniquely qualified.

The Church does not exist to help any particular groups, whether "haves" or "have-nots," to achieve their own special interests. It exists for the sake of the Kingdom of God, and in service to the Kingdom it must invite all persons and collectivities to repentance and conversion. Not satisfied with a reshuffling of power and wealth, to be accomplished by social revolution, the Church looks forward to a total transformation of humanity and all creation, to be accomplished by the power of God. A reshuffling of earthly resources may at times be called for, but this will not achieve justice in the long run unless human hearts are renewed by God's grace in Jesus Christ. Recognizing this, Hartford in no way disapproves of the Church's involvement in the quest for justice, but insists that such involvement must be informed by the full resources of the Christian tradition. In this way, as Pannenberg has perceived, the Hartford Appeal points the way toward a livelier liberation theology than has yet emerged.[61]

The Church, then, does not exist to accede to the demands placed upon it by any social or economic class. Even the popular notion that the Church ought to reply to the questions put to it by the "world" is profoundly misleading. Jesus refused to answer many of the questions addressed to him, especially those prompted by curiosity, hypocrisy, or a vain desire for self-justification. Instead he put questions to his questioners. The Church, likewise, must question the world's questions, and in this way challenge the values and priorities on which those questions are based.

Drawing its inspiration, then, from the gospel, and fully conscious of its specific mandate, but at the same time closely in touch with the actual human situation, the Church must chart its own course. Far from responding to all the requests made upon it, the Church must be prepared to say no, to swim against the stream, to seize the initiative, to set its own agenda. This it can do if the leaders of the Church are both deeply committed to Christ's lordship and deeply engaged in the life of the communities to which they belong.

To conclude and summarize these reflections on the Hartford Appeal, I should like to address myself to four common objections. The first of these—that Hartford sounds a call to retreat from social involvement and blesses a return to private piety—has already, perhaps, been sufficiently discussed. Admittedly, the Appeal does insist that the Christian vocation is not exclusively political. As Richard

Neuhaus has said, the political task, as ordinarily defined, must be seen as one vocation among many in the mission of the Church. Few Christians accept the idea that the meaning of Christian existence is found exclusively, or even predominantly, in effecting social change. This idea, as Neuhaus observes,

> . . . does not comprehend the mystery of communion with God, the knowledge of tragedy and redemption while holding the hand of a husband terminally ill, the awesome encounter with infinity in a snowflake, the ecstasy of great art that has no purpose but to glorify God in its very being, the devastating finality of one's own death.[62]

When told that politics is what Christianity is all about, the run-of-the-pew Christian knows in his heart that the speaker must have "a very barren and truncated experience of what it means to be a Christian."[63]

Without denying the social imperatives, therefore, the Hartford Appeal seeks to set these in the context of a larger view of the Christian commitment. This wider context actually gives support to the Church's social mandate, for loving dedication to the service of those in need cannot be successfully sustained in the long run except in the perspectives of a more universal hope and a more comprehensive vision of God's Kingdom than a purely political theology can offer. Ironically, those who portray political action as the be-all and the end-all of the Christian life must accept some responsibility for the retrenchment and disillusionment of the 1970s. Committed Christians are repelled by a movement that allows no scope for contemplation and worship except as methods of raising the believer's revolutionary consciousness. In resisting such reductionism, Hartford places Christian social action on a more solid footing.

The second objection is that Hartford is untimely. Although it might have been appropriate in the 1960s, as a protest against the excesses of secular theology and social activism, it is just what we do not need amid the new conservatism of the seventies. Were not some of the Hartford signers—it is asked—issuing a belated *mea culpa* for their own previous infatuation with "romantic radicalism"? Have they too not shifted with the mood of the times, so that now, under the guise of prophetic denunciation, they are simply echoing the resurgence of interest in the transcendent? According to Martin Marty, the Church by 1975 "needed help in separating the faith from the explosion of 'transcendences'"—help which Hartford presumably failed to supply.[64] What is the point of appealing for a recovery of transcendence at a moment when our whole nation is positively wallowing in vague religiosities including everything from astrology to Zen?

This objection, in my estimation, rests more upon the journalistic reporting of Hartford than upon the actual text. The secular press, especially, was inclined to present Hartford as though it were a recall to "spiritual" religion. Actually the Appeal is as much directed against the religiosity of the new cults as against the social activism of the mid-sixties. Hartford explicitly warns against a "false transcendence" that would lead to a withdrawal into "religious privatism or individualism" (Theme 11). Also, as we have seen, it deplores the current tendency to "remove religious statements from the realm of reasonable discourse" (Theme 2). By refusing to separate religious faith from the rigorous pursuit of truth, the Appeal calls attention to one of the fundamental weaknesses of the new irrational spiritualities. The passionate search for psychological "peak experiences" (which may be found in some sectors of the Christian charismatic movement as well as in the cults of Esalen) is an unauthentic form of the quest of the transcendent. Privatistic religion, with its orientation to inwardness, is a byproduct of the bureaucratization of public life and is integral to the secularization syndrome.[65]

Thirdly, it is objected that the Hartford Appeal is directed against phantom heresies. According to Harvey Cox, the authors have "conjured up a list of thirteen caricatures, straw men so easily toppled that the genuinely troublesome issues of contemporary theology never appear.[66] And Martin Marty, as quoted in *The New York Times*, echoes the same charge. "Hartford sets up straw-man modernisms that I haven't heard anyone in the church ever say."[67]

From the preceding pages it should be evident that influential persons within the Christian community have in recent years set forth every one of the positions repudiated by Hartford, often in the precise form repudiated. Still it is true that the themes attempt to spell out in words what appears more often as latent heresy—and latent heresy, as already stated, tends to resist explicit formulation. As soon as one articulates the principles or premises that seem to be implied by the way people consistently speak, feel, and act, almost everyone begins to deny holding any such thing.

An example may clarify this point. In spite of the passages cited above from Gilkey, Tracy, Johnston, and Ogden, few Christians explicitly say that the question of life beyond death is marginal or irrelevant (Theme 13). Yet many seem to act as if they believed that the only salvation worth considering must be attainable in this world, before death, if not by ourselves, at least by some future generation. Once we explicitly set forth the implied heresy, we are alerted to the ambiguity of our previous behavior. We attend for the first time to the real significance of our silences and omissions, our enthusiasms and our boredoms, our approvals and disapprovals. Sometimes, when we advert to the discrepancy, we are shaken out of our previous inconsistency and compelled to change either our professed beliefs or our course of action.

This brings us to the final objection—that the Hartford Appeal is, in Cox's terminology, an act of "ecclesiastical triumphalism."[68] It is accused of settling the Church proudly above the world and above history. This impression can only rest upon a hasty and inaccurate reading. The whole point of the Appeal is to call attention to errors that are genuinely pervasive, in the sense that they affect practically everyone, whether Christian or non-Christian, Protestant or Catholic, Anglican or Orthodox. The introductory paragraph explicitly declares that the debilitating themes are at work within the Church, undermining its ability to perform the tasks to which God calls it. Far from being an act of self-congratulation, the Hartford Appeal is a summons to the Church to return to the authentic sources of its own life.

The signers of the Hartford Declaration have repeatedly made this point. Dr. Ralph McInerny of Notre Dame has been quoted as saying that the statement should be applied to the drafters as well as any other audience.[69] George Tavard, another signer, confesses that he himself holds the rejected themes "whenever I let my professional sense of the comfortable overshadow my sense of the risk of faith in the world in which I live."[70] A third signer, Carl Peter, points out that the Hartford themes, like the gospel parables, are open-ended, and intend to leave the application to the reader himself. They are phrased in language calculated to make the reader ask, "Is it I, Lord?"[71] Immersed in the modern world, today's Christian lives on several different levels. Even if we have not come down with an acute case of "latent heresy," we are more or less infected with its bacteria and viruses.[72] We hardly know whether our orthodox professions or our quasi-heretical attitudes represent, more fundamentally, our real selves. By a keener awareness of the dangers, we may more easily escape them.

Although written by an ecumenical group and addressed to an ecumenical audience, the Hartford Appeal perhaps has special pertinence to Roman Catholics. There is real danger that the Catholic Church, after a decade of severe self-scrutiny, could lose sight of its message and surrender its sense of mission. In part this has already happened. The postconciliar period witnessed an extraordinary collapse of institutional self-confidence, amounting almost to a corporate failure of nerve. So self-critical did Catholics become that it was most difficult for anyone to articulate the faith or mission of the Church. Whenever anyone tried to specify what the Church really stood for, he was accused of triumphalism and greeted by a storm of protest from other Catholics and Christians. Pope Paul VI's "Creed of the People of God" was negatively received by many prominent theologians. At the synod of 1974, the representatives of the world episcopate were unable to reach an agreed statement on the Church's mandate to evangelize. Yet their reflection did prepare the way for Pope Paul VI's Apostolic Exhortation "On Evangelization in the Modern World," which unequivocally declares the transcendent and eschatological character of the salvation preached by the Church. The salvation offered to all, according to the pope, is

> not an immanent salvation, meeting material or even spiritual needs, restricted to the framework of temporal existence and completely identified with temporal desires, hopes, affairs, and struggles, but a salvation which exceeds all these limits in order to reach fulfillment in a communion with the one and only divine Absolute: a transcendent and eschatological salvation, which indeed has its beginning in this life but which is fulfilled in eternity.[73]

Without such convictions the Church would not be able to maintain itself. While secular accommodationism is still a live option for some Christians in England, Canada, and the United States, it is a luxury that can no longer be afforded in many other portions of the globe. In the spheres of influence of Soviet Russia and the Chinese People's Republic, and under the violent dictatorial regimes of many African and Latin American countries, a more intransigent posture is demanded, as was the case several decades ago in Nazi Germany. Secular accommodationism blends easily with the optimism of the Camelot mentality or with the irresponsible self-cultivation of pampered American college drop-outs. But it is not the training ground of prophets, heroes, and martyrs. In situations of political, economic, and military oppression, the Christian must be made of sterner stuff. The Church, if it is to be at all effective, must find a leverage beyond the elite of the intellectual establishment. In a subhumanized society, Christianity must have a message of hope and courage to those whose lives can never be, by worldly standards, humanly fulfilling. It must find strength to denounce the reigning powers in the name of Power beyond this world. Only by breaking through in faith to a transcendent that is universally present, yet never immersed in time and history, can Christianity bear its unconquerable witness. The Hartford Appeal, since it calls for a more robust and disciplined faith, may speak to larger audiences than do the voices of humanistic reductionism and optimistic developmentalism, though these systems may still be dominant on American secular campuses.

The Hartford Appeal, therefore, comes at the right time. It can help arm the Church against the new demons unleashed in our age. Although predictably deplored by many who wished to prolong the ecclesiastical masochism and disarray of the previous decade, it has helped others to regain confidence in "the Church's ability to address with clarity and courage the urgent tasks to which God calls it." Negative in form, the Hartford Appeal is thoroughly positive in scope and in intent. It is, quite simply, "An Appeal for Theological Affirmation."

For Catholics today, the task of theological affirmation is intimately linked with the question who has authority to speak for the Church, and under what conditions. In the next chapter, therefore, we may appropriately consider certain problems connected with the teaching office in the Church today.

V. Doctrinal Authority for a Pilgrim Church

Enlightenment, according to Immanuel Kant, is the overcoming of self-caused immaturity. "Immaturity is the incapacity to use one's own intelligence without the guidance of another. The motto of the Enlightenment is 'sapere aude!'—have the courage to use your own intelligence."[1] Through laziness or cowardice, Kant goes on to say, a large portion of humankind gladly remains immature. It is more comfortable to be a minor, under the guardianship of others.

Kant recognized that in certain official functions one may take on an obligation to refrain from speaking according to one's own convictions and to abide by the teaching of an institution. For example, he notes, a pastor is obliged to teach his congregation according to the doctrine of the Church he serves. He has to state faithfully what the Church teaches, regardless of his own personal views. If he felt that the teaching of the Church were seriously wrong, he would no doubt have to resign his post. But as long as he is a priest he remains unfree, for he is executing the mandate of others.

Quite different, according to Kant, is the position of the scholar. He writes for the general public and in that capacity he is entitled, even obliged, to employ his own reason and to speak with complete candor.

Kant is typical of rationalism insofar as he presumes that reason is the best tool we have for getting at the truth, and that reason operates more effectively when unchecked by authority. Authority, he holds, is for the sake of the immature. It is only provisional. True personal conviction depends not upon authority but upon rational insight.

The rebellion against authority at the time of the Enlightenment was a time-conditioned reaction against the excesses of ecclesiastical authoritarianism, which was carried to unprecedented lengths in early modern times. When authority becomes oppressive and violates the integrity of honest inquiry and conscientious decision, it generates the kind of negative image reflected in the writers of the Enlightenment. The rejection of authority, however, is scarcely a sign of adulthood. Rather, it is a mark of adolescence. In practically all the affairs of daily living, mature persons rely upon authority in the sense that they depend on the advice of experienced and knowledgeable persons—those whom they have reason to regard as experts in the particular field. If we do this in law, in medicine, in history, and art criticism, why not in religion? In the case of a religion which, like Christianity, claims to rest on a definite revelation given in the past, belief is essentially linked with the acceptance of the testimony of those who, allegedly, were the prime recipients of the revelation. There is no way in which reason can prove by universally cogent arguments the truth of the interpretation that the New Testament and the creeds give to the figure of Jesus. If we antecedently refuse to take anything on authority, we cut ourselves off from the benefits of historical revelation. Christianity ceases to have any value except as a set of symbols for interpreting our own experience.

The acceptance of authority, as I understand it, does not mean the abandonment of reason. As I have explained more fully elsewhere, reason and authority are dialectically intertwined throughout the process of religious inquiry and the life of faith.[2] Reason is a necessary instrument for assessing the rival claims of various claimants to authority. Reason is also necessary to interpret authoritative statements, to judge whether the authority is speaking within its competence, and to reinterpret past statements to grasp their significance for new situations. Reason may at times detect false emphases or errors into which the authorities may have fallen. The critical thinking developed by Kant and the great philosophers of the Enlightenment can thus be helpful in guarding against the absolutization of authority. Contemporary Christians are indebted to the Enlightenment for having developed defenses against an unhealthy authoritarianism.

While acknowledging the importance of relativizing authority, I would contend, against certain liberal theologians, that authority has a central place in the Christian religion. For the vitality of the faith it is essential that the authorities function properly. If the authorities fail to speak with truth and power, the whole community of faith is in danger of disintegrating. The right question for Christians is not whether to accept authority but rather how to identify and relate to the authorities. Many Christians make the mistake of overlooking some authorities and of absolutizing others.

The standard loci of authority in the Christian system are well known: the Bible, the pastoral office, the sense of the faithful, the judgment of theologians, and the testimony of prophetically gifted individuals. Certain groups of Christians have traditionally accented some of the instances as against others.

Classical Protestantism at one time coined the slogan, "The Bible alone."[3] The position was a protest against the teachings that had been cumulatively built up by the Scholastic theologians and the popes in the Middle Ages. The Reformation was, under one aspect, a radical call for simplification—for a return to primitive purity. The word "alone" in the formula has to be taken with a grain of salt, for no Protestants really ignored tradition. Luther and Calvin were scarcely less eager than the Roman Catholics to square their doctrine with the early ecumenical councils. In their controversies they drew heavily on the church Fathers and even, at times, on the medieval doctors. But they insisted that any Christian teaching—including that of councils and church Fathers—had to be aligned with Scripture. If anything could not be shown to agree with Scripture, it had for them no authority. Very many contemporary Protestants hold approximately this position.

From a Catholic point of view we may agree that the Bible, taken as a whole, is the word of God. It is the fundamental document of Israelite and Christian revelation. The Bible, we believe, is the fundamental touchstone of our faith. No teaching that contradicts the Bible, taken as whole, could be true.

On the other hand, the Catholic will have many difficulties against the catchword "Scripture alone." Let me put some of the familiar difficulties under three headings:

1. The Bible did not collect itself. It is a selection of Jewish and early Christian writings made in the early centuries by the Church—and more specifically by the leaders of the local and regional churches, and ultimately by councils. To put one's trust in the Bible, therefore, inevitably implies a certain trust in the Church that gathered up these writings and declared them to be authoritative for Christians. One cannot drive a wedge between the authority of the

Church which canonized the Scriptures and that of the Scriptures which it canonized. To say "Bible alone" with the negative implication "not Church" is therefore unacceptable.

2. The Bible is not self-interpreting. It is a very complex collection of writings from different ages and situations. One can pick out sentences here and there that seem to teach error—things we know to be false from science, from history, or from faith. To gather up the meaning of the Scripture as a whole is an act of creative interpretation, in which all sorts of skills and funds of information are brought to bear. If the Bible is to speak to us today, its meaning must be mediated to us through other authorities—the exegete, the pastor, the believing community, or whatever. If the individual reader were handed a Bible outside of any ecclesial context, he would probably find it uninteresting, unintelligible, or seriously misleading.

3. According to the New Testament, Jesus has promised to remain forever present with his Church. The Holy Spirit, who previously "spoke by the prophets," remains at work in the Christian community to the end of time. Thus it may be presumed that Christians since biblical times have spoken with the special assistance of the Spirit. We should therefore make an effort to identify the occasions on which God may be judged to be speaking through persons who have lived since Christ and the apostles. To accept no authority but the Bible would be to reject, in part, the teaching of the Bible, which refers us to Christians who speak by the Spirit.

Among Catholics it is undisputed that the Holy Spirit who inspired the Scriptures is also at work in the Church, and therefore that there is living authority in the Church. But there are differences of opinion regarding the loci in which the presence of the Spirit is to be found: pastoral office, people of God, or a variety of charismatic leaders.

Since the Reformation, and especially since the eighteenth century, the Catholic emphasis has been upon the pastoral office and, more specifically, upon the papal and episcopal offices. In the Roman textbooks out of which most of the present clergy were taught in their seminary days, practically no other form of authority than that of the office-holder was acknowledged. The term "magisterium" came to be used to designate the teaching authority of popes and bishops—and the tendency was to reduce every other kind of theological authority to this one font.

According to the theory of apostolicity then prevalent—and still prevalent in some circles—the bishops and they alone were successors of the apostles. Apostolic succession was conceived as giving the bishops a special "charism of truth" proper to themselves. The pope, as head of the whole Church, was thought to have in himself as much authority as the entire body of bishops. Thus he was the supreme and universal teacher of all Christians, equipped with that infallibility with which Christ had endowed his Church.

This theory of authority, which may be called institutional or hierocratic, has real assets that should not be overlooked. For one thing it helps to safeguard the unity of the Church and its doctrinal continuity with the Church of apostolic times. If the Church is to cohere as a society, it must have ways of assembling a body of clearly identifiable, self-consistent, and certified teachings—qualities that are clearly fostered by the hierocratic model.

On the other hand, this model, taken in isolation, has certain liabilities.[4] By insisting as it does upon the formal and juridical aspects of authority, it encourages a kind of doctrinal extrinsicism, sometimes referred to as the "blank check" theory of assent. Furthermore, it does not sufficiently attend to the fact that the official teaching would not have power or credibility except that it emanates from a community of faith and is, so to speak, inscribed within this community. Official teaching has no force unless it somehow expresses the faith of the believing Church, and unless the teachers are bound by conviction to the community of believers. The doctrine of infallibility, in particular, becomes incredible if set forth in an automatic or mechanistic way, without taking account of the human and Christian character of the process by which faith is gathered up and distilled into doctrine.

Some modern ecclesiologists, seeking the limitations of the hierocratic model, have attempted to substitute what may be called a democratic view of authority.[5] Without saying explicitly that the Church is a democracy, they lean in that direction. They speak of the common priesthood of all the faithful, and are uncomfortable with the idea that the priesthood, or authority, of the ordained would be essentially different from this. They would see the official teachers simply as those who publicly announce what is already the conviction of the faithful, or at least of a large majority of them. These democratic ecclesiologists strongly emphasize the "sense of the faithful" (*sensus fidelium*), which, according to Vatican II, is so assisted by the Holy Spirit that the people of God as a whole is infallible in its unanimous understanding of what constitutes a matter of faith.[6]

I am not sure whether any Catholic ecclesiologists go so far as to say that the pope can be bound by a majority vote of the bishops or that the bishops can be bound by a majority vote of the priests and faithful of their diocese. Such a view would be difficult to reconcile with Vatican I and with the whole tenor of the Catholic tradition. But because of the doctrine that the Holy Spirit is present in the whole Church as well as the rulers, majorities do have to be taken seriously. In actual practice, popes and bishops very rarely if ever seek to impose doctrines unless they believe those doctrines are already accepted by a large majority.

The attention given in modern theology to the active role of the faithful is in many ways a welcome development. It corrects certain exaggerations to which the hierocratic model is prone—especially the unhealthy concentration of all active power in the hands of a small ruling class, with the corresponding reduction of the lower classes in the Church to a state of passivity scarcely consonant with lively Christian commitment.

The main weakness of the democratic theory is that, like the hierocratic, it labors under a certain juridicism. Concerned with the formal aspects of authority, it overlooks the authority of the gospel or the content of revelation, which could conceivably be opposed to the drift of public opinion in the Church. Preoccupied with juridical structures, this theory leaves insufficient room for the inspirations and special graces bestowed by the Holy Spirit, who can raise up powerful voices of prophetic protest.

In contrast to some contemporary theologians of the Western world, I tend to be distrustful of majorities. I am fond of Kierkegaard's aphorism "The majority is always wrong." The *sensus fidelium*, as a theological font, should never be confused with the public-opinion poll. Not all in the Church are equally close to Christ and to the Holy Spirit. Many members of the Church are as much influenced by the mass media and the secular fashions of the day as they are by the gospel and Christian tradition. This does not mean, of course, that by taking power from the people and transferring it to a power elite one gets closer to the truth. The officials can easily make decisions in the light of their class interests and professional biases rather than the gospel itself. Where the teaching of the magisterium fails to resonate with the consciousness of the faithful at large, one has reason to suspect that the power of office has been incorrectly used.

In contradistinction to the hierocratic and democratic theories in their crude form, I should like to propose, as theologically more acceptable, a pluralistic theory of authority in the Church. The Church, I would maintain, depends for its health and vigor upon the coexistence of several distinct organs of authority, and hence on multiple groups of believers.[7] These authorities serve as mutual checks and balances. They exist in a state of natural tension and dialogue, and only when they spontaneously converge can authority make itself fully felt. The great French ecclesiologist Yves Congar has put the matter well:

> . . . if the question is to be considered theologically, it is impossible to restrict oneself to *a single* criterion, or to ancient texts without the "living magisterium," or to the living magisterium without the ancient texts, or to authority without the community, or to the latter without the former, or to the apostolicity of the ministry without the apostolicity of doctrine, or *vice versa*, or to the Roman Church separated from catholicity, or to the latter detached from the former. . . . All these criteria together should ensure a living faithfulness and identity in the full historicity of our lives and our knowledge. The fullness of the truth is associated with that of the means that God has given us to enable us to live by it; and with the totality of Christian existence.[8]

Among the authorities in the Church one must unquestionably include the documents which it recognizes as constitutive of its own beliefs. The canonical Scriptures, as we have said, serve as the basis and reference point of all Christian teaching. Anyone who seeks to impose beliefs and norms of conduct that evidently contravene the Scriptures will meet with deserved resistance. Even the magisterium of the Church, according to Vatican II, is not above the Word of God, but serves it.[9] A sound historicocritical approach, as cultivated by the community of biblical scholars, can prevent the Bible from being misused to support whatever anyone wants to maintain on nonbiblical grounds.

A second constitutive norm, which Catholics place on a par with the Bible, is sacred tradition. Tradition is known through various sedimentations, technically called the "monuments of tradition." They would include, most importantly, the solemn decisions of ecumenical councils. Unlike the Scriptures, these expressions of tradition, in Catholic theology, are not normally called the "word of God," but they bear witness to the word of God, and as such are authoritative.

Among the living voices that have authority in the Church I would mention, in the first place, the general sense of the faithful. This is to be obtained not simply by counting noses but by weighing opinions. The views of alert and committed Christians should be given more weight than those of indifferent or marginal Christians, but even the doubts of marginal persons should be attentively considered to see if they do not contain some prophetic message for the Church. The sense of the faithful should be seen not simply as a static index but as a process. If it becomes clear that large numbers of generous, intelligent, prayerful, and committed Christians who seriously study a given problem change their views in a certain direction, this may be evidence that the Holy Spirit is so inclining them. But there is need for caution and discernment to avoid mistaking the influences of secular fashion for the inspirations of divine grace.

In addition to the general community of the faithful, there are persons who by reason of their particular gifts or positions in the Church have special qualifications to speak with authority. Here I think one must consider three sets of factors: first, learning and other natural personal endowments, such as prudence and common sense; second, spiritual gifts such as faith and prophetic insight, attributable to prayerful intimacy with God; third, regular appointment to an office in the Church with the graces, concerns, and experiences that go with the office in question.

These three sets of qualifications can be brought into some kind of

loose correspondence with three types of ministry that have been recognized in the Church since biblical times: the doctoral, the prophetic, and the pastoral. For the first, the human gifts of intelligence
and learning are of chief importance; for the second, docility to the
Holy Spirit; for the third, regular appointment to office. It would be
a mistake to overlook the special authority of each of these three
types of witness.

The three classifications of ministry are not, of course, mutually
exclusive. A qualified teacher in the Church must be something
more than an intelligent and learned person; he must be open to the
movements of the Spirit and sensitive to pastoral concerns. So, likewise, the prophet may stand to gain if he is theologically educated
and pastorally responsive. The pastor, finally, should be sensitive to
the demands of sound doctrine and to the promptings of the Holy
Spirit. It is possible for teachers and prophets, as well as pastors, to
have a recognized office in the Church, as they would seem to have
had in New Testament times, at least at Antioch. It would be a mistake, therefore, to identify the official Church exclusively with pastoral administration or to look upon prophecy and teaching as merely
private charisms. The three types of ministry, while remaining distinct, should somewhat overlap and interpenetrate.

Is there a hierarchy of dignity among teachers, prophets, and pastors? To judge from the listings of charisms in the New Testament
(1 Cor 12:27–31; Eph 4:11), one would conclude that the highest of
the three in dignity are the prophets, who rank immediately after the
apostles in both listings.[10] The administrators (*kybernēseis*) in First
Corinthians rank not only after prophets and teachers, but after
wonder-workers and healers. In Ephesians, however, the pastors
(*poimenes*) rank after prophets and before teachers, or perhaps, according to another interpretation, the pastors in this text are the
same persons as the teachers. The presbyters (*presbyteroi*) and
bishops (*episkopoi*) do not appear in either list, but they are perhaps
to be equated with the administrators and/or pastors. The New Testament *episkopoi* are the ancestors of the modern bishops, but are
not identical.[11] They seem to have been something like an executive
board of the presbyters, and combined in their persons some administrative and pastoral roles together with certain functions of pro-

claiming, teaching, and supervising doctrine. Like all the other officers, the *episkopoi* were subordinate to the apostles, so long as the apostles were still alive. Their authority, moreover, appears to have extended only to the local church.

Since biblical times the *episkopoi* have risen in status so as to occupy the highest rank in the ecclesiastical hierarchy. The term "successors of the apostles" is sometimes applied to the bishops and the bishops alone. This title could be misleading for three reasons: First, the apostles were founders of the Church, and as such they have no successors. Second the apostles, as wandering missionaries, did not have regular administrative responsibility for any particular local church. Third, we have no clear biblical or historical evidence that the apostles designated any particular class of persons in the Church to take over their transmissible functions. Still, the expression "successors of the apostles" can, if necessary, be defended.[12] For the bishops, in modern ecclesiastical polity, have a kind of general supervision, on the highest level, of all the functions of the Church, and in this way they resemble the New Testament *apostoloi*, at least as portrayed in the early chapters of Acts.

The precise reasons for the emergence of the *episkopoi* as a kind of ruling class in the Church need not concern us here. Presumably the power shift had something to do with the necessity of strong organizational structures to ward off heresies such as Gnosticism, Marcionism, and Montanism and to equip the Church to stand up under the pressures of persecution. It seems likely, too, that religious leaders imitated, consciously or unconsciously, the civil structure of government in the Roman Empire.

In the post-Tridentine Church, and in the Neo-Scholastic theology of the nineteenth and twentieth centuries, the dialectical tension between the charisms in the Church is virtually eliminated. All authentic teaching power is simply transferred to the episcopal order. The main disadvantage in this system is that the bishop is given an almost unbearable load of responsibility. He becomes in his diocese —at least theoretically—not only the highest administrator but also the chief priest and the supreme teacher. In this last capacity he is supposed to be in a position to settle intellectually all disputed doctrinal questions. To illustrate this awesome doctrinal responsibility, one may refer, for example, to the Ethical and Religious Directives for Catholic Health Facilities issued by the United States bishops in 1971, which state:

> The moral evaluation of new scientific developments and legitimately debated questions must be finally submitted to the teaching authority of the church in the person of the local bishop, who has the ultimate responsibility for teaching Catholic doctrine.[13]

In order to encourage the vigorous exercise of this responsibility, and to facilitate compliance with the bishop's doctrinal decisions, the authors strongly emphasize the grace of the episcopal office. They frequently quote St. Irenaeus to the effect that the bishops have the "sure charism of truth" (*charisma veritatis certum*).[14] But they neglect to mention that Irenaeus in this passage acknowledges that presbyters as well as bishops have this "charisma." Furthermore, according to many commentators, *charisma veritatis* in this passage signifies not a subjective grace for discerning the truth but the objective deposit of faith, "the precious and spiritual gift entrusted to the Church."[15] Irenaeus, speaking to the situation of his own time, was presumably referring to the fact that the apostles had thoroughly instructed the persons to whom they turned over the leadership of the apostolic churches.

The Neo-Scholastic theory, in my opinion, is very unconvincing. It fails to give a rationale for the kind of collaboration between bishops and theologians that has normally existed in the Church. There are ample resources for a better theory both in the New Testament and in the earlier theological tradition.

From the Acts and the Pauline letters, one has the impression that there was a special class of individuals in the early church recognized as having received from the Holy Spirit the gift of teaching Christian doctrine.[16] The *didaskaloi* could teach in their own right, and were not viewed as mere representatives of *episkopoi* or *presbyteroi*. The *episkopos* was primarily an administrator or, perhaps better, a pastor—a true shepherd of the flock. The presbyter-bishop was expected, among other things, to be "an apt teacher" (1 Tim 3:2; cf. Tit 1:9), but he was not expected to be a paragon of learning or to appropriate all doctrinal functions to himself. In many passages the *didaskaloi* are seen as a distinct class. According to Paul's ecclesiastical polity, as set forth in First Corinthians, the various ministries in the Church are bound together by mutual interdependence, as are the organs in a living body. Just as the eye and the ear cannot say to each other, "I have no need of you," so the teacher, the prophet, and the administrator must recognize their dependence upon one another for the sake of better service to the entire Christian community.

If this is true, it would seem to follow that those who have the specialization of teaching in the Church should have a voice in doctrinal decisions. In the words of a contemporary New Testament scholar:

> . . . if there is any group in the church which has the right to be heard when the church makes decisions it is that composed of those to whom the charism of teaching has been given, the *didaskaloi*, who, in the list of 1 Cor 12:28 rank third after the apostles and prophets. If this charism now exists in the Church apart from the hierarchy—and to deny that it does is utterly arbitrary—it is surely possessed by the theologians. If the "whole church" is to have a part in the making of decisions, particularly in the making of decisions which bear upon the content of faith, the proper authority of the theologians must be given much more weight than is often the case in the present functioning of the church.[17]

In the early centuries the concentration of authority in the episcopal office did no great harm because the bishops of those times were less heavily burdened with administrative responsibilities than are their modern successors. Many of them were charismatic leaders and theologians. Irenaeus and Cyprian, Augustine and Leo, Athanasius and Chrysostom, Cyril of Jerusalem and Cyril of Alexandria, Gregory of Nyssa and Gregory of Nazianzus—these and many other great patristic theologians were also bishops.

In the Middle Ages, the doctoral function once again had a certain autonomy. As the cathedral schools outgrew the personal control of the bishops and evolved into universities with theological faculties, the *magistri* and *doctores* were seen as the primary teachers. Thomas Aquinas, for instance, makes a sharp distinction between the *officium praelationis* (prelacy), possessed by the bishop, and the *officium magisterii* (magisterium), which belongs to the professional theologian.[18] In one text he does speak of a magisterium of

bishops, but only in a qualified sense; for he draws a distinction between the *magisterium cathedrae pastoralis* (pastoral magisterium),
which belongs to the bishop, and the *magisterium cathedrae magis-
tralis* (magisterial magisterium), which pertains to the theologian.[19]
The former, he holds, is concerned with the regulation of preaching
and public order in the church rather than with the intricacies of
speculation.[20] The *magistri*, according to St. Thomas, teach by
learning and argument rather than by appeal to their official status.
The conclusions are no more valid than the evidence they are able to
adduce. In this sense, therefore, the magisterium of the theologians
is unauthoritative.[21]

In the course of the thirteenth century we see the beginnings of
what Yves Congar calls a "magisterium of doctors" in the Church.[22]
Over and above the task of scientific teaching, doctors and university
faculties begin to acquire a certain decisive role, especially in judging
cases of alleged heresy. The *studium* thus gradually takes its place as
a third force in Christendom, alongside the *sacerdotium* and the *reg-
num*. By order of Pope Clement V, the decrees of the Council of
Vienne (1311–12) were not made official until they had been submitted to the universities for approval. At a number of councils in
the later Middle Ages, including Constance and Basel, the theologians were given a deliberative vote even though they were not
bishops.[23] Facts such as these call into question the correctness of
the statement, so often made in the past century, that theologians
do not belong to the magisterium.

I recognize, of course, that theologians, whose energies are so often
taken up with subtle speculative questions, are not always well suited
to make decisions of a practical nature concerning the government
and public preaching of the Church. It is necessary that there be pastoral authorities whose main concern is to supervise the mission and
good order of the Church as a community of faith and witness. On
the other hand, it is important that questions touching on the order
of revelation and theology should not be settled without regard for
the demands of truth and scholarship. In questions of a mixed nature, involving both pastoral and academic considerations, there is
need for close collaboration between bishops, as holders of the chief
pastoral power, and theologians.[24]

In making this recommendation I feel that I am merely articulating what is in practice developing. At Vatican II the theologians had considerable visibility, and in some cases it was well known that they were the real authors of certain speeches given by bishops and of certain sections of conciliar documents. Since the Council Pope Paul VI has set up an International Theological Commission that, even with limited autonomy, speaks in its own name. In the United States, as elsewhere, efforts are being made to establish regular working relationships between the bishops and learned societies such as the Catholic Theological Society of America, the Canon Law Society of America, and others. Groups of theologians collaborate closely with the National Conference of Catholic Bishops, especially through its Commission for Ecumenical and Interreligious Affairs. Both in the United States and abroad, it is common for consensus statements emanating from ecumenical dialogues to be signed by bishops and by theologians as coauthors. This practice might in the course of time be extended to other statements, more properly magisterial in character.

The tendencies represented by these new initiatives are in my opinion signs of closer collaboration, without confusion, between the scholarly and the pastoral functions in the Church. As this process continues, it may become possible for scholars to have a greater initiative in selecting their colleagues who are to be in contact with the pope and the bishops, lest those who do collaborate come to be labeled "court theologians." I would hope also that there could be regular consultations in which theologians would have an appropriate input into the agenda.

The proper balance of authority demands that theologians should not be merely apologists for what the pastoral leaders decide, nor mere consultors to the pastors (though they may well be this *also*), but that they have a recognized voice in the Church, with a certain relative autonomy to develop their own positions by their own methodology and to seek to gain acceptance for these positions by the pastoral magisterium.

In speaking of the scholar's independence I am by no means returning to the position of Kant, rejected at the beginning of this chapter, but I am, I would hope, recognizing what is sound in the Kantian thesis. With Kant I would hold that it is possible and necessary to assess authoritative pronouncements in the light of rational criteria, but against him I am maintaining that theology is as much concerned with truth as are philosophy and the natural sciences. The theologian can be a true scholar—one who asks the hard questions and honestly expresses his real convictions—without on that account being less bound to the community of faith or less respectful toward the authorities recognized in the Church. In fact the Catholic Christian, reflecting on the faith, will find positive aids to truth in all the types of authority discussed in the preceding pages—the Bible, the "sense of the faithful," and the decisions reached in previous ages through interaction among pastors, prophets, and theologians. None of these instances, in my opinion, is a peremptory authority in isolation from the others, but in combination they afford the guidance needed for the sustenance of Christian faith and the progress of theology. Christian theology, as I understand the term, presupposes a commitment to the saving truth disclosed in the Christian sources.[25]

To give a somewhat practical turn to what I have been saying about teaching authority, I should like to conclude with some observations on dissent. This problem is, I suspect, one that will never cease to recur both in civil society and in the Church. There will always be painful conflicts between some who are sincerely convinced that certain ideas are intolerable within the community of faith and others who believe these same ideas are true or at least compatible with Christian commitment. I cannot propose a full solution, but pastors and theologians can, I think, fruitfully ponder together the sources of the difficulty and the best ways of treating conflicts so that they do not become destructive.

Dissent, in the sense in which we are using the term, is a matter internal to the society in which the opposite position is normative. Dissent in the Church means that a member of the Church takes exception to the position that has become official. Dissent therefore cannot be absolute. It occurs within the context of a larger agreement—namely, the acceptance of Christ as the supreme revelation of God and of the Church as the place where Christ is made specially present and accessible.

Generally speaking, dissent pertains not to fundamental articles of faith, which are regarded as constitutive of membership, but to relatively secondary teachings. Dissent can exist within the Church because it is not usual, nor would it be proper, to impose the supreme penalty of excommunication for views not infallibly proclaimed as pertaining to the very substance of the faith. Thus it is possible to be a Christian and a member of the Church even when one disagrees with certain official teachings.

The problem of dissent has always existed in the Church, but has not always been equally acute. In the "fortress Church" of the past several centuries, dissent was kept to a minimum. Catholics felt a strong obligation to stick together for the sake of survival, and were therefore willing to subject their personal judgment to that of the ruling authorities. The ecclesiology of nineeenth-century Neo-Scholasticism, with its heavy stress on "official charisms," tended to reinforce the authority structures. Dissent was handled by essentially the same moral principles as were applied to the case of an erroneous conscience, and thus insufficient consideration was given to the possibility that dissent might be a corrective force in the Church.[26]

The phenomenon of dissent has been intensified in recent years by all the factors that have tended to weaken the "hierocratic" view of authority and to substitute the kind of pluralistic or dialogic view I have attempted to sketch. Three aspects of the general climate of ideas may be singled out for special mention.

1. Under the influence of psychological and philosophical currents, our age has become particularly sensitive to the values of freedom and authenticity, and to the dignity of conscience as the ultimate norm for moral choice. Typical of our times is an abhorrence of laws and institutions that inhibit personal freedom, and a deep conviction that true religion should help its adherents to become mature, responsible persons. As previously explained, this does not mean a rejection of authority but it does involve a certain relativizing of authority.

2. Thanks to modern means of travel and communications, the believer almost inevitably lives in a pluralistic situation, at the intersection of many different cultures and traditions. This pluralism was sanctioned by Vatican II, which invited the Church to seek out new forms of solidarity with the various cultures of humankind. There are increasingly few protected havens in which the mind of the faithful is predominantly formed by official Catholic teaching.

3. The Freudian and Marxist critiques of ideology, combined with

evident abuses of power on the part of leaders in the political and economic world, have made us acutely aware that officeholders are under a constant temptation to employ their power to bolster up their position. When popes and bishops insist very heavily on apostolic succession, divine right, and the special graces attached to their office, they leave themselves open to the suspicion that ideology is at work.

Vatican II, in its formal discussion of the teaching authority of popes and bishops, did not directly challenge the reigning Neo-Scholastic theory. Article 25 of the Constitution on the Church may be interpreted as supporting the standard position of the day. It affirms the obligation to assent to the ordinary noninfallible teaching of the Roman pontiff without any explicit mention of the right to dissent. Several bishops at the Council submitted a proposal that allowance should be made for the case of an educated person who for solid reasons finds himself unable to assent internally to such teaching. To this the Doctrinal Commission replied that "approved theological explanations should be consulted."[27] Thus the Council in its formal teaching did not advance the discussion of dissent beyond where it had been in the previous generation.

Indirectly, however, the Council worked powerfully to undermine the authoritarian theory and to legitimate dissent in the Church. This it did in part by insisting on the necessary freedom of the act of faith and by attributing a primary role to personal conscience in the moral life. By contrast, the Neo-Scholastic doctrine of the magisterium, with its heavy accentuation of "blind obedience," minimizes the value of understanding and maturity in the life of faith.

Most importantly for our purposes, Vatican II quietly reversed the earlier positions of the Roman magisterium on a number of important issues. The obvious examples are well known. In biblical studies, for instance, the Constitution on Divine Revelation accepted a critical approach to the Bible, thus supporting the previous initiatives of Pius XII and delivering the Church once and for all from the incubus of the earlier decrees of the Biblical Commission. In the Decree on Ecumenism, the Council cordially greeted the ecumenical movement and involved the Catholic Church in the larger quest for Christian unity, thus putting an end to the hostility enshrined in Pius XII's *Mortalium animos*. In Church-state relations, the Declaration on Religious Freedom accepted the religiously neutral state, thus reversing the previously approved view that the state should formally profess the truth of Catholicism. In the theology of secular realities, the Pastoral Constitution on the Church in the Modern World adopted an evolutionary view of history and a modified optimism regarding secular systems of thought, thus terminating more than a century of vehement denunciations of modern civilization.[28]

As a result of these and other revisions, the Council rehabilitated many theologians who had suffered under severe restrictions with regard to their ability to teach and publish. The names of John Courtney Murray, Pierre Teilhard de Chardin, Henri de Lubac, and Yves Congar, all under a cloud of suspicion in the 1950s, suddenly became surrounded with a bright halo of enthusiasm.

By its actual practice of revision, the Council implicitly taught the legitimacy and even the value of dissent. In effect the Council said that the ordinary magisterium of the Roman pontiff had fallen into error and had unjustly harmed the careers of loyal and able scholars. Some of the thinkers who had resisted official teaching in the preconciliar period were among the principal precursors and architects of Vatican II.

As a result of the conciliar experience, together with the general climate of ideas previously alluded to, dissent is today perceived by many sophisticated Catholics as an inevitable and potentially beneficial phenomenon. Many would not wish to have a situation, even if it were possible, in which every Catholic agreed with every stated position of the hierarchy. On the other hand, dissent can be a source of confusion and discord; it is not something to be desired for its own sake. To alleviate the harmful effects of dissent, I would submit the following recommendations:

1. The pastoral magisterium should keep in close touch with the theologians and other intellectuals in the Church. Popes and bishops would do well not to act without benefit of the best available scholarship, as happened, to the detriment of the Church, when the Biblical Commission issued some of its less enlightened decrees. Conversely, scholars in the Church should try to cultivate greater sensitivity to pastoral considerations.

2. Generally speaking, the pastoral leaders should not speak in a

binding way unless a relatively wide consensus has first been achieved. For authentic consensus to develop, there is need of free discussion. Only when it becomes clear through such discussion that the weight of responsible opinion decisively favors one side over the other can true consensus arise.

3. Where no such consensus exists, it is well to acknowledge publicly that good Christians do in fact disagree. Such disagreement will hardly be scandalous in our times, when open clashes of opinion are common in the scientific and political worlds. It would, however, be scandalous for the holders of pastoral power to suppress freedom of expression and debate on issues where there is as yet no agreed solution.

4. Even where there is no consensus, popes, bishops, and others in authority may clearly and candidly state their convictions on matters of pastoral importance and seek to win assent for their own positions by giving testimony and adducing arguments. If they do this without trying to impose their views by juridical pressures, they will generally meet with a favorable response on the part of the faithful who are hungry for pastoral leadership.

5. When members of the Church find themselves sincerely unable to give assent to a given teaching of the pastoral authorities, they should not feel that they are on that account disloyal or unfaithful. Noninfallible teaching, as Richard A. McCormick has pointed out, does not bring with it an immediate obligation to assent. Rather, it calls for "religious docility and deference—always on the assumption, of course, that authority has proceeded properly."[29] In view of such deference, the dissenter will be reluctant to conclude that the official teaching is clearly erroneous; he will carefully reassess his own position in the light of that teaching; and he will behave in a manner that fosters respect and support for the pastoral magisterium, even through he continues to strive for a revision of the current official teaching.

6. Provided that they speak with evident loyalty and respect for authority, dissenters should not be silenced. As already noted, experience has shown that in many cases those who dissent from church teaching in one generation are preparing the official positions of the Church in the future. Vatican II owes many of its successes to the

very theologians who were under a cloud in the pontificate of Pius XII. The Church, like civil society, should cherish its "loyal opposition" as a precious asset.

These principles, although they seem quite evident in the light of the general ecclesiology governing this study, will be contested by some. There are still those who look upon the Church as an institution that must give oracular responses to all really important questions, and who consequently regard dissent as tantamount to disloyalty. My own point of view is governed by the vision of the Church as a pilgrim community renewing itself by creative interaction with its changing environment. The Church, "like a pilgrim in a foreign land," receives from the risen Lord not a clear vision of ultimate truth but the power "to show forth in the world the mystery of the Lord in a faithful though shadowed way, until at last it will be revealed in total splendor."[30] Thus the Church may in some sense be called a "Society of Explorers"—to borrow a term from Michael Polanyi's prescription for the scientific community.[31] The Church, like any other society, needs outside criticism, and depends on all the help that its thoughtful members can provide in the task of discerning the real meaning of the gospel for our time. Faith, then, is not simply a matter of accepting a fixed body of doctrine. More fundamentally, it is a committed and trustful participation in an ongoing process. In the course of responsible discussion, certain previously accepted doctrines will be modified. For progress to be achieved, there must be discussion, and for there to be discussion, all must be assured of their "lawful freedom of inquiry and of thought, and of the freedom to express their minds humbly and courageously about those matters in which they enjoy competence."[32] Without such freedom, and thus without the possibility of dissent, the Church would be deprived of that creative interaction which, as we have seen, is the key to authentic renewal.

VI. Toward a Renewed Papacy

Among the symbols of Catholic identity, none is more focal than the papacy. The life of the Catholic Christian is by no means centered on the papacy; it ought, at least, to be centered on God and on Jesus Christ. But belief in the central Christian mysteries concerning the triune God and the redemptive Incarnation is something that Roman Catholics happily share with other Christians. When asked what makes them different, what is distinctive to themselves, Catholics point, first of all, to the papacy. Because of its importance as a symbol of Catholic identity, the papacy is, for Catholics and for others, laden with much emotion.

In the present age of revisionism, the papacy, like many other Catholic symbols, has become a sign of contradiction. Some Catholics, strongly committed to the specifics of their own tradition, look upon the pope as the guardian and cornerstone of faith. To them, any questioning or limitation of papal authority is treasonous; it plays into the hands of the enemy and damages the Catholic cause. Others, committed to a thoroughgoing renewal of the Church, hold that for the effectiveness of renewal it is essential that the papacy be rethought and restructured. "Papal primacy," some assert, "as presently exercised, constitutes a block both to further development of the ecumenical movement and to reform movements within the Catholic Church."[1] In this chapter I shall consider the papacy chiefly as an inner-Catholic problem, but at the end I shall add some reflections on the ecumenical dimensions of the problem.

The Roman Catholic doctrine of the papacy, as we know it today, is a product of the nineteenth century. More specifically, it belongs to the pontificate of Pius IX, and it received its most authoritative expression at Vatican Council I (1869–70). That Council, in *Pastor aeternus*, defined under anathema that the papacy is of divine institution, that the pope enjoys a primacy of jurisdiction (and not simply of honor) over all particular churches, pastors, and believers; and that, when he speaks *ex cathedra* as successor of Blessed Peter, he is gifted with infallibility.

The definitions of *Pastor aeternus* depend for their full intelligibility on the historical situation of the Church in Western Europe in the second half of the nineteenth century.[2] It was an era of legitimism and restorationism, when many religious thinkers were in full reaction against the excesses of the Enlightenment and of the French Revolution. Liberalism was seen as the archenemy of the Christian spirit, and faith was extolled as an obedient submission of the mind of man to the revealing word of God. The Church was esteemed as the chief bulwark of divine truth and order against what Newman called "the wild living intellect of man."[3] In some countries, such as Germany and the Austro-Hungarian Empire, efforts had recently been made to give the national hierarchies virtual autonomy from Roman authority. Many Catholics, disturbed by these efforts, and viewing the relative weakness of the Church of England under Queen Victoria, felt the necessity of a strong ecclesiastical government on the international level. They looked to the papacy to give splendor and dignity to the Christian religion and to prevent the Church from being fragmented and manipulated by ambitious political rulers. The idea of a powerful papacy appealed to those who wanted to see the Church prophetically denounce what were thought to be the chief evils of the time—liberalism, nationalism, secularism, relativism, and the like.

It is scarcely surprising, therefore, that the work of Vatican I manifests a rather negative attitude toward the modern world with its glorification of liberty and progress. The council documents are by our contemporary standards highly authoritarian in tone. Vatican II, meeting almost a century later, reflects a vastly changed situation. By the middle of the twentieth century the Catholic Church felt itself, in the words of Charles Davis, "culturally estranged from the modern world."[4] For its own vitality and enrichment, as well as for the effectiveness of its mission, the Church saw a real need to participate more fully in the struggles and experiences of the whole human family and to assimilate into its own thinking and practice whatever was healthy in the modern mentality.

In comparing the pronouncements of the two Vatican Councils, one finds clear points of contrast. Vatican I shows a concern for the unchanging identity of the Church and gives little play to historical change and inner pluralism. Vatican II, on the other hand, reflects an acute historical consciousness and a sensitivity to the variety of human cultures. Vatican I speaks in categories that are abstract, scholastic, metaphysical, and juridical. Vatican II prefers to speak in more vivid and concrete language, using historical and empirical categories. Vatican I sees divine truth as coming to the faithful through the mediation of their appointed hierarchical leaders; it suggests a pyramidal model, in which revelation descends from the pope through the bishops to the pastors, who then mediate it by their preaching to the laity. Vatican II accents the value of lay initiatives and the freedom of the Holy Spirit to bestow his charisms as he pleases. Vatican I emphasizes the sufficiency of the Catholic Church as the authorized mediator of the gospel. Vatican II acknowledges the necessity of openness to values present in the teaching of groups external to the Roman Catholic community. For the authoritarian, defensive stance of Vatican I, Vatican II substitutes a posture of friendliness, self-criticism, and adaptability.

For the contemporary Catholic who fully accepts the attitudes of Vatican II as here characterized, the doctrine of Vatican I concerning the papacy seems in need of considerable explanation. Many would speak, with Gustave Thils, of the necessity of revision.[5] Revision, however, is a delicate operation since Vatican I laid such heavy emphasis on the irreformability of the divinely given structures and teachings of the Church. In view of the claim of divine institution made for the papacy, it might seem that any significant modification of the doctrine of primacy would fly in the face of the clear teaching of the Council.

A full solution to this difficulty would require a lengthy discussion of the subtleties of hermeneutics. For present purposes, it may suffice to recall that dogmatic statements are not immune to hermeneutical treatment. They need to be reinterpreted so as to bridge the gap between the era when they were written—with its own concerns, presuppositions, conceptuality, and literary and linguistic conventions—and the interpreter's own era, in which all of these variables will have changed. *Mysterium ecclesiae*, the previously mentioned 1973 declaration on infallibility issued by the Congregation for the Doctrine of the Faith, recognizes the historically conditioned character of dogmatic pronouncements and calls attention to the need of updating them according to the exigencies of the times.[6] The process of reinterpretation is, self-evidently, an unending one. No one interpretation can be imposed as definitive for all future time.

In the following paragraphs an attempt will be made to explore the need and possibility of reinterpreting three of the key assertions of Vatican I: the divine institution of the papal office, the pope's primacy of jurisdiction, and his infallibility.

The question of divine institution became central in the Protestant-Catholic polemical exchanges of the sixteenth century.[7] By and large, both sides agreed that divine institution meant establishment through God's special intervention in history. With reference to the Church this meant, in effect, establishment by the historical Jesus Christ. The assumption was that Jesus had equipped the Church of the first generation with everything essential for its mission to the end of time. Protestants and Catholics, while they were at one in holding that the divine patrimony was permanently sufficient for the Church, disagreed about whether certain ecclesiastical doctrines, offices, and rites belonged to this patrimony. They disagreed also regarding the criteria. Protestants generally held that the criterion of divine institution was an explicit dominical injunction contained in Scripture, such as was given in favor of baptism in Matthew 28:19. Catholics replied that there were many things taught by our Lord not written in Scripture but handed down, at least in the early generations, by oral tradition.

With regard to the papacy, Catholics maintained that its divine institution was attested by certain Petrine texts, such as Matthew 16:17–19, Luke 22:32, and John 21:15–17. These texts, as interpreted in the Catholic tradition, referred not simply to the historical Peter but to his successors to the end of time. The Protestants often denied that these texts established a genuine primacy of Peter among the apostles; quite universally, they denied that these texts could properly be understood as applying to the bishops of Rome.

Today the interconfessional polemics regarding these Petrine texts have considerably abated. Scripture scholars of all traditions are inclined to agree that, while many texts, such as those cited above, portray Jesus as conferring upon Peter a certain pre-eminence among the apostles, nevertheless there is no direct biblical proof for the institution of the papacy as a continuing office in the Church.[8] The idea of an abiding primatial office, or papacy, does not seem to be clearly demanded by Scripture. On the other hand, such a primacy is in no way contrary to Scripture; it is rather favored by those texts which attribute a universal pastoral ministry to Peter.

Can it be maintained that in spite of the lack of any clear biblical attestation, the papacy was specifically instituted by the historical Jesus Christ? The idea that Christ's establishment of this office was known from the beginning and was continuously handed down in oral tradition runs up against the great difficulty that no one seems to have thought of the papacy as a permanent office until about the middle of the third century. Rome did indeed have a certain preeminence among Christian churches, but this status was not ascribed to the fact that Peter had been bishop of Rome or that the pope was Peter's successor in that office. Rather, the emergence of the Roman "primacy" was apparently due to the convergence of a number of factors—most importantly, the dignity of Rome as the only apostolic church in the West, the tradition that both Peter and Paul had been martyred there, the long history of Rome as capital of the Empire, and its continuing position as the chief center of commerce and communications. These and other factors helped to confer prestige, wealth, vigor, and influence upon the Roman Church.

Historical investigation shows that the claims made by and on behalf of the bishop of Rome developed very gradually.[9] The crucial period was from the middle of the third century to the middle of the fifth. Even by that time, Rome had a very different relationship to the churches of the West than to those of the East, which had their own apostolic or patriarchal sees to which they looked for direction. As the Eastern churches were subsequently weakened by mutual rivalries, Rome was increasingly called upon to play the role of judge or arbiter. The rise of the Frankish empire in the West and the Muslim pressure on the Eastern churches brought the primacy of Rome to a culmination.

In view of this complicated process of development—all too briefly summarized in the preceding paragraph—it seems simplistic to speak of the papacy as having been "divinely instituted" in the sense that the term would have had in the sixteenth century. Of course it may plausibly be held, from within the Roman Catholic tradition, that the process of development was divinely intended, or even that it was brought about by some kind of special divine providence; but this is not to claim divine institution for the papacy in the traditional sense. The idea of a providential development, even if admitted, leaves open the question of a possible further development that would leave the papacy behind.

For the modern mind, steeped in historical consciousness, the ancient category of "divine institution" has become problematic. Historically, it is most difficult to ascertain just what Jesus did intend for his Church. The New Testament already gives us a picture colored by the theology of the community in a post-Resurrection situation. Even if it can be established that Jesus organized his community in some definite way, it does not necessarily follow that he intended to impose that order as an immutable law binding on all future generations. The presumption is rather that he would have intended the Church to be capable of modifying its polity as might be necessary to meet the needs of later centuries. The best order for the infant Church might differ radically from the order most suitable for the Church of the nineteenth or twentieth century. Interest today focuses less upon what Jesus "instituted" than upon what form of church order is most viable for our time.

Not surprisingly, therefore, in both the international and American Lutheran–Roman Catholic dialogues, the panels agreed that the concept of "divine institution," so prominent in the sixteenth-century debates, is no longer a helpful category.[10] Divine institution implies a rather static or nonevolutionary view of the Church, today rejected by many sophisticated theologians, both Protestant and Catholic.

For a contemporary approach to the problem of papacy, a more fruitful notion would seem to be that of the "Petrine function" or "Petrine ministry."[11] As already mentioned, many New Testament passages attribute to Peter a particular responsibility for the mission and unity of the Church as a whole. This function, it is argued, is permanently necessary, for if no one is charged with the universal direction of the Church, fragmentation and anarchy cannot be avoided —a consequence to which history bears abundant witness. In theory, the Petrine function could be performed either by a single individual presiding over the whole Church or by some kind of committee, board, synod, or parliament—possibly with a "division of powers" into judicial, legislative, administrative, and the like. Vatican I seems to argue that dissidence will be most effectively precluded if a single individual performs the Petrine function. While this may be true as a general rule, it must also be admitted that ecumenical councils have often had a status in the Church at least equal to that of the popes. In certain crises—e.g., when there is no pope or when there is an unresolved doubt about the identity of the true pope—some other agency than the pope must play the decisive unifying role. Vatican I, which situated supreme authority in the pope, left some uncertainty regarding the relations between the papacy, the universal episcopate, and ecumenical councils (which are not necessarily mere meetings of bishops). Since this uncertainty was not fully cleared up by Vatican II, the question of the supreme directive power in the Church still requires further discussion within the Roman Catholic communion. At present the prevalent assumption seems to be that the pope should have supreme power in the ordinary administration of the Church, but that, in crisis situations, he should convoke ecumenical councils at which all the bishops deliberate and decide with him what course should be pursued. The absence of any constitution or "fundamental law" in the Catholic Church preserves a large measure of vagueness and flexibility regarding the rights and duties of various officers and agencies.

Even the meaning of the term "papacy" is not as clear as might be thought. Catholics generally speak of it as if it were identical with the pope himself, for the pope, at least in theory, has unlimited power over all the Roman congregations, secretariats, and the like. In practice, however, these agencies partly escape the pope's control and operate according to their own principles. The inevitability that there be a certain division of labor in the papacy could at some future time call for changes that would make the papacy more like a "constitutional" government, with a legally sanctioned separation of powers. The Catholic Church might experience a constitutional evolution somewhat similar to that of England, for example, in modern times.

It is often asked whether it is absolutely necessary, according to Catholic doctrine, that the successor of Peter should be the bishop of Rome. Vatican Council I did not wish to condemn the opinion of Bañez and others that the primacy could for good reason be separated at some future time from the Roman see.[12] When the Bishop of Granada requested that the connection between the primacy and the Roman see be defined as being *de iure divino*, he received the reply: "The most reverend Father has spoken learnedly and piously, but not every pious opinion can be inserted into a Dogmatic Constitution."[13] In principle, therefore, it remains open to discussion whether someone other than the bishop of Rome might someday be the primate of the Catholic Church. It would be conceivable, for example, that the bishop of another city might hold the primacy, or that the papacy might rotate among several sees, somewhat as the presidency of the Security Council in the United Nations rotates among representatives of various nations.

From the Roman Catholic point of view, the essential would seem to be that the Petrine function should be institutionalized in some way so that there is in the government of the universal Church an effective sign and instrument of unity. For symbolic efficacy, there are many advantages in having a single person as the bearer of this august office, and in view of the long tradition in favor of Rome as the primatial see, Catholics would be reluctant to see the primacy transferred elsewhere. While understandably attached to the good things in their own tradition, Catholics would be well advised not to assume too easily that the forms of government to which they have become accustomed will necessarily survive to the end of time. For the renewal of the structures of their own Church, Catholics would do well to attend to the experiences and reflections of other Christian groups who have had to wrestle with the problem of worldwide spiritual authority in their own traditions. Common consultations about such matters can redound to the advantage of all who take part in them.

According to Vatican Council I, the pope, as successor of Peter, has received by divine right a primacy not of honor alone but of true and proper jurisdiction.[14] The jurisdiction of the pope, according to the Council, is universal, ordinary, immediate, truly episcopal, supreme, and full.[15]

Quite apart from the question of divine institution, already discussed, these statements are ecumenically difficult, for they run directly counter to the teaching not only of Protestants but also of Anglican and Orthodox Christians, many of whom would be willing to concede that the pope has, at least by human right, a primacy of honor. Increasingly, Roman Catholics themselves have found difficulty in the claim of papal jurisdiction, with all the resounding adjectives attached to it by Vatican I.

"Jurisdiction," as currently employed, is a legal term derived from the Roman juridical tradition. It referred initially to relationships within a sovereign state. On the basis of a certain analogy between the kinds of power exercised in the Church and in the state, the term gradually came to be applied to the Church also. In point of fact, the Roman Catholic Church, especially in the late medieval and early modern periods, took on many of the features of the secular state. But this political model does not seem particularly helpful for describing the primitive Church, as understood by John or Paul, and it is of diminishing applicability to the Church in our own times, when the Church, as we shall see in our next chapter, is taking on many of the features of a voluntary society.

Historically, the attribution of jurisdiction to the bishop of Rome was a gradual development. As Batiffol and others have pointed out, papal influence in the first three centuries had a different character in various zones.[16] In Italy the bishop of Rome exercised strict jurisdiction over all the bishops, whose metropolitan he was. In the remainder of the West (except for certain privileged areas such as Africa), the bishop of Rome was a supermetropolitan, intervening only in *causae majores*. In the East, the churches enjoyed full canonical autonomy under their own metropolitans and supermetropolitans (the future patriarchates). These Eastern churches, however, admitted a certain primacy in the Roman see, to which they accorded what was called a *"praecellentia fidei."* The churches outside the Roman Empire, such as those of Persia and Abyssinia, had a still more tenuous relationship to Rome.

Only in the Middle Ages, when the Church reacted defensively against the encroachments of the Frankish empire, did something like universal spiritual jurisdiction begin to be claimed for the popes. To St. Thomas in the thirteenth century and Suárez in the sixteenth, it seemed obvious that the Church was a strict monarchy, in which all bishops depended for their jurisdiction on the positive action of the pope. In the context of opinions such as these, Vatican I maintained that Jesus had conferred on Peter "true and proper jurisdiction" over the entire Church. From the standpoint of the contemporary scholar, it is questionable whether the term "jurisdiction" was a felicitous one, since it seems to juridicize unduly the authority given to Peter. The New Testament, for instance, gives no clear indication that Peter was empowered by Christ to make laws in the Church, and without this power the modern concept of jurisdiction would not be verified.

Even at Vatican I the concept of jurisdiction was hotly debated. The language of *Pastor aeternus*, in chapter 3, is unquestionably taken from Roman canon law, but the intention, as explained at the Council, was to express a properly theological and scriptural reality. In the course of the debate Bishop Krementz, the future Cardinal Archbishop of Cologne, emphatically declared:

> The notion of *plenitudo potestatis* is not to be sought from the analogy of worldly powers, or arbitrary and highly subtle explanations of terms, in which everyone finds what he is looking for, but is to be derived from the constitution that Christ the Lord gave to his Church, and the government of this Church cannot be adequately compared to a monarchy, whether absolute or limited, or to an aristocracy or any such thing.[17]

Bishop Federico Zinelli, the official reporter for chapter 3 of *Pastor aeternus*, made the point that the meaning of the term "jurisdiction" in this chapter is qualified by its adjectival modifiers. In particular, he contended, the term "episcopal" should make it clear that the pope's authority is that of a pastor, whose mission it is to feed the flocks entrusted to his care. Just as individual bishops are commissioned to feed the particular flocks committed to them, so Zinelli argued, the pope is commissioned to pasture the whole flock of Christ.[18] Following this line of thought, we may conclude that the universal jurisdiction of the pope as Peter's successor, grounded in Jesus' promises to Peter, is in a very different category than the jurisdiction exercised by a patriarch or metropolitan over some group of churches as a matter of human and ecclesiastical law.

Even with all these qualifications, some Catholics continue to question the appropriateness of the term "jurisdiction" as applied to the kind of authority that the pope should have over the other bishops. As Cornelius Ernst points out, Vatican I posed the question in terms of an opposition between two types of primacy—honor and jurisdiction—so that the term "jurisdiction" was used to exclude a mere primacy of honor.[19] Seen from the perspective of our own day, this dichotomy is unsatisfactory. The authority of Jesus, which according to Matthew 16:17-19 was in some sort transmitted to Peter, cannot be suitably called either honorary or jurisdictional. There is a third kind of primacy, properly theological in nature, to which Ernst gives the name ontological or, in a wide sense, sacramental. In the writings of Leo the Great, he maintains, sacramental themes of primacy predominate over the juridical themes that later became so prominent. In a sacramental view of primacy, the notion of papal power moves away from jurisdiction in the legal sense toward a style of leadership based on charism and moral authority. "What is more, in the providence of God, we have actually had an historical Pope in recent years, John XXIII, who has given us a personal expression of that original unity, perhaps because personal sanctity alone is the only valid means of discovering and disclosing it."[20]

Some careful scholars, since Vatican II, maintain that the notion of a "primacy of honor" is capable of being defended, even from within the Roman Catholic tradition. The pope, like a patriarch, is not a superbishop; he is a bishop among bishops. He exercises a primacy not over bishops but rather among bishops and is, in that sense, a first among equals. He may be said to have a primacy of honor, provided it be recognized, as Père Duprey reminds us, that there is no honor in the Church except in view of a service.[21] The special service of the universal primate, viewed in the ecclesiological perspectives of Vatican II, is "to preside over the assembly of charity"[22] and to foster collegial relationships among the regional bishops and particular churches. This idea, suitably explained, might remove some of the difficulties continually raised, especially in the East, against the concept of a primacy of jurisdiction. It would permit the concept of papal primacy to be interpreted less legalistically and more in accord with a collegial or conciliar vision of the Church.

For one member of a college to exercise jurisdiction, in a political sense, over all the others would seem to destroy the fundamental equality that is the very basis of collegial relationships.

From the standpoint of our times, the most offensive of all the definitions of Vatican I is the dogma of papal infallibility. The idea that the truth of revelation could be pinned down in a dogmatic formula, binding on all future generations, seems to many of our contemporaries quite intolerable. The scandal is increased by the Council's affirmation that papal statements enjoy such infallibility "by themselves and not by the consent of the Church."[23]

Once again, we are faced with the effects of a cultural shift. At the time of Vatican I, infallibility as such was not a crucial problem. The Council saw no necessity to explore the notions of infallibility and irreformability, for it was taken for granted by all parties in the Church that the supreme magisterium, as the decisive organ of revelation, must be able to speak infallibly, in such a way that its pronouncements would be "irreformable." The main question under debate was the locus of the supreme, infallible teaching power. Did the pope have it by himself, or did he have it only—as the Gallicans had contended[24]—when the national hierarchies or the universal episcopate concurred? In answer to this question the Council affirmed that the pope himself, under certain conditions, enjoys "that infallibility with which the divine Redeemer willed his Church to be equipped in defining the teaching of faith and morals."[25] This statement leaves open the tremendous question: What kind and measure of infallibility did Christ choose to confer upon his Church?

In the twentieth century, and especially since Vatican II, the nature of infallibility has come up for very serious re-examination within the Catholic Church.[26] Everyone is now aware of the difficulty of pinning down the exact meaning of religious statements, and of the ways in which words change their meanings according to the cultural situation and point of view of the reader. We are aware, likewise, that the truth of the gospel is never definitively given, but that it must be won anew through continual efforts to reread the gospel with the help of the "signs of the times." The doctrine of infallibility seems to suggest that the statements of previous generations can be definitive and adequate, so that we would be dispensed from further inquiry.

These objections do not show that the teaching of Vatican I on infallibility is untenable, but rather that it demands a sophisticated interpretation, according to the methods of modern hermeneutics. As previously mentioned, such reinterpretation is encouraged by the Declaration *Mysterium ecclesiae*.[27] Even infallible statements do not escape the limitations inherent in all human speech. Dogmatic statements, insofar as they bear upon the divine, contain an element of special obscurity. The formulations of faith necessarily fall short of capturing the full richness of the transcendent realities to which they refer. Furthermore, as already stated, dogmatic pronouncements are inevitably influenced by the presuppositions, concerns, and thought categories of those who utter them, as well as by the limitations in the available vocabulary. Without contradicting Vatican I's teaching on infallibility, therefore, one may admit that all papal and conciliar dogmas, including the dogma of papal infallibility, are subject to ongoing reinterpretation in the Church.

There remains the problem how the pope can be infallible by himself, without dependence on the consent of the Church. Vatican I, in asserting this, was rejecting the Gallican view that papal teaching did not become irreformable until it had been juridically approved by the national hierarchies. The Gallican view was seen by Manning and others as imperiling the independence of the Church from national parliaments and kings. Vatican I, however, had no intention of cutting the pope off from the rest of the Church. Indeed, it stated that his infallibility is nothing other than that with which Christ had been pleased to endow the *Church*.

Vatican II, operating in a changed historical context, was eager to bring papal infallibility into a positive, organic relationship with the infallibility of the whole Church in believing and that of the universal pastorate in teaching.[28] In this new perspective it becomes unthinkable that the pope could infallibly teach anything contrary to the faith of the Church or the general teaching of the bishops. In the words of *Lumen gentium*: "To the resultant definitions the assent of the Church can never be wanting, on account of the activity of that same Holy Spirit, whereby the whole flock of Christ is preserved and progresses in unity of faith."[29] According to the *relatio* of the Theological Commission on this passage, infallible definitions of popes and councils "carry with them and express the consensus of the whole community."[30]

It would not be correct to regard the pope as a mere mouthpiece for voicing what had previously been agreed to by the whole Church. As supreme pastor and doctor he has a special responsibility and charism to teach. But, for the reasons given above, it seems evident that definitions, if they authentically flow from the charism of the papal office (which is to express the faith committed to the whole Church, rather than the pope's personal convictions), will find an echo in the ranks of the faithful and will therefore, at least eventually, win assent. If in a given instance the assent of the Church were evidently not forthcoming, this could be interpreted as a signal that the pope had perhaps exceeded his competence and that some necessary condition for an infallible act had not been fulfilled.

Understood in this way, there is nothing magical about papal teaching power. In order to teach infallibly the pope must align himself with the faith of the whole Church—a faith already objectified in Scripture and in the documents of tradition. If he were to separate himself from this faith, which lives on in the body of the faithful, the pope could well become a heretic or, to use the harsh term of some reformers, an Antichrist. *Corruptio optimi pessima.*

Many Catholic theologians contend that divine Providence will never permit the pope to fall into error in making a solemn definition.[31] We may piously believe this to be so, but there is no strict proof. In fact there are several objections. For one thing, it is always dangerous to set limits to what divine Providence will permit. With or without God's "permission"—as it is anthropomorphically called —many things go awry, even in the Church. For instance, there have been uncertainties, over a relatively long span of years, as to who was the legitimate pope. Then again, we cannot lightly set aside the common view of medieval theologians and canonists (down to the time of Albert Pighius, if we may accept the authority of Bellarmine) that it is possible for popes, in their public teaching, to fall into heresy.[32] I do not find this view incompatible with the teaching of Vatican I on papal infallibility, since the Council recognized that the pope's infallibility was limited and conditional.

The moderates at Vatican I managed to get many restrictions written into the text and into the explanations given to it on the council floor. As a result, the celebrated definition of papal infallibility really commits one to very little. Minimalistically, or even strictly, interpreted, it is hardly more than an emphatic assertion that the pope's primacy, as previously set forth in the first three chapters of *Pastor aeternus*, extends also to his teaching power. He is not only the first pastor but also the first teacher in the Church. In view of his special responsibility for the unity of the whole Church in the faith of the apostles, it is antecedently credible that in him the infallibility of the whole Church may come to expression. If this be a generally correct interpretation of the basic meaning of chapter 4 of *Pastor aeternus*, that chapter is not likely to be rejected by anyone who accepts primacy along the lines we have sought to explain it.

Early in this chapter I remarked that the papacy is a distinctively Roman Catholic religious symbol. It might seem, then, that the subject matter of this chapter would have no interest for other Christians. That might almost be the case were it not for the ecumenical movement, which has caused the papacy to become a subject of intense concern, both as an obstacle and as a possible resource for Christian unity.

It has become almost a commonplace to say that the papacy, in its present form, is the prime barrier to reconciliation. Paul VI himself, in a frequently quoted remark, admitted, "The pope, as we all know, is undoubtedly the gravest obstacle in the path of ecumenism."[33] If this were all that could be said on the subject, we should be forced to make a choice between loyalty to the pope and devotion to ecumenism.

Fortunately, however, there is more to be said. For the ecumenical movement to succeed, the presently divided Christian groups must find signs and instrumentalities that will bring them together in universal unity. For Roman Catholics, the papacy has proved itself, over many centuries, an effective symbol of the unity of the whole people under the one chief shepherd. The pope is understood not, of course, as a replacement for Christ but as a sign or sacrament of Christ, exercising universal pastoral responsibility in the name of

Christ and in continuity with Christ's commission to Peter. The question therefore arises whether there is not a demand for a pastoral office that transcends the present barriers between Christians. Although the papacy, under present circumstances, cannot fully perform this Petrine function, we must consider whether, under changed conditions, it might not in some way do so.

In recent years a number of Anglican, Orthodox, and Protestant theologians and several official bilateral consultations have indicated the possibility that a renewed papacy, far from being a mere obstacle, might be a singular asset in bringing about worldwide Christian unity.[34] For example, a distinguished team of American Lutheran theologians, in 1974, found it possible, in a bilateral statement, to ask their own churches "if they are prepared to affirm with us that papal primacy, renewed in the light of the gospel, need not be a barrier to reconciliation."[35] And in 1976 a symposium was published, with contributions by theologians of seven different denominations, bearing the title, A Pope for All Christians?[36] "Of all the non-Catholic theologians only the Baptist C. B. Hastings writes that his tradition could not accept reunion with a Pope or with any centralized authority since it would do violence to Baptist understanding of the autonomous local church."[37]

At the very outset it must be admitted that the idea of a pope for non–Roman Catholic Christians is fraught with difficulty. If the papacy is the distinctive symbol of Roman Catholicism, how could it serve as an organ of ecumenical unity? If the pope remains a Roman Catholic, and the spiritual head of the Roman Catholic communion, how could other Christians look to him as their supreme pastor and teacher? And if he ceased to be the spiritual head of the Roman Catholic communion, how could he continue to be pope at all?

I have no full solution to these apparent dilemmas, but perhaps some suggestions may be made that will make them less acute. Some of the suggestions are admittedly rather utopian, but even a utopian suggestion can sometimes help to point the way beyond a present impasse.

First of all, the other Christian churches might consider whether they have taken as seriously as they might what I have here called the "Petrine function." Some Orthodox and Protestant communities, to all appearances, are content to be churches of particular national or cultural groups. This is unobjectionable provided they also recognize, as is increasingly the case, that the Church of Christ is catholic (in the sense of universal). Regional churches should be encouraged to look upon themselves as partial realizations of a Church that knows no national or ethnic boundaries. They must reactivate their concern—if this has not been vigorous—for the dimension of catholicity, in order that the Church may in truth become, in the words of the Uppsala Assembly of the World Council, "the sign of the coming unity of mankind."[38]

While the Roman Catholic Church has perhaps been too centralized in recent centuries, other churches and confessional families have tended rather to err in the opposite direction. Churches that exist only as national or ethnic groupings can hardly be called signs and instruments of the unity of all in Christ. As the non-Roman churches develop more adequate universal structures, it is possible that a kind of parity may develop between them and the Roman Catholic communion. They may come to see more importance in having an international spiritual head equipped with an appropriate ceremonial mystique—such as the Archbishop of Canterbury and the patriarchs of the Eastern churches have never ceased to enjoy, at least for their own constituencies.

This suggestion, by itself, would not bring Christians to the point of having on earth one visible head as a sign and source of unity. But it might lead to a further stage in which the spiritual primates of worldwide communions or confessional families might act in concert. Occasionally in the recent past there have been dramatic manifestations of solidarity between the pope and the Patriarch of Constantinople, the pope and the Coptic Patriarch, the pope and the Archbishop of Canterbury. These occasions have helped to invest the papacy with an import that transcends confessional differences. The occasional joint undertakings of the Holy See and the World Council of Churches have a similar significance, although they are marred by a certain lack of parity between the Catholic Church, which is a confessional body, and the World Council which, strictly speaking, is not. Regular meetings between Christian world leaders could help to fill the void created by the absence of any officer or office that can presently speak to and for the whole community of Christians.

In this connection, one should not belittle the ecumenical benefits that might follow if the Roman Catholic Church were to enter the World Council of Churches.[39] The exact status of the papacy in such a body would have to be carefully worked out with a view to the concerns of all. It would not be inconceivable, as Karl-Heinz Ohlig proposes, that the pope as *primus inter pares* might serve as the "permanent chairman" of the World Council.[40] If something along this line were done, the papacy would have a vastly enhanced ecumenical significance, since the pope would wear, so to speak, a "second hat" as a World Council official.

Quite apart from any relationship to the World Council, the papacy might have some kind of spiritual authority for certain non–Roman Catholic communions. It is not out of the question that certain churches might be willing to enter into communion with Rome as "sister churches" without becoming, in the full sense of the word, Roman Catholic. In such a case, the strictly jurisdictional powers of the pope might be limited to his Roman Catholic constituency, somewhat as, in the patristic Church, the pope exercised ordinary jurisdiction only over certain Western churches. Like the preceding suggestion, this would amount to giving the pope an additional function without detracting from any of the functions he now has. He could be a kind of symbolic head of the larger communion of sister churches, exercising such powers as they would be prepared to invest in him.

This possibility would open up some interesting speculation regarding the structures of government of the new ecclesiastical coalition. One could imagine that the other member churches might be given a voice in the election of the pope, possibly by means of a bicameral process in which only one chamber would be composed exclusively of Roman Catholics. So likewise, for the running of the papacy, there might be, in addition to the Roman Catholic congregations, secretariats representing the insights and concerns of the other sister churches, thus assuring a creative interaction between them and the Church of Rome.

These organizational changes are, to be sure, very hypothetical and doubtless far from realization. Even without any such changes the pope could act, even more than in the past, as a kind of moral leader for many Christians beyond the visible limits of the Roman Catholic communion. Many of the social encyclicals, as well as many conciliar documents of Vatican II, have been received with great respect by non-Catholic Christians. Many felt able to identify with Pope John XXIII when he pleaded for Christian unity, or with Paul VI when he spoke on peace at the United Nations.

Several recent authors, sensing the exciting possibilities of this kind of informal moral influence, have recommended that the pope should distance himself somewhat from the responsibility of the day-to-day operations of ecclesiastical government and thus liberate himself for a more inspirational role. Some speak of a more "affective" behavioral mode, which would serve to underscore the purposes of the organization rather than to run the ecclesiastical machine.[41] Andrew Greeley, in a similar vein, argues for a papacy that is predominantly symbolic and interpretive, and for this reason, he declares, more powerful than one that would be purely administrative. "The papacy," he contends, "is not merely an essential sacred symbol for the Christian Church, it also is or at least can be an extraordinarily important institution for facilitating the proclamation of the Gospel and for speaking to the conscience of the world from the Christian perspective."[42] It is easy to imagine that a charismatic papacy, such as Greeley here envisages, might assume profound ecumenical importance.

If the Petrine ministry could from time to time be implemented on an ecumenical level even by transitory actions, this would be a major step toward a situation in which it might be meaningful to speak of a "pastor and teacher of all Christians." Such occasional acts of single or joint ecumenical leadership would be tokens of the day when all Christians could be visibly gathered under a single spiritual head who would perform for the Church of the future what Peter, according to certain New Testament texts, was chosen to do for the Church of the first generation.

VII. Changing Concepts of Church Membership

In our reflection on the papacy we have already seen how closely connected, in the circumstances of today's world, are the inner dimensions of church renewal and the outer dimensions of ecumenical relationships. By seeing how our own church is perceived from the perspective of other traditions, we can often find new light for grappling with "domestic" difficulties. Among the problems which are inseparably both intradenominational and ecumenical a prominent place should be given to that of church membership. The same sacramental process of initiation is commonly considered to incorporate the new member into the Church of Christ and into a particular communion, such as the Roman Catholic. Are these two incorporations separable? Are Christians of other communions members of the Church of Christ and yet not members of our own particular church?

Church membership is pivotal to the sense of identity of Catholic Christians. Typically they identify themselves simply as "Catholics," using this term as a substantive. For their sense of identity, therefore, it is important for them to have a clear notion of what it means to be a Catholic. Growing confusion in this area has plunged numerous Roman Catholics into a crisis of religious identity. When asked what they are religiously, some answer vaguely that they were "raised Catholic," but they do not know what more to say. According to George Gallup, Jr., more than a quarter of the adult Roman Catholics in the United States say that they are not members of a church.[1] Are they correct, or are they church members—even perhaps members of the Roman Catholic Church without knowing it? The answers to these and many like questions depend upon what church membership means.

The ecumenical importance of our present theme is manifest. The World Council of Churches, in the Report on Unity accepted by the New Delhi Assembly of 1961, listed "membership accepted by all" as one of the essentials of a visibly united Church. In the divided Christianity of the past few centuries, it has been common to deny that members of other communions are truly members of the body of Christ. In the more irenic climate of the present century, efforts are being made to give due recognition to the Christian status of members of other churches, and proposals of multiple membership, or of mutual recognition of members, are frequently made. Such proposals, however, demand a careful rethinking of the meaning of membership.

In the literature from various centuries, three basic concepts of membership would seem to be operative: the organic, the juridical, and the participatory. Each of these three concepts, in my judgment, presupposes a different ecclesiology, evokes different images, and has different practical and logical consequences. Hence they must be separately analyzed.

The first understanding of membership, well founded in the New Testament, is based on a biological analogy. In several Pauline letters (Rom 12:4-5, 1 Cor 12:12-27) the Church is pictured as an organism, the Body of Christ, in which all Christians are incorporated by faith in Christ and by baptism in the one Spirit. Within this body they are mutually linked by complementarity of callings and of functions. According to a further development of this theory, found in Ephesians and Colossians, Christ is the head of the Body; Christians are the other members. Patristic and medieval theologians, pondering on this imagery, brought out more explicitly the idea that the Holy Spirit, the Spirit of Jesus, is the soul of the Body. In the High Middle Ages the Church came to be called the "mystical" Body of Christ—an expression still in use today. Membership, in this theory, comes down to incorporation—being taken into the body.

Who, then, are the members of the Church? According to a medieval theologian such as Thomas Aquinas, everyone who is animated by the Holy Spirit, everyone in whom the grace of Christ is at work, is to that extent a member of the body.[2] In the opinion of Aquinas, the saints of the Old Testament, since they lived by the grace of the Holy Spirit, were already members of the Body of Christ, but in the present stage of salvation history, since the Incarnation, the normal way of being joined to the Church is through the sacraments. The basic sacrament of incorporation is baptism, the sacrament of faith, but incorporation is perfected and completed by the Eucharist, the sacrament of charity. Aquinas also maintains that in the present phase of salvation history the visible head of the Church on earth is by divine appointment the bishop of Rome, the successor of Peter. All the baptized are in principle obliged to subject themselves to the pope, and a contumacious refusal of subjection may be grounds for excommunication. Thus St. Thomas does not stick entirely to the biological analogy. He introduces some juridical or societal elements into his notion of the Church, but these, in my judgment, are secondary features of his ecclesiology. His dominant notion of the Church would seem to derive from the organic or biological analogy, according to which membership is primarily constituted by a relationship to the Holy Spirit, who vitally incorporates us into the body of the living Christ.

In comparison with other theories, this mystical-organic conception gives particular emphasis to the divine elements in the Church and to the passive or receptive aspects of membership. The Church is seen as a divinely established community, equipped by Christ himself with a threefold deposit of sacraments, doctrine, and ministry. The members are recipients of the ministrations of the Church rather than, as such, active participants in the work of the Church. The life of the Christian, to be sure, is seen as including intense activity. Having become members of the Church, the faithful are obliged to respond actively to their particular vocation to ministry and mission, according to the grace of the Holy Spirit imparted to them. Membership, however, does not consist in such active cooperation but rather in reception of the sacraments of initiation and in submission to the teaching contained in the deposit of faith and to the directives of the divinely appointed hierarchy.

To clarify the concept of membership that goes with this type of ecclesiology, it may be helpful to refer to the distinction between "church" and "sect" made early in the present century by the great German sociologist of religion, Ernst Troeltsch. The "organic" view of membership is the quintessence of Troeltsch's church-type. It presupposes that the Church is an objective organ of redemption having a divine endowment of grace and truth. The individual has to submit himself to its influences—the sooner the better. In this view, which attaches relatively little importance to individual activity, the practice of infant baptism is fully intelligible.[3] Normally the infant is baptized into the Church by the decision of his parents or the community into which he is born. He remains in the Church for life unless he voluntarily withdraws from the body or is expelled from it.

According to theologians who consistently follow this model, a person cannot get out of the Church except by a seriously sinful act, whereby he rejects the grace offered him in the Church. Unless he is proud, he will without recalcitrance accept the divine teaching handed down in the Church; he will be subject to its authorities and will humbly obey its commandments as the commandments of God. If it should happen that through ignorance some individual should come to have ideas at variance with the teaching of the Church, the mistake would not be fatal. He would revise his opinions as soon as his deviance had been brought to his attention. He would not be cut off from the body unless he sinned against the light, rejecting the grace that had been given him in baptism.

The incorporation theory of membership, as developed in the classical theological tradition, highlights the unity of the Church. There can be only one Church, since there can be only one Body of Christ. The Church is larger than any sociological organization—for, as we have seen, it includes all the just souls of the Old Testament, beginning with Adam or Abel. In fact, according to St. Thomas, it includes the holy souls in purgatory, the blessed in heaven, and even in some sense the angels, for they have Christ as their head. On earth today, however, there is only one Church, and the pope, according to Christ's will, presides over this entire assembly.

The strength of this theory consists, first of all, in its basic conformity with the New Testament doctrine of the Body of Christ and in its ability to bring out the divine and supernatural elements that distinguish the Church from all merely human societies. Its weakness is that it tends to absorb the individual too much into the organism, giving too little scope for human freedom and creativity. Such a theory may have seemed almost self-evidently true in an age when the majority of Christians were living in a peasant-type of society, dominated by tradition. They would have assumed spontaneously that the truth of revelation must have been handed down from the ancients and that the permanent form of the Church must have been given to it by its divine founder. In modern times, history, if nothing else, has taught us that the doctrines, structures, and liturgical rites of the Church are variable, and depend very much on the free initiatives of men. This means that our concept of the Church has to take greater cognizance of the human element than is allowed for by this organic model.

The inadequacies of the classical organic theory became manifest at the Reformation. From the earliest times there had been sectarians who took small groups of enthusiastic partisans outside the great Church—but the sects were small and generally short-lived. There had also been schisms based on a temporary disagreement between different parts of the one Church. Only in the sixteenth century, however, does one find the emergence of large, internationally organized churches, competing on the same soil for the allegiance of the same persons, appealing to the same basic Christian documents, and denying true churchly status to one another. Lutheran and Reformed Christianity could not be satisfactorily analyzed in the old categories of schism and heresy. The problem of religious dissent took on a new form, at least in those countries where the competing churches existed side by side.

In this new situation it was no longer possible to assume that, in the great majority of cases, the baptized believer remained a member of the Church in which he was born unless he arrogantly set himself up against its authorities. Different sets of authorities, with their own body of confessional and polemical literature, found themselves in mutual confrontation. The believer had to exercise an option to come into, and remain in, some one church.

This altered situation forced a change in the theory of membership. The new vision is typified by the seventeenth-century Roman Catholic, Robert Bellarmine, for whom

> The one and true Church is a group of men bound together by the profession of the same Christian faith and by the communion of the same sacraments, under the rule of the legitimate pastors, and especially of the one vicar of Christ on earth, the Roman pontiff.[4]

Applying Troeltsch's dichotomy, one would still have to classify this theory as belonging to the church-type rather than the sect-type, for the Church is seen as something essentially constituted by the action of God in Christ and not by the free institution of the believers themselves. But the stress is no longer on the organic and sacramental elements, nor even on the interior element of grace. Rather it is on the external, juridical elements, including especially government by the legitimate pastors. One becomes a member of the society chiefly by subjecting oneself to the officers. They have a threefold function: As teachers, they tell the faithful what to believe; as priests, they officiate at divine worship and administer the sacraments; as governors, they shape the discipline and common life of the churches over which they preside.

This theory, although characteristically Catholic, has near equivalents in the Protestantism of the early modern period. In Protestant Germany, for instance, the ruling princes forcibly imposed the Lutheran symbolic books as norms of belief and practice.[5] Juridicism and authoritarianism were the order of the day.

How is membership terminated according to this juridical theory? From the side of the individual, one may cease to be a member by rejecting the teaching, ministrations, or ruling authority of the pastors. From the side of the group, one may be ejected by a formal act of excommunication. Since the Church is seen as an essentially visible society, membership is determined by empirically verifiable factors. A baptized person who externally conforms to the standards of the group is a member, even though he subjectively believes none of its teachings; conversely, a person who is juridically excommunicated ceases to be a member, even though the excommunication is unjust. [6] On this point, the juridical theory, with its insistence on institutional visibility, gives answers quite different from the mystical-organic theory, which looks upon the interior or spiritual element as primary. For St. Thomas and the Thomists, excommunication does not cut a person off from the Church unless he has already withdrawn by heresy or schism.[7]

The juridical theory had real plausibility at a time when Christianity in the West was divided into hostile blocs, in fundamental disagreement about the basic content of the Christian message. Each group had to claim for itself, in effect, that it was the one true Church, and that the members of rival churches were outside the una sancta. Where there were several sets of authorities, each claiming to present the genuine and complete message of Christ, everything depended on which authorities one was prepared to follow. Christians were in fact divided into internally homogeneous groups, and the beliefs of each individual were almost a carbon copy of the beliefs of his coreligionists.

Pope Pius XII, in his encyclical on the Mystical Body of Christ (1943), sought to integrate a predominantly juridical theory of membership, heavily indebted to Robert Bellarmine, into a predominantly organic vision of the Church. He identified the Mystical Body exclusively with the Roman Catholic Church and made the full acceptance of Catholic doctrine a necessary condition for incorporation into the Body of Christ. The crucial paragraph reads as follows:

> Only those are really to be included as members of the Church who have been baptized and profess the true faith and who have not unhappily withdrawn from the Body-unity or for grave faults been excluded by legitimate authority. "For in one Spirit," says the apostle, "were we all baptized into one Body, whether Jews or Gentiles, whether bond or free." As, therefore, in the true Christian community there is only one Body, one Spirit, one Lord and one baptism, so there can be only one faith. And so if a man refuse to hear the Church, let him be considered—so the Lord commands—as a heathen and a publican. It follows that those who are divided in faith and government cannot be living in one Body such as this, and cannot be living the life of its one divine Spirit.[8]

Quite predictably, this paragraph provoked some dismay in Protestant and Orthodox circles. Even Catholic commentators found defects in it. Scripture scholars, committed to the Pauline notion of the Body of Christ, felt that the encyclical did not sufficiently respect faith in Christ and baptism as the essential constituents of incorporation. Canon lawyers complained that the encyclical was in conflict with the Code of 1917, which seemed to make baptism sufficient for membership.[9] Thomistic theologians, faithful to their master, continued to teach that baptized Christians who had committed no sin of schism or infidelity were members of the Body of Christ even if they were not professing Roman Catholics. Catholic ecumenists, such as Cardinal Bea, strongly concurred with many of these objections.[10]

Without explicitly contradicting the doctrine of Pius XII, Vatican II in effect corrected it. The Council made an important distinction between the Church of Christ and the Roman Catholic communion.[11] It held that valid baptism has the effect of incorporating the recipient into Christ, and thus conjoining him to the Body of Christ, even if not to the Roman Catholic Church.[12] For full incorporation into the Body of Christ, according to the Council, one would have to accept the complete reality of the Church, including the papal office.[13] Basic incorporation, however, could be achieved by faith and baptism outside the Roman Catholic communion.

In some respects Vatican II could be interpreted as a move back toward the older organic theory of membership. But it would not be adequate to characterize its doctrines as a simple return to the past. In many ways Vatican II was an accommodation to the third theory, to which we now turn.

In the nineteenth and twentieth centuries, especially in Western Europe and the United States, the Church ceased to be the monolithic power it had previously been. The alliance between throne and altar broke down, and the state achieved a clear superiority of power over the Church. Sociologically speaking, the churches, mutually divided by dissension, sank to the level of voluntary groups or movements within the larger framework of civil society. It became increasingly difficult to credit either the organic theory, according to which one is simply born into the Church of one's fellow countrymen, or the juridical theory, in which the Church is seen as a legally autonomous "perfect society."

As the Church lost its objective solidity over against its own members, the members began to understand their relationship to the Church in a new way. Under the impact of new modes of education, communications, and political life, Christians began to look upon themselves as playing a more active role in the determination of their own religious beliefs and behavior. They used the Church as a help in arriving at their personal religious stance, but did not unconditionally subject themselves to its teaching and direction. Rather they considered it their duty to contribute, in some way, to the teaching and life of their own Church, much as the citizens of a free society contributed to the welfare of the body politic. Membership, then, came to be viewed as a form of active participation in the shaping of the Christian community.

According to this participatory theory, one is not born a member of the Church, but one freely joins the church of one's choice.[14] In a certain sense, the members are prior to the Church; they constitute the Church by setting up an organization that corresponds to their religious convictions. In the United States, where this vision of the Church obtained the widest acceptance, hundreds of new sects and denominations were spawned. For the most part, they did not claim to be the one true Church, outside of which there was no salvation, but simply to be viable Christian organizations for those who wanted to belong. If anyone found that he did not share the convictions and priorities of the group, he might seek to remold it according to his own ideas, and if he failed in his efforts, he could always transfer his allegiance to a group that suited him better. In the highly mobile society of our time, people rather frequently change their religious affiliation, and this becomes progressively easier to do as the last traces of legal and social sanctions die away.

What we are here describing is the "denominational society," a term increasingly applicable not only to the United States but to many other countries.[15] In such a society it is scarcely possible for one religious group, such as the Roman Catholic Church, to make a serious claim that it alone is the one true Church. Under the influence of the prevalent denominationalism, Vatican II attributed to the Catholic Church many of the features of a free society.[16] It emphasized that faith, by which one comes to the Church, is a free and voluntary act. It discountenanced the coercion of consciences, whether in favor of religion or against it. It called upon the faithful to participate actively in the liturgy and in the day-to-day government of the Church through pastoral councils and lay organizations. It depicted the role of popes, bishops, and pastors in terms of service rather than domination, and gave some scope for the faithful to practice conscientious disobedience and dissent toward the official leadership.

I would not go so far as to say that Vatican II placed the Catholic Church in the sociological category of the denomination. It continued to teach—albeit with many reservations—that the Catholic

Church and it alone is the fully authentic Church, in some sense necessary for salvation.[17] The Council's doctrine of magisterium, the priestly ministry, and the sacraments retains many features of the ancient organic view, together with reminiscences of the authoritarianism of Trent and Vatican I. But these elements are set side by side with certain principles of "voluntarism," so that the Church, as presented by Vatican II, takes on some features of the denomination.

In this denominational theory of membership, as contrasted with the other two theories, the individual is by no means immersed in the group. Even after joining it, he retains a certain autonomy vis-à-vis the church authorities. He does not necessarily endorse all the decisions of the highest officeholders; he may feel entitled or conscientiously obliged to protest. His participation may sometimes assume the form of docile collaboration with the hierarchy—as in the older style of "Catholic action"—but it may also be a more independent type of activity. It may even at times demand a measure of disaffiliation. Thus in the denominational model full participation and identification with the group is not necessarily viewed as the ideal. A good Christian may at times marginalize himself with respect to the institutional authorities of his own church. Even a justified revolt or withdrawal does not seem completely out of the question.

Membership, on this theory, is a many-faceted reality. There are many degrees and kinds of membership—active membership or dormant membership, full membership or associate membership. Some distinguish within active membership degrees such as nuclear, modal, and marginal.[18] In religious statistics today it is often questioned whether infants and minors, who have not yet made a personal commitment to the church, ought to be listed as members. In fidelity to "voluntarist" principles, certain churches delay baptism until such a time as the individual feels prepared to make a full personal commitment. In many Protestant churches, moreover, a person is stricken from the rolls unless he attends church services or contributes financially to the organization. Consequences such as these are logical enough once membership is viewed in terms of participation rather than in terms of incorporation or subjection.

This third vision of membership has the advantage of a certain sober realism. Putting aside the false comforts of mythology, it does not assume that the official Church is always in the right. It puts the responsibility for Christian faith and practice squarely on the shoulders of the faithful themselves.

For all the obvious realism and practicality of this third approach, I cannot feel that it is fully satisfactory. I find it depressing to dissolve Christianity, as this theory seems to do, into a multitude of competing denominations, no one of which can dare to address its members in the name of Christ or impose any genuine obligations. In this spectacle of competing groups, seeking to outbid each other for members, the grand vision of the unity of the Church almost vanishes from sight. Small, ephemeral private groups are obviously incapable of effecting the kind of universal reconciliation that has traditionally been regarded as the Church's mission. Not surprisingly, the denominations themselves have felt their own weakness and have periodically sought to recapture the vision of the one, holy, catholic Church. Occasionally they have banded together in councils, federations, or mergers. Many Protestants have cast envious glances at the Catholic Church with its ancient ceremonies, its worldwide unity, and its strong hierarchical authority. But the problem remains: can the Catholic Church, which inherits these elements from an earlier period, preserve them in the rapidly moving civilization of our time? Can it hold on to the organic or juridical theories of membership in an age of flux and pluralism?

Although I can well understand, and in part share, the nostalgic desire of some Catholic groups to restore the glories of the past, I am also convinced that it is no longer appropriate to look upon the Church primarily as a great biological organism, in which the identity of the individual would be submerged, or as an absolutistic society in which all power is lodged in the governing class. If we cannot be satisfied with the alternatives provided by the denomination theory—as I believe we cannot—we shall have to search for some fourth option that escapes the difficulties of the three theories already examined.

According to the vision espoused in this book, the Church is essentially a mystery. In its visible aspect, it is the sacrament of Christ—that is to say, a real and efficacious symbol of the divine-human reconciliation that flows from the redemptive mediation of Christ.[19]

The Church, therefore, is not a merely human organization but a graced response to the divine initiative. In conformity with its nature as sacrament of reconciliation, the Church cannot be content to take people as they are. It must inwardly transform its members and open them up to communion with one another. This mutual communion, and thus also the Church itself, may be realized on different levels —the family, the basic worship group, the parish, the regional church, and the worldwide community of Christians. This theory, therefore, does not limit the Church to the status of a club of like-minded individuals. It makes them reach out to their brothers and sisters across the face of the globe. It recognizes that a necessity is laid upon the Church to share in Christ's mission of universal reconciliation, and that the individual Christian must seek to translate into visible actuality the mysterious union that binds together all those who live by God's grace in Jesus Christ.

Once it has come to understand itself as a living symbol of God's reconciling work in Christ, the Church is driven by an insatiable impulse to build up a true and holy fellowship in the entire human family. It reaches backward and forward in time. Those who have been accepted into the fellowship are said to be "in communion" with those of all generations into whose fellowship they enter. Fellowship or communion is thus a reciprocal relationship that may be realized either among individuals in the Church or among particular churches.[20]

Communion, thus understood, is a valuable category for bringing together the aspects of membership proper to each of the three preceding approaches. In the first place, as we have seen in our discussion of the organic theory, Christian fellowship is founded in the sharing of faith and charity and is mediated by the external signs or bonds of baptism and Eucharist, which efficaciously symbolize these interior virtues. Secondly, communion is intensified and sealed by the societal bonds of obedience and solidarity that are the special concern of the juridical approach. Thirdly, fellowship is expressed and fulfilled through the voluntary commitment and common effort that constitute the principal theme of the participatory theory of membership.

The doctrine of communion, on the other hand, does not labor under the particular difficulties we have noted in the preceding three theories of membership. Implying freedom and reciprocity, the notion of communion is untainted with the biologism that plagues the organic approach to membership. Implying personal responsibility and friendship, it escapes the rigidities associated with the juridical approach. Implying a profound inner transformation wrought by God's mysterious approach to his people, communion avoids the superficial functionalism that can easily vitiate the participatory theory. Communion is a highly flexible concept, admitting of an indefinite variety of degrees and modalities. This flexibility is a valuable asset in an age of instability, pluralism, and ecumenism.

Each local church may be evaluated from the standpoint of the communion it achieves. Does it bind together its faithful, or at least some of them, in a deep personal fellowship—a fellowship centered on Christ, expressed and reinforced by credal, liturgical, and social bonds? To the extent that the faithful are drawn into a truly Christian communion, they may be said to have become "members of one another" (Rom 12:5). Communion reaches its sacramental high point in the Eucharist, where a particular local community celebrates its own internal unity and its solidarity with the other churches and communities with which it is in fellowship.

The doctrine of the Church as communion puts the question of membership in a different perspective. In common usage the term "member" refers chiefly to the relationship between an individual or part and an encompassing whole. Communion refers rather to the mutual relationship among individuals or among particular churches. In other words, membership generally denotes a nonreciprocal relationship; communion is reciprocal. It is established by the interaction whereby each enters into communion with the other. Excommunication, according to this style of ecclesiology, is normally a mutual action by which each group severs relations with the other.

Vatican II, recognizing the ambiguities and inadequacies of the term "member," avoided that term in all passages dealing with the question of who is in the Church. On some occasions, as we have seen, the Council used the language of incorporation and in several important texts it spoke of communion. The Decree on Ecumenism, for example, in its treatment of the status of non–Roman Catholic Christians, said that through their faith and baptism they are brought into a certain, though imperfect, communion with the

Catholic Church.[21] In the following sentence the Decree goes on to speak of differences among the traditions as creating obstacles to full ecclesiastical communion.

From an ecumenical point of view, this approach, I submit, is a very fruitful one. The Christian world is seen as a multitude of churches and communities, each of which is in full communion with certain Christian groups and in an imperfect or partial communion with others. The ecumenical task, then, is to strive for the mutual understanding and accommodation that will make it possible for the separated Christian bodies to pass from partial to full communion with one another.

The same idea may be restated in terms of another category—that of tradition. The Church may be seen as a variety of traditions, coming down from Christ and the apostles, undergoing constant development and adaptation. In the course of this development the traditions are sometimes enriched, sometimes impoverished, sometimes contaminated, sometimes purifed. Each of the Christian communions has its own stream of traditions, questioned or rejected or simply not shared by those who stand in another stream. To be a Christian is to accept, at least in general, the Christian heritage as handed down within some particular communion which one recognizes as one's own. It does not require a closed or polemical attitude toward the traditions of other groups. Ecumenism strives to achieve the mutual understanding that will make it possible for each church to recognize the validity of the traditions of the others. This may require serious study, criticism, and debate; it may require the correction of certain distortions and the supplying of certain lacunae; but it does not mean the destruction of anything sound in any of the traditions.

Understood in these perspectives, the apostolate of Christian unity is not a spiritual tug of war. The churches in dialogue do not seek to weaken or destroy each other but to build each other up in Christ. The aim of the dialogue is to receive what is sound and assimilable from other traditions, and in return to give whatever is good and communicable. So conceived, dialogue would seem to offer only benefits to every church that engages in it.

In the recent ecumenical literature proposals of common or "general" membership have occasionally been advanced, with the idea that the members of a given denomination might be recognized as having membership in a larger group made up of several denominations.[22] Alternatively, some propose that a single individual might on his own application become a member of two or more denominational churches at the same time. Such proposals do not seem wholly fantastic, in view of the less polemical relationships presently developing among different denominations.

To suggest a possible case, one might imagine the situation of a family who have a winter residence in a large city and a summer residence in the countryside. During the winter months they regularly worship at a church of the denomination to which they have always belonged. In the country, however, they cannot find a church of that denomination. They regularly worship in the summer months, therefore, at a nearby church rather similar in polity and doctrine. After some years, they wish to join the country church without ceasing to be members of their city parish. They are perfectly capable of meeting the standards for membership in both churches, and of fulfilling their duties to each by way of financial support and participation.

In terms of the organic theory of membership, such proposals of common or dual membership would make little sense, for the theory presupposes that membership is total absorption in a single divinely founded institution. So, too, in the juridical theory there would be severe problems, for on that theory membership is unconditional obedience to a single organization that anathematizes all its rivals. In the participatory theory, common membership might be a meaningful option, for there seems to be no good reason why one individual could not partially identify with, and actively participate in, several churches just as he can belong to several social or athletic clubs. But the adequacy of the participatory theory, taken alone, may be questioned.

If one were to understand membership in terms of the notion of communion, multiple membership would be problematic but not unthinkable. The question would be: Can a person in full communion with one group establish the same relationship with other groups with which the first is not in full communion? Generally speaking, it would seem best for a church member to act in such a way as to express by his behavior the partial but imperfect communion that exists among the groups, while seeking, at the same time, to bring the groups themselves into the desired full communion. But if the groups are so similar that there are no serious barriers between them, it might be possible for an individual to express complete solidarity with more than one of them, even though the groups have not yet officially achieved full solidarity with one another. For example, it might be possible for a member of one of the churches in the Consultation on Church Union to be allowed to become a member of another church in the Consultation without renouncing membership in the first. Provided that the individual continues to take both memberships seriously, dual membership could be a help in drawing the denominational churches closer together.

A Roman Catholic will be acutely conscious that his own church makes unique claims and does not accept the Christianity of any other church as being fully in accord with the Lord's will. For a Catholic to join another church would appear to weaken, if not destroy, his affiliation with his own. But he could without any infidelity to his own Catholic identity share many things with these other groups, and through a process of mutual giving and receiving help all concerned to grow closer to Christ the Lord. In this way he could help both his own church and the others to work toward a fuller mutual recognition that might make common membership normal.

Proposals for plural simultaneous membership in several churches could be unhelpful in solving the general ecumenical problem unless accompanied by serious efforts on the part of the denominations themselves to recognize the theological significance of faith and sacramental life among Christians of other groups. Perceiving this situation, the Consultation on Church Union—a movement among ten Protestant churches in the United States seeking to form a new "Church of Christ Uniting"—has come up with an important proposal. The Plenary Meeting of the Consultation in Cincinnati in November 1974 adopted an eighteen-point affirmation "Toward a Mutual Recognition of Members."[23] The Cincinnati Affirmation, as it is called, states that "all who are baptized into Jesus Christ are members of His universal Church" and that "membership in a particular church is membership in the whole People of God." Further, it acknowledges that in the present divided state of Christianity the word "membership" is used to refer to enrollment in a particular church and that incorporation into the one Church of Christ through baptism does not abolish membership in a particular church or imply simultaneous plural membership in several churches. Seeking to hasten the day when every member of each of the churches participating in the Consultation can be fully recognized as a member by all the participating churches, the Cincinnati Affirmation asks these churches to consider nine questions designed to bring out the implications of mutual recognition of membership with reference to baptism, confirmation, eucharistic sharing, and mutual recognition of ministries as well as with reference to the obligation to work together against social and racial injustices.

Since the Cincinnati Affirmation concludes with the recommendation that churches outside the Consultation should be invited to share in the affirmation of mutual recognition of members, a response may eventually be sought from the Roman Catholic side. I cannot anticipate in detail what that response might be. On the basis of the documents of Vatican II, one may foresee a fundamentally positive response. The Constitution on the Church and the Decree on Ecumenism make it possible for Catholics today to distinguish between membership in the Church of Christ and membership in the Roman Catholic Church. The Catholic Church in practice already recognizes the baptism practiced in Protestant churches such as those presently involved in the Consultation on Church Union, and it understands baptism as the fundamental sacrament of incorporation into the Body of Christ.

The Cincinnati Affirmation, however, raises several problems from the Roman Catholic perspective. In the first place it seems to imply that baptism by itself fully constitutes a person as a member of the Church. I cannot say that this is contrary to Catholic doctrine, since, as already indicated, some biblical texts and some canons from the 1917 Code of Canon Law seem to say the same. On the other hand the liturgical and doctrinal tradition of the Catholic Church favors the view that baptism is only the first of the sacraments of initiation, and that it is to be completed by confirmation and Eucharist, as complementary sacraments of initiation. For full incorporation in the Church, the Constitution on the Church and the Decree on Ecumenism seem to demand profession of the full faith of the Church, acceptance of all its essential structures, and a relationship of communion with others who are fully incorporated. In the words of the Decree on Ecumenism:

> Baptism, of itself, is only a beginning, a point of departure, for it is wholly directed toward a complete profession of faith, a complete incorporation into the system of salvation such as Christ Himself willed it to be, and finally, toward a complete participation in Eucharistic communion.[24]

A second problem arises from the statement in the Cincinnati Affirmation that "Membership in a particular church is membership in the whole People of God." This statement perhaps gives excessive status to the denominations. Granted that the denominations, even in their presently divided condition, have a genuinely ecclesial character inasmuch as they are the places in which Christian preaching and worship are generally conducted, still one may question whether membership in the Church of Christ is actually constituted by membership in a particular denomination. An astute Roman Catholic critic has written:

> Is recognition of juridic memberships a strong enough theological base for recognizing churches' confirmation and eucharist and ordained ministry? Furthermore, exaggerated emphasis on the concept and practice of "enrollment" in particular denominations involves the theological inconsistency of a baptized person not becoming an enrolled church member until he makes his confirmation–confession of faith, thus apparently holding in abeyance his prior incorporation into the Church of Christ through baptism; emphasis on "enrollment" can also involve such practical problems as churches competing for members and congregations overstressing financial giving.[25]

Third, a Roman Catholic might have some problems about the implication, evident in the nine questions attached to the Cincinnati Affirmation, that wherever there is valid baptism there must necessarily be valid ordination and a valid Eucharist, with the result that full eucharistic sharing becomes desirable. According to the view presently in possession in the Roman Catholic Church—and I see no sign that it will be changed—all the sacraments of the Church and papal-episcopal ministry in the apostolic succession are constitutive of the Church, so that where any of these is lacking the Church itself is only deficiently present. From this point of view, membership would be seen as an analogous and multifaceted reality. The minimal membership given by baptism is indispensable, indeed, but it demands development and enrichment in the numerous dimensions already set forth in the present chapter.

The three questions I have raised from a Roman Catholic perspective are not intended to discredit the Cincinnati Affirmation but simply to open up the kind of discussion for which the Affirmation seems to call. The Cincinnati Affirmation should be reckoned as one of the most constructive recent developments in the ecumenical movement. While recognizing the significance of membership in particular denominations, the Consultation on Church Union rightly subordinates this to membership in the Church of Christ, thus seeking to overcome the exaggerated denominationalism that has led so many churches in the past to act, in practice, as though they and they alone were the Church of Christ.

In the present divided state of Christianity it may be impossible to draw up a completely clear and consistent theology of membership, for the actual divisions within the Body of Christ are a living contradiction of the essential nature of the Church. For an even more vivid illustration of the dilemmas arising out of the present ecclesiastical predicament we may now turn to some ecumenical reflections on the Eucharist.

VIII. Eucharistic Sharing as an Ecumenical Problem

Throughout the centuries great theologians and churchmen have reiterated the idea that the Eucharist is the sacrament of the unity of the Church.[1] Reception of holy communion, therefore, is not simply an act by which the individual soul is united to Christ. "Because there is one bread," declares St. Paul, "we who are many are one body, for we all partake of the one bread" (1 Cor 10:17). By receiving the Eucharist the faithful both express and deepen the many-faceted ecclesial unity in which they already share.

As we know, the one Church of Christ is present today in a number of mutually divided churches. Although these churches are not in full communion with one another, they have in recent decades achieved a greater degree of mutual recognition and may be said to exist in what I have already called "partial" or "imperfect" communion. The members of these divided churches often have deep bonds of spiritual kinship. Frequently Christians of different communions unite in sacramental marriage. The Faith and Order Commission of the World Council of Churches, at its Louvain meeting in 1971, approved a study entitled "Beyond Intercommunion," and added:

> In the light of this theological work, we urge church authorities, each in their own way and in line with their own ecumenical commitments, to work towards full eucharistic communion and meanwhile to consider adapting their eucharistic disciplines, so as to allow the appropriate ecumenical advance at this time—e.g., by extending admission to communion under certain circumstances.[2]

In the present chapter I should like to comment as a theologian on the current eucharistic discipline of the Roman Catholic Church, especially with regard to eucharistic sharing with Protestants.

Recognizing the profoundly ecclesial character of eucharistic participation, Catholic theology has been reluctant to admit intercom-

munion. The basic governing principle was stated as follows in an
Instruction issued by the Secretariat for Promoting Christian Unity
in 1972:

> The strict relationship between the mystery of the Church and the
> mystery of the Eucharist can never be altered, whatever pastoral
> measures we may be led to take in given cases. Of its very nature,
> celebration of the Eucharist signifies the fullness of profession of
> faith and the fullness of ecclesial communion. This principle must
> not be obscured and must remain our guide in this field.[3]

If this were the only principle to be taken into account, intercommunion would be entirely excluded. For all practical purposes, it was
ruled out in the 1917 Code of Canon Law. Some churches today
take a similarly rigorous stand. The Standing Conference of Canonical Orthodox Bishops in America, for example, has thus stated the
position of the Orthodox Church:

> To the Holy Communion the Church admits only her baptized
> and chrismated children who confess the full Orthodox Faith,
> pure and entire, and by it she shows forth their oneness with her
> and with her Divine Spouse. Holy Communion is the sign and evi-
> dence of right belief and of incorporation in the Israel of
> God. . . . The Standing Conference would at this time remind
> the children of the Church as they pray, study and work for Chris-
> tian reunion that the Eucharistic Mystery is the end of unity, not
> a means to that end, and that therefore, the decisions regarding
> Holy Communion reached by Christian bodies outside the Ortho-
> dox will have no significance or validity for the Orthodox Church
> or her members. Holy Communion will not be sought by Ortho-
> dox Christians outside the Church, nor will it be offered to those
> who do not yet confess the Orthodox Church as their mother.[4]

Quite apart from the question of the exclusive claims of one or another of the churches to possess the only "valid" Eucharist, it stands
to reason that the Eucharist, as the high point of ecclesial life,
should normally be the celebration of those fully united to the community. To use an admittedly deficient yet helpful analogy, we
might say that the Eucharist is generally viewed as a family meal to
which only acknowledged members of the family have a right to

come. If we regard the members of other ecclesial families as friends, however, the question arises whether it may not be proper on occasion to give and accept invitations to participate in the Eucharist of a Christian family other than one's own. Is the meal of its very nature reserved to the family, or are occasional acts of eucharistic hospitality admissible? If so, under what conditions?

For Roman Catholics, the door was opened to occasional intercommunion by the Decree on Ecumenism:

> As for common worship, it may not be regarded as a means to be used indiscriminately for the restoration of the unity among Christians. Such worship depends chiefly on two principles: it should signify the unity of the Church; it should provide a sharing in the means of grace. The fact that it should signify unity generally rules out common worship. Yet the gaining of a needed grace sometimes commends it.
>
> The practical course to be adopted, after due regard has been given to all circumstances of time, place, and personage, is left to the prudent decision of the local episcopal authority, unless the Bishops' Conference according to its own statutes, or the Holy See, has determined otherwise.[5]

Taken literally, these sentences seem to say that the sign aspect of the Eucharist—to signify unity—and the efficacy of the Eucharist—to be a means of grace—can point in opposite directions. This would be difficult to accept, for the Eucharist, like other sacraments, is held to be a cause insofar as it is a sign. If the Eucharist, then, were a false sign, it could scarcely be a means of grace, and if it were causing grace it would have to be a true sign. If the Church were to withhold a means of grace out of respect for the esthetics of the sign, one would wonder what kind of sign the Church itself was becoming.

I interpret the paragraph therefore as probably meaning that in the case of churches not fully in communion with one another, both the sign value and the efficacy of the sacrament tend to be impaired by the lack of ecclesial unity, thus rendering common worship questionable. But even within a single denomination—it may be observed—the unity of the congregation in faith and love will always fall short of the ideal. Thus the lack of ecclesial unity among different confessions is not an absolute bar to intercommunion. Eucharistic sharing may at times be an appropriate sign of a growing, though still imperfect, unity, and may under such circumstances confer a corresponding grace to move toward greater unity.

According to the Decree, eucharistic sharing is not to be used indiscriminately as a means to restore union. The unity among confessionally divided churches is not so great as to call normally for a commonly celebrated Eucharist or for mutual eucharistic hospitality. The difficulty is not simply that the esthetics of the sign would be marred, but rather that the grace of the sacrament might be impeded. Intercommunion could do spiritual harm if the reception of communion in a church other than one's own were to result in cheapening the meaning of the sign, or weakening the intensity and purity of one's own faith, or rupturing the intimate unity of a family of believers engaged in a most sacred act of celebration.

In a later article, the Decree on Ecumenism applies these principles to the separated churches of the East.[6] Since these churches, it declares, possess a true priesthood and true sacraments, reciprocal eucharistic sharing between them and the Roman Catholic Church under certain circumstances "is not merely possible but is recommended." In the Decree on the Eastern Catholic Churches, the conditions are spelled out in greater detail: the approval of competent ecclesiastical authority, spontaneous request, right dispositions, some necessity or spiritual urgency—besides certain negative conditions such as the unavailability of a priest of one's own communion, the absence of scandal and of danger of indifferentism or deviation in the faith.[7]

As may be seen from the previous quotation from the Standing Conference of Orthodox Bishops in America, the unilateral action of Vatican II in encouraging eucharistic sharing with the Orthodox was not well received on the part of the latter, who make a very strict equation between the sacraments and the Church, understood as the Orthodox Church. Roman Catholicism, at least today, is willing to interpret the ecclesial character of the Eucharist more broadly, in accordance with the long-standing tradition by which it has recognized the validity of certain sacraments administered in other Christian churches.

From the Roman Catholic point of view, the more painful decisions regarding eucharistic sharing have to do with Catholic-Protestant relations. Can Protestants ever appropriately receive communion at a Roman Catholic service, and can Catholics ever appropriately receive at Protestant services? These two questions will be discussed in the light of certain postconciliar decrees issued by Roman Catholic ecclesiastical authorities.

As regards the admission of Protestants to receive at a Roman Catholic service, the Ecumenical Directory issued by the Secretariat for Promoting Christian Unity in 1967 states that this may be proper in cases of danger of death or urgent necessity, such as might occur during persecution or imprisonment. Even in these urgent cases, however, four conditions must be fulfilled: that the Protestant in question have no access to a minister of his own faith; that he spontaneously ask for communion from a Catholic priest; that his eucharistic faith harmonize with that of the Catholic Church; and that he be rightly disposed. Then the Decree adds that in other cases the judge of the "urgent necessity" is to be the diocesan bishop or the episcopal conference.[8]

In its Instruction of 1972, the Secretariat issued a further clarification. It gave a more lenient interpretation to the notion of "urgent necessity," making it clear that this is not confined to situations of persecution or danger of death. The Instruction speaks of "serious spiritual need," which it defines in terms of what is required for personal spiritual growth and, inseparably connected with this, deeper involvement in the mystery of the Church and its unity. In another respect, however, the 1972 Instruction is more stringent than the Directory. It specifies that the unavailability of a minister of one's own community must extend "for a prolonged period." It also underlines the standard precautions that the admission of non-Catholics to the Catholic Eucharist should never be allowed to endanger or disturb the faith of Catholics.[9]

A "Note" explaining the 1972 Instruction was issued in October 1973, with the purpose of correcting excessively lax interpretations. This note reminds local ordinaries that they have no discretion to dispense from any of the conditions set forth in the Instruction, but that they may, in particular cases, judge whether the conditions are verified.[10]

Comparing the Vatican II Decree, especially the two paragraphs quoted above, with the postconciliar documents from the Secretariat, one may note a movement toward greater strictness. The Decree implies that because of the anomalous situation of a Church divided against itself, there are inevitable ambiguities. It is impossible, therefore, to lay down precise and binding legislation. Intercommunon is viewed as a matter for discernment by those in touch with the concrete situation on the local scene. The Directory and the subsequent Roman clarifications are more legalistic in tone. They greatly restrict the discretion of local authorities, including the local bishop. The Directory and the Instruction seem to emanate from a mentality that looks upon intercommunion not as an ambiguous and partly desirable phenomenon, but as an evil not be to permitted without serious justifying reasons. This represents, in my opinion, a recession toward the preconciliar theology of "communicatio in sacris" and a closer approach to what I have described as the Orthodox position.

If one were to see occasional intercommunion not simply as a concession to weakness but as an appropriate sign of the partial but growing unity among separated churches, one could take a more positive view than these Roman documents do. A certain liberalization would have the advantage of bringing the directives into closer alignment with what many conscientious and committed Christians are now doing, and would thus tend to make such persons better disposed toward church authority and toward ecclesiastical legislation. From this point of view one may question the necessity of some of the conditions presently laid down.

1. The term "urgent need" suggests that a prohibition is being relaxed because of some extraordinary pastoral situation, such as imprisonment, persecution, or danger of death. Even the term "spiritual need," used in the Instruction, is no great improvement, because it likewise connotes the mere avoidance of evil. Such negative language, I believe, ought to be dropped, in view of the fact that, as the decree indicates, intercommunion may be positively desirable. The practice is commended by the grace to be gained—especially, I would say, the grace of showing forth and fostering the partial but growing unity among churches that are as yet imperfectly in communion with one another.

2. On the same principle, it is difficult to see why the unavailability of ministers of one's own community should be laid down as a

requirement. Granted that it would be anomalous regularly to receive communion in a church to which one did not wish to belong, there might be reasons for doing so on certain specific occasions, even when one could approach ministers of one's own church. This might be the case, for example, on the occasion of a mixed marriage, an interdenominational retreat, an ecumenical conference, or a special service for Christian unity.

3. Certainly Protestants or others should not be subjected to any moral pressure to receive communion in the Catholic Church, but does the demand that they "spontaneously ask" preclude the possibility of their being told on some special occasion that they would be welcome to approach the altar? If so, it is difficult to see the reason for this prohibition.

4. That the faith of the non-Catholic should be in harmony with Catholic teaching concerning the Eucharist seems to me to be a correct principle—even one that might be extended to include beliefs in harmony with Catholic teaching on other central matters of faith. One may also agree with the remark in the Note of 1973 that a mere affirmation of faith in the "real presence" of Christ in the Eucharist would not suffice. On the other hand, it would be too strict to insist on the ability of the communicant to subscribe to a technical theological formulation, such as "transubstantiation." The demands should not be so stringent that believing Catholics would be excluded by the same tests. A correct worshipful attitude is more important than an exact theological expression.

5. That the communicant be rightly disposed is, of course, always desirable. Among these dispositions should be included, most importantly, a sense of needing God's pardon for one's sins. When receiving the Eucharist under ecumenical circumstances, one should be penitent especially for those personal and corporate sins that have divided, and continue to divide, Christian communities. The right disposition should include a sincere concern to promote greater unity in the truth. The "right disposition," however, should never be so rigorously interpreted as to make it appear that communion is a reward for merit rather than a remedy for weakness.

6. The principle that Catholics should be protected from being scandalized or led into indifference and error, often mentioned in the directives, is itself perfectly sound. In applying this principle, how-

ever, one must keep in mind that it is a two-edged sword. Although some are perhaps shocked by the practice of intercommunion, others are scandalized by the refusal of communion to a baptized Christian who approaches the sacrament with sincere faith and devotion. Indifference is fostered not only by indiscriminate eucharistic sharing, but also, and perhaps more virulently, by the inability of Christians, even on exceptional occasions, to share in altar fellowship. Bigots who resent it when anyone outside their own denomination is treated as a Christian should not be confirmed in their obsessive attitudes, but should, on the contrary, be educated to appreciate better the real and growing unity of which we have spoken.

I conclude, therefore, that the present instructions could suitably be liberalized to include the idea that suitably disposed baptized Protestant believers who feel spiritually united to the Catholic Church and to its leaders, and who recognize the sacramental presence of the Lord in a Catholic Eucharist as Catholics do, might on certain special occasions be permitted or invited to receive Holy Communion at a Roman Catholic service. The determination of the kind and number of occasions might be further specified by the regional conference of bishops or by the local episcopal authority. Considerable discretion in applying the directives might appropriately be left to the local pastor or celebrant.

In the very complex religious situation of the United States, it would be most difficult to draw up specific rules applicable to all cases. To preserve any kind of discipline, the directives would have to be simple and easily understood. It would be impossible in such documents to make fine distinctions among the various Protestant denominations, although their mutual differences are great and important. Thus we may have to live with general rules that are not fully applicable to individual cases. For this reason, it seems to me that directives, rather than laws, are in order.

As a corrective to the liberal bias of some contemporary ecumenists, one should bear in mind that excessive laxity in eucharistic sharing may be at least as harmful as excessive strictness. A penitent abstention from intercommunion may be an appropriate and grace-filled sign of the existing disunity among Christians. Care must be taken to prevent holy communion from degenerating into a mere expression of courtesy, civil friendship, or solidarity in some secular cause. It should always be positively related to the Church as a sign of God's redemptive and reconciling love.[11]

The most complex and sensitive question about eucharistic sharing concerns the action of Roman Catholics receiving at Protestant services. This problem clamors for attention because such intercommunion occasionally occurs in practice. Moreover, in the absence of some reciprocity, the action of the Catholic Church in extending eucharistic hospitality to Protestants is often felt to be triumphalistic and humiliating.

The Decree on Ecumenism did not specifically recommend eucharistic sharing between Catholics and Protestants. Referring to the Protestant churches, it declared:

> The ecclesial Communities separated from us lack that fullness of unity with us which should flow from baptism, and we believe that especially because of the lack of the sacrament of orders they have not preserved the genuine and total reality of the Eucharistic mystery. Nevertheless, when they commemorate the Lord's death and resurrection in the Holy Supper, they profess that it signifies life in communion with Christ and they await His coming in glory. For these reasons, dialogue should be undertaken concerning the true meaning of the Lord's Supper, the other sacraments, and the Church's worship and ministry.[12]

The Ecumenical Directory of 1967, in articles 55 and 59 (taken together) seems to say that it is never permissible for Catholics to receive at a Protestant service, apparently because the Catholic Church does not recognize Protestant ordinations as sacramental.[13] The same line of thinking reappears in the Note on Intercommunion released by the Secretariat in 1973, which asserts that "the question of reciprocity arises only with these Churches which have preserved the substance of the Eucharist, the Sacrament of Orders, and apostolic succession."[14] The study on Apostolic Succession issued in 1974 by the International Theological Commission states that intercommunion between Roman Catholics and Protestants is impossible for the present "because sacramental continuity in apostolic succession from the beginning is an indispensable element of ecclesial communion both for the Catholic Church and for the Orthodox churches."[15] A second reason frequently given for prohibiting Catholics from receiving communion in Protestant churches is that the latter do not have a correct eucharistic faith.

The postconciliar Roman documents, therefore, seem to forbid Catholics ever to receive communion at a Protestant service. There are, however, a number of documents issued by individual bishops and episcopal conferences that designate situations in which a Catholic could conscientiously decide to receive the Eucharist at a Protestant service. These documents claim to be in harmony with Vatican II, though they are difficult to reconcile with the letter of the postconciliar directives from Rome.

The most important of these more liberal documents are those emanating from Léon Arthur Elchinger, the bishop of Strasbourg. His instruction of November 30, 1972, was a very important breakthrough in postconciliar Catholic ecumenism.[16] He was here speaking—as he has repeatedly pointed out—to his own diocese, which is unique because of the large number of French-speaking Lutheran and Reformed Christians and because of the numerous confessionally mixed households (*foyers mixtes*) in which Protestants and Catholics meet to meditate together on the word of God. Deepening their faith as they ponder the significance of their life together, couples in mixed marriages frequently feel a deep spiritual need to nourish their love by receiving the Eucharist jointly. Elchinger's directives are an attempt to meet this spiritual need and to avert underground or wildcat liturgies that could lead only to a deterioration of the sense of the Church.

Before giving a positive response, Elchinger makes two limiting statements. In the first place, he says, there can at present be no question of general intercommunion. To open one's Eucharist habitually to members of other churches would be a false sign, masking the important differences that still exist and obscuring the length of the road that still lies ahead. Second, one cannot presently authorize intercelebration—that is, a eucharistic service at which ministers of several churches jointly preside. Such a service would be premature, since it presupposes an agreement that has not been reached with regard to ordination and the role of the ordained minister with regard to the Eucharist. The bishop therefore limits himself to discussing the permissibility of "eucharistic hospitality," here defined

as "the occasional admission of a baptized person to a Eucharist celebrated in a church other than his own."

As an underlying principle, Elchinger maintains that every Eucharist is both the sign of a lived reality and a sign of hope and expecta-
tion of a reality not yet achieved. Church and Eucharist are always
linked, but each of them is inscribed in a living tension between
what is already given in Christ and what will come about only when
God is fully "all in all."

In this dynamic perspective, Bishop Elchinger addresses two questions: Under what conditions may a Protestant, by way of exception,
be admitted to Roman Catholic Eucharist? And under what conditions may a Catholic exceptionally participate in the Eucharist of a
Protestant community? The first of these questions he answers very
much along the lines in the preceding pages. He departs from the
Secretariat's 1972 Instruction in two main respects. He extends the
notion of "serious spiritual need" to include the need to foster the
growth of an ecumenical community; and he omits the requirement
that a minister of one's own community should in every case be
unavailable.

Turning to the second question, Bishop Elchinger maintains that
under four conditions the participation of Catholics in a Protestant
communion service could be a meaningful action:

1. The Catholic must not have to renounce anything of his own
faith or membership in his own church. (This condition, he adds,
implies a substantial agreement in eucharistic faith.)

2. The Catholic must recognize in the Protestant minister a duly
constituted representative of the Protestant community, ordained to
dispense the word and the sacraments in fidelity to the teaching of
the apostles.

3. The Catholic should have real bonds of life and faith with
those in whose Eucharist he or she desires to participate (as might
be expected in the case of members of confessionally mixed households sincerely seeking to develop a joint Christian life).

4. The request must express a spiritual need arising out of the
common life of the confessionally mixed family.

With regard to the state of mind of the Catholic receiving communion under such conditions in a Protestant church, Bishop

Elchinger makes a statement that, in my mind, admirably coincides with the teaching of Vatican II:

> He would recall that certain deficiencies exist—greater or lesser according to the particular church—on the plane of the sacramental organism by which the Church visibly constitutes itself as the Body of Christ.
>
> He would know, however, that in spite of these deficiencies, those who celebrate the Eucharist in faith and fidelity to the Lord's testament may really share in the life of Christ who gives himself as food for his own for the building up of his one Body.[17]

Such a Catholic, then, would receive communion at a Protestant Lord's Supper with the conviction "that this celebration—in a mysterious manner, difficult to specify precisely—gives him a share in the unique eucharistic reality which he is certain, according to his faith, of approaching in all its sacramental plenitude in his own church."[18]

Since Bishop Elchinger's courageous initiatives, some other individual bishops and groups of bishops have begun to follow suit. Bishop Schmitt of Metz, on July 10, 1973, authorized certain Catholics to receive communion at Protestant services "under the conditions anticipated in the Guidelines of the Bishop of Strasbourg, Msgr. Elchinger."[19] The French Bishops' Committee for Christian Unity, in a recent commentary on a document from the Groupe des Dombes, accepts the possibility of limited reciprocal intercommunion with Protestants.[20] We have not yet reached the day, they declare, when eucharistic hospitality, and especially reciprocity, present no problems. In the present ambiguous situation it is important to avoid an "all or nothing" mentality. It is the responsibility of the local bishop to exercise discretion in particular cases.

Even more significant for its detail is the Pastoral Instruction adopted on March 1, 1975, by the Swiss Interdiocesan Synodal Assembly and subsequently approved by the Swiss Episcopal Conference.[21] This Instruction holds, in conformity with the Decree on Ecumenism (§ 22), that any church which has not retained the episcopate and the sacrament of orders lacks the "full reality of the eucharistic mystery." In such cases the general rule is that of the Ecumenical Directory (§ 55), that a Catholic may not ask to receive the Eucharist from a minister who has not validly received the sacrament of orders. But if a Catholic in an exceptional situation arrives at the conviction that his conscience authorizes him to receive the Eucharist, "this step should not be interpreted as necessarily implying a rupture with his own church, even though common sharing of the Eucharist remains problematical as long as the separation of the churches continues."

Summarizing the current state of Catholic opinion as reflected by the official statements noticed in this chapter, we may note both agreements and disagreements. All apparently agree that Protestant churches which have no episcopate or sacramentally ordained ministry lack "the genuine and total reality of the eucharistic mystery," as the Decree on Ecumenism puts it. This fact alone makes it inappropriate for Catholics, at least normally, to receive communion in these churches. But there is disagreement about whether a Catholic, by way of exception, might occasionally be justified in receiving communion in such a church. The Roman documents seem to rule this out. Bishop Elchinger and those who follow his general line of thought allow this as a possibility, under a number of conditions which they are careful to specify.

The disagreements appear to be rooted in different answers to two questions: First, is there a sufficient agreement in eucharistic doctrine so that a Catholic, faithful to the beliefs of his own church, can also share in the beliefs of the Protestant church in which he is receiving? Second, can the Catholic believe that the Protestant church in question has a genuine Eucharist so that he can receive with the attitudes of worship deemed appropriate for holy communion?

Of the two difficulties, that arising from the disparity of eucharistic doctrine is generally regarded as the more tractable. The discussions of the Eucharist in the Faith and Order Commission of the World Council of Churches and in the bilateral consultations of the decade following Vatican II have produced a remarkable series of consensus statements. As a result it has become apparent that the doctrinal barriers between Roman Catholics and certain Protestant groups (Anglican, Lutheran, and Reformed) are not nearly so great as was commonly supposed.

The two doctrinal issues most fiercely contested at the time of the Reformation were the sacrificial nature of the Eucharist and the doctrine of the real presence. On both there has been significant progress, even though the dialogue groups have not broken out of the sixteenth-century questions and categories of thought.

With regard to sacrifice the Catholic Church has succeeded in making it clearer to other Christians that it does not defend the superstitious positions repudiated by the sixteenth-century Protestants. In part, these charges seem to have been due to a misunderstanding of what Catholics were teaching at that time; also, Catholic theology has undergone further and needed clarification since the Reformation. In any case, Catholics today have explained to the satisfaction of many Protestants that the Eucharist is not regarded as another sacrifice added to that of Christ. On the other hand, many Anglicans and Protestants, drawing on modern biblical studies, have become convinced that the Eucharist is the sacrifice of Christ re-presented and re-enacted through effectual proclamation. Some scholars refer in this connection to the biblical idea of "memorial" (the Hebrew *lezikkaron* or the Greek *anamnesis*) as an efficacious recall. Others appeal to the fact that Christ, as the one who died for our sins and rose for our salvation, is still living and present to his community and making intercession for them as they celebrate his redemptive act. This heavenly intercession of the risen Christ, it is pointed out, pertains to the integral notion of sacrifice.

Is there full consensus with regard to sacrifice? This might be too strong a term, especially since the evangelical Protestants have not been much heard from on the subject. In this connection it is noteworthy that the Windsor Statement of the International Anglican–Roman Catholic Commission (1971) did not unequivocally call the Eucharist "sacrifice."[22] Catholic signers (e.g., Bishop Christopher Butler) said that this was implicitly asserted, but an evangelical signer (Julian Charley) strongly denied this. The Windsor Statement can be read as affirming that Christ, who is the one full and sufficient sacrifice, makes the *fruits* of his sacrifice available in the Eucharist.[23] It seems certain that many Protestants, especially those in the more "evangelical" tradition, would deny that the Lord's Supper is a sacrifice except in some wide or metaphorical sense—for instance, as a "sacrifice of praise." They would not subscribe to the teaching of the Council of Trent, which defined under anathema that the Mass is a true and propitiatory sacrifice.[24]

The question of real presence is even more complex and difficult than that of sacrifice. Among the groups that have been directly involved in the ecumenical discussions concerning the Eucharist, there seems to be a rather general consensus that Christ is really and truly present in the celebration of the Lord's Supper, which accordingly is not just a bare sign or commemoration in the psychological sense of remembering. The living Lord makes himself graciously present to his people according to his covenant.

Real presence, however, is a very wide term. It can be applied to Christ's presence among those who gather in his name (cf. Mt 18:20), to his presence in the Scriptures and in the proclaimed word, and to his presence in other sacraments such as baptism.[25] Regarding the Eucharist, there is a wide consensus that Christ is present whole and entire (and thus in his "body and blood"), though not in a material way. Some refer to the manner of presence as sacramental or spiritual, and this should cause no difficulty if these terms are understood in a spiritual sense.

That is about the extent of the consensus. When efforts are made to specify how the real presence of Christ is related to the eucharistic elements (the bread and wine) there are sharp differences of doctrine, which tend to follow along confessional lines. In Western Christianity there are three main schools of thought, well summarized by Max Thurian, whose analysis I follow at this point[26]:

1. *Transubstantiation.* The bread and wine are converted into the body and blood of Christ. This conversion is not in the physical order (and thus involves no chemical change), but it does affect the profound reality (substance) of the elements, so that they are no longer substantially what they were—bread and wine. This is the Roman Catholic doctrine defined at Trent[27] and reasserted by Pope Paul VI as late as 1965.[28]

2. *Consubstantiation.* The profound being of the bread and wine subsists, but is closely united to the profound being or substance of the body and blood of Christ, which becomes present in and under the elements, somewhat as fire is present in heated metal. Luther was inclined toward this view, and it appears in some of the official Lutheran confessional writings.

3. *Concomitance.* The bread and wine remain what they were, but they become the vehicle of Christ's presence, so that when we

eat the bread and drink the wine we also spiritually receive Jesus Christ. This has frequently been the view of Calvinists and other Reformed Christians. Some have held that the real presence occurs only at the time of communion and is dependent on the faith of the recipient (receptionism).

In view of the continuing conflicts among these three schools, it is doubtful whether we can speak today of a full or even a substantial consensus regarding real presence. Yet there have been significant convergences. Roman Catholics in the past decade have made it clear that transubstantiation, in its status as a binding dogma, does not involve any particular metaphysical explanation of the real presence. Many Catholic theologians would be willing to say, as does a footnote in the Windsor Statement:

> The word *transubstantiation* is commonly used in the Roman Catholic Church to indicate that God acting in the eucharist effects a change in the inner reality of the elements. The term should be seen as affirming the *fact* of Christ's presence and of the mysterious and radical change which takes place. In contemporary Roman Catholic theology it is not understood as explaining *how* the change takes place.[29]

In the light of explanations such as these, there is today a widespread disposition to treat the differences between the first two schools as a matter of theological opinion rather than of binding doctrine. Even though the concept of consubstantiation has not appealed to Catholics nor that of transubstantiation to most Protestants, still many Lutherans, Anglicans, and Catholics can agree that Christ becomes substantially or objectively present in the elements themselves, which truly "become" his body and blood, according to Jesus' words in the Gospels, "This is my body. . . . This is my blood." Some Reformed Christians, such as Max Thurian, would surely share this consensus, but it is not clear, at least to me, that this may be said of Reformed Christians generally. Many seem to insist that although Christ is really present in the eucharistic celebration he is not substantially present in the consecrated elements; they do not become his body and blood. With such Christians Roman Catholics will have to say that they have an important disagreement within an even more important agreement. As Lutherans and

Reformed Christians continue to work out their differences, they may point the way toward a wider and deeper Christian consensus. I believe that, as each group rethinks its traditional positions in the new context of our times, there is reason to hope that consensus can be reached by the path of mutual enrichment and convergence, without any major Christian constituency simply capitulating to the others.

In cases where a Christian community's present eucharistic doctrine is not in accord with the Roman Catholic understanding of the sacrament, there is a serious obstacle to intercommunion. The act of receiving communion in a Protestant church seems to convey the significance of being able to accept in substance the teaching of that church concerning the Eucharist.

A further complicating factor, as mentioned above, is the question whether the Protestant church in which one is receiving has a genuine Eucharist. This is quite different from the question of eucharistic doctrine, just discussed, although the two questions are often confused. The Decree on Ecumenism, as we have noted, states that, especially because of the lack (*defectum*) of the sacrament of orders, the Protestant churches do not possess "the genuine and total reality of the eucharistic mystery." None of the catholic documents to which I have referred contests this negative judgment. The Decree does not say, to be sure, that Protestants have no true ministry of word and sacrament. Nor does it say that they have nothing of the eucharistic mystery. The rest of the paragraph seems to me to imply rather that the Lord does in some way make himself present in response to the devout worship which these communities conduct in obedience to the biblical mandate, "Do this in commemoration of me."

Why should the Eucharist of a Protestant church be regarded as defective? The difficulty in the eyes of Catholic theologians would seem to lie not so much in the area of eucharistic doctrine as in the area of ministry. There is a widespread conviction that the eucharistic mystery is not fully present unless celebrated under the presidency of a minister sacramentally ordained in the apostolic succession. This is the difficulty to which the Decree on Ecumenism apparently alludes in the passage just quoted; and the same difficulty is spelled out even more clearly in the International Theological Commission's 1974 paper on apostolic succession, already mentioned in this chapter. Further work by Catholic theologians is needed to determine more clearly the requirements for sacramental ordination in the apostolic succession and to clarify whether this necessarily involves ordination by a bishop who stands within that succession.

If it be true that the Eucharist of Protestant churches is defective (as even Elchinger seems to admit), there are problems for the Catholic receiving it. Can the Catholic approach the Lord's table with the same spiritual attitudes that are expected to be present in members of these churches? Paradoxically, the more "orthodox" by Catholic standards is the eucharistic doctrine of such a church, the more difficult will it be for the Catholic to participate. For if the Catholic accepts the teaching of his own church that the Protestant Eucharist is defective, he will probably be unable to credit the claim these churches sometimes make to a "substantial presence" of Christ in the consecrated elements. And if the Catholic does not share the faith of the Protestant community, his reception of communion would seem to be a false sign—one possibly offensive to the church in which he is a guest, and in any case highly ambiguous.

It would be easy to dismiss these points as the scruples of a professional theologian whose specialization inclines him to be cautious and even hypercritical. In these pages I am intentionally speaking as a theologian, not as a legislator. I am convinced, however, that my professional scruples may have significance for the nontheologian. One's understanding about what is happening at Mass and communion has a vital impact on one's spiritual attitudes. Is one partaking in a sacrifice? Does one inwardly reverence the host that one receives? The recipient at the service will have to take a responsible attitude in accordance with what he believes. And the Church, in its official directives, will seek to guide the believer in forming his attitudes.

The pastoral guidelines set forth by Bishop Elchinger and the Europeans who follow his general approach display fine ecumenical sensitivity and are probably well adapted to the local situations envisaged. Similar directives could perhaps be appropriate in a country such as Uganda, where most Christians are either Roman Catholic or Anglican, and where all Christians are currently under great pressure. In North America there seems to be no tendency on the part of bishops to favor reciprocal eucharistic sharing with Protestants, and the reason for this reluctance is no doubt the extreme complexity of the religious situation in the United States and Canada, where there are so many varieties of Protestantism. While one may anticipate exceptional cases calling for a departure from the general rule, such exceptions, as the Secretariat for Promoting Unity has declared, are to be examined individually. "Hence a general regulation cannot be issued which makes a category out of an exceptional case, nor is it possible to legitimize on the basis of *epikeia* by turning this latter into a generalized rule."[30] The existing prohibitions of reciprocal intercommunion should weigh heavily with the individual seeking to make a conscientious decision. To violate the known discipline of one's own church, it would seem, is rarely a source of edification or of spiritual blessings.

In the past some enthusiasts have promoted intercommunion as though it were a panacea for division among Christians. If the Eucharist is an efficacious sign of unity, some reasoned, Christians ought always to celebrate an "open" Eucharist. Otherwise, the sacrament of unity would become a symbol of division. In practice, however, eucharistic promiscuity has not proved the remedy that was foreseen. Especially when done in violation of official directives, its main effects would seem to be those of detaching the communicant from any particular church and of fostering indifference to all ecclesiastical structures. In this way the Eucharist loses its ecclesial significance and is impoverished.

In the present state of divided Christianity, there is room for liturgical symbolization of the existing disunity. In a situation of division, we cannot eucharistically celebrate a unity we do not have. At the Eucharist more than elsewhere, Christians have the opportunity to experience, as is fitting, the pain of disunity. By reverent and prayerful abstention, they may perhaps impetrate the grace to work effectively for the unity that we await as God's will and God's gift to his Church.

IX. Ecumenical Strategies for a Pluralistic Age

In the last three chapters we have seen how the inner revitalization of the Catholic Church is closely interconnected with ecumenical openness. The literature on Vatican II, and indeed the Decree on Ecumenism itself, has often recognized the intimate relationship between the projected updating of the Church and the new dialogue among the separated Christian communities. The historical experience of other Christian traditions, with which Rome has regained friendly contact, suggests new and fruitful paths for the renewal of Catholicism. Conversely, as the Decree explicitly recognized, authentic renewal of the Catholic Church "has notable ecumenical importance,"[1] for it overcomes many unnecessary and harmful barriers among Christians. It is no mere coincidence, then, that the council of *aggiornamento* was also the great council of ecumenism.

During and immediately after the Council there was a general feeling throughout the Christian world that the twofold movement of reform and ecumenism was rapidly picking up momentum. But institutional reform, as we have noted in an earlier chapter, quickly ran into obstacles, as a result of which it has been slowed down. We must therefore ask, has the same happened to ecumenism? If so, is it important and possible to get the ecumenical movement under way again?

During the fifty years from 1910 to 1960 ecumenism seemed very sure of its basis and its goals. Inspired by the prayer of Jesus that all his disciples might be one, it aimed to bring all Christian communities into a single church with an agreed doctrinal basis and agreed forms of polity and worship. Fidelity to the demands of unity, it was assumed, would at some point demand that each denomination accept an "obedience unto death"—to use the phrase of the Evanston Assembly.[2] In their more enthusiastic moments, some dared to speak of the day when ecumenism itself would be superfluous, since all

Christians would be organically united in a single visible communion.

Ecumenists of the past two generations have been divided not so much about the ultimate goal of the movement as about the strategies for attaining this goal. A number of different strategies have been simultaneously pursued, and these may be conveniently grouped under four major headings:

1. Operating on the premise that doctrinal disagreements are among the chief obstacles to Christian unity, many theologians have been working to establish a wider measure of agreement. In the Faith and Order movement, since its Lausanne Conference of 1927, multilateral conversations have been conducted at the world level and these have in fact led to major breakthroughs such as, for example, the statements on Scripture and Tradition accepted at the Fourth World Conference on Faith and Order at Montreal in 1963. Vatican II, meeting in the wake of these successes, called for "dialogue between competent experts from different churches and communities" with a view to overcoming the obstacles to perfect ecclesiastical communion.[3] It proposed bilateral consultations among theologians,[4] both between Catholics and Orthodox[5] and between Catholics and Protestants,[6] and suggested a number of specific themes for dialogue. Since the Council, numerous bilateral consultations have been set up both on the international and on the national level, not least in the United States.[7] The Anglican–Roman Catholic international consensus statements on the Eucharist and on the ministry, and the American Lutheran–Roman Catholic accords on the Eucharist, the ministry, and papal primacy have been among the more outstanding fruits of these dialogues. Profiting from the results of the bilateral consultations, the Faith and Order Commission of the World Council of Churches, now with Roman Catholic participation, has produced major statements on baptism, on the Eucharist, and on a mutually recognized ministry.[8]

2. Christians of different churches or denominations have found it possible to engage in co-operation for nonecclesiastical objectives, especially for social and humanitarian goals. This kind of interchurch co-operation was strongly promoted by the Swedish archbishop Nathan Söderblom in the early years of the century, and by the Life and Work movement which he helped to initiate. The Decree on

Ecumenism encouraged Roman Catholics to collaborate with other Christians in social action, adding that "co-operation among all Christians vividly expresses that bond which already unites them, and it sets forth in clearer relief the features of Christ the Servant."[9] During the late sixties Catholics and Protestants in the United States were drawn together in the civil rights movement, the war on poverty, and the peace movement. On the international level, the World Council of Churches and the Pontifical Commission for Justice and Peace jointly established in 1968 an organization known as SODEPAX (acronym for Committee on Society, Development, and Peace). High hopes were set on "secular ecumenism" to achieve the kind of lived unity that had eluded the theologians in their more theoretical approaches.

3. Participation in the ecumenical movement has been formalized by the establishment of Councils of Churches on the world level (the World Council of Churches), on the national level (e.g., the National Council of Churches in the United States), and on the local level (state, regional, and metropolitan councils or conferences). The World Council of Churches comprises some 250 member churches, the vast majority of which are national bodies. According to its new Constitution, the prime purpose of the World Council is "to call the churches to the goal of visible unity in one faith and in one eucharistic fellowship expressed in worship and in common life in Christ, and to advance towards that unity in order that the world may believe."[10]

The World Council, according to the Uppsala Assembly of 1968, understands itself as "a transitional opportunity for eventually actualizing a truly universal, ecumenical, conciliar form of common life."[11] Recognizing that the present ecumenical conciliar bodies have no real power to speak for their member churches and are not as yet truly ecclesial fellowships, the Uppsala Assembly and the 1971 Louvain meeting of the Faith and Order Commission called for preparations for a "genuinely universal council" that might be able to "speak for all Christians and lead the way into the future."[12]

4. The final strategy is that of church unions leading to "united churches." The following definition has been proposed: "A united church is one which is born out of the acceptance of one another of two or more denominations which have had varying and distinct tra-

ditions and developments, and thus decide to cease to exist as two or more entities and from a point of time begin to live and function as one visible body or fellowship."[13] Advocates of these union churches see them as the key to the worldwide united church of the future. The Salamanca Consultation of the Faith and Order Commission, meeting in 1973, offered the following vision of the goal of the ecumenical movement:

> The one Church is to be envisioned as a conciliar fellowship of local churches which are themselves truly united. In this conciliar fellowship each local church possesses, in communion with the others, the fullness of catholicity, witnesses to the same apostolic faith and therefore recognizes the others as belonging to the same Church of Christ and guided by the same Spirit. . . . To this end, each church aims at maintaining sustained and sustaining relationships with her sister churches, expressed in conciliar gatherings whenever required for the fulfillment of their common calling.[14]

In June 1975 there was held at Toronto an important Consultation of United Churches and Committees on Union, with representatives of fifteen united churches, including those of Canada, North India, Pakistan, South India, Japan, and Zaire, as well as of many church-union committees from various countries. These united and uniting churches are setting up closer bonds among themselves and developing an aggressive program for the future.

As might be expected with different groups of people applying different strategies to achieve the same goals, there has always been some tension among ecumenists. Prior to World War II the most obvious tension was a kind of rivalry between the more doctrinally oriented Faith and Order movement and the more practically oriented Life and Work movement. Today tensions exist among all four of the strategies listed above. Proponents of each strategy find themselves ranged against champions of the other three, and as a result certain weaknesses have been found in each of the four strategies.

Against the bilateral theological consultations it is often objected that the progress is very slow and that the agenda tends to concentrate on historically debated points far removed from the concerns of contemporary "grass-roots" Christians. This type of consultation is well suited to churches whose identity is founded on a specific doctrinal stance, as are the Lutheran churches and some of the "confessional" Reformed churches emanating from the sixteenth-century Reformation. But these theological discussions do not fully meet the specific concerns of other Christian bodies, such as the more "organic" churches found in the East and the more "denominational" churches that have arisen in the West since the eighteenth century. Further, it is objected that while the dialogues have achieved a measure of consensus among the participating theologians, this consensus has rarely been more than partial, and even the partial consensus has not always gained acceptance with the official leadership or the general membership of the respective churches. The attention given to distinctively confessional issues has tended rather to enhance than to diminish the attachment of each group to its specific doctrines and traditions.

The main difficulty raised against the second strategy—collaboration for social goals—is that it has very little impact on the structural relations among the churches themselves. The social activists from different denominations often establish excellent rapport among themselves, but fail to carry their communities along with them. To some extent they create new divisions among Christians by tending to pit social progressives against conservatives, and radicals against moderates. While strong arguments can no doubt be made for "conflictual" theology, it scarcely furthers the traditional goals of the ecumenical movement.[15]

As a remedy for the isolation of Christians social activists from their churches, efforts have been made at times to set up agencies rather closely linked with the official leadership of the churches. But the agencies in such cases find their hands tied by the necessity of making their programs generally acceptable to the authorities and membership of the respective churches, some of which have widely divergent traditions in the area of social thought. The effort to overcome these divergences and to find a theological rationale for the social mission of the churches leads back again into the doctrinal debates discussed above.

The third strategy—the establishment of "councils" of churches such as the World Council, the national and local councils, and the projected "genuinely universal council" has not proved very helpful in overcoming the inveterate divisions. If anything, membership in interchurch councils appears to solidify the existing divisions by institutionalizing them. Once established, the councils tend to turn into immense bureaucracies, seeking to engage the services of experts on innumerable questions drawn from a wide spectrum of traditions. These unwieldy bureaucracies find it very hard to make pointed statements or to implement specific policies lest they alienate their member churches and thus destroy their own effectiveness as advocates.

The call of the Uppsala Assembly for a universal conciliar fellowship might seem to offer an alternative vision of growing into unity by a type of association less bureaucratic than the present interchurch councils and yet less drastic than organic union. The World Council, however, has rejected any such interpretation. The Nairobi Report on "What Unity Requires" states clearly that conciliar fellowship is not to be understood as an alternate model of unity but simply as an "aspect of the life of the one undivided Church." Conciliar fellowship, it adds, presupposes the organic unity of the Church.[16] Thus Uppsala's project of a universal conciliar fellowship, it would seem, could be carried out only after the establishment of the kind of "united church" envisioned in the fourth strategy.

The fourth strategy, more than the other three, can claim definite attainments to its credit. United churches have sprung into existence in many countries, and many projected church unions are now in the process of negotiation. But it is not clear that these unions have been helpful to the cause of ecumenism. A regional union, such as the Church of South India, may bring together Christians who had previously been divided. But in a sense it also divides some who had previously been united, because the members of the newly founded church are drawn outside the tradition of their ancestors and separated from their previous confessional family. For this reason John Macquarrie strongly contests the proposal that there should be in Great Britain three autonomous churches—English, Scottish, and Welsh—each uniting in itself the denominations previously found in each of the three countries. Why should the tolerable differences, he asks, be limited to those that can be defined in national or regional terms?

> The type of ecumenism that aims to bring into being national united churches in each country seems to me quite misguided. The last thing the world needs is a series of national churches reduplicating the political divisions that already exist, and in some cases breaking up the international Christian communions (Roman, Anglican, Lutheran, etc.) which transcend national and racial borders.[17]

An additional danger in such unions is that the resultant church tends to be a rather colorless mixture, lacking the characteristic traits of each of the parent bodies. In many cases episcopacy and high sacramentalism are conserved in appearance, but are in fact deprived of their force by ambiguous formulas and qualifications introduced to placate Christians of Presbyterian, Congregational, or other low-church background. As Macquarrie observes: "The different Christian traditions—Orthodox, Lutheran, Methodist, Anglican and so on—has each a certain integrity and, like an art style, cannot be mixed up with other traditions without loss of its distinctive appeals."[18]

Finally, it deserves to be noted that union churches flourish only among a certain spectrum of Christians, generally those coming from an English-speaking Reformed tradition. Thus far, such "united churches" have normally failed to include Pentecostals, conservative evangelicals, Lutherans, Orthodox, and Roman Catholics. Since there is almost no likelihood of national or regional union churches truly including all Christians in a given area, the Salamanca projection of a future *una sancta* made up of internally united local churches seems rather gratuitous.

The ecumenical movement of the twentieth century has brought about many good results, but I find it difficult to believe that it has in the slightest degree advanced the day when we may expect to see the vast majority of Christians united in a single visible fellowship. No one of the four strategies described above may be said to hold great promise of achieving this goal.

Classical ecumenism, therefore, would be in difficulty even if Christians were generally enthusiastic about merging all the existing communions into a single visible church with its own forms of doc-

trine, polity, and worship. But in point of fact this supposedly ultimate goal of the ecumenical movement has been rapidly losing its
appeal. The widespread lack of enthusiasm becomes in some quarters
a positive distaste, based on grounds that may be set forth both negatively and positively.

Negatively, there is fear of homogenization. We live in the age of
the supermarket, when goods are mass-produced to suit the desires of
the average consumer, as determined by techniques of market
research. What the supermarket has done to the grocery business,
ecumenism could, if unchecked, do for the churches. A single united
church, though it might boast many millions of members, would be
bland and unexciting. Constrained to satisfy an enormous and
widely diverse constituency, the mass-church would be even less capable of speaking out prophetically than are our presently divided
confessions. If the official leadership of such a Christian conglom-
erate were to take any controversial positions, many of the members
would have just cause for resentment. Caught up in this gargantuan
organization, they would have no escape from its determinations except by fleeing into the outer darkness of a churchless existence.

The same difficulty may be positively formulated from the other
side. Emerging from several centuries of rationalism, our generation
is convinced that truth is too complex to be attained by a single
route. We see clear advantages in maintaining a number of different
options, even though some of them are logically incompatible with
others. History has frequently demonstrated the validity of ideas and
movements that were disapproved when they first arose. Where
orthodoxy has reigned unchallenged it has commonly fallen into
decay. Hence we acknowledge the value of preserving even that of
which we cannot presently approve. We would all stand to lose if
the world contained only people who thought and acted like ourselves.

In opposition to classical ecumenism, which threatened to become
the orthodoxy of the early sixties, we have witnessed in the past decade a resurgence of ecclesial particularism. In our homogenized society, people feel an increasing hunger for local color, tradition, glam-
our, poetry, and distinctiveness. In the Catholic Church, this
yearning has bolstered the traditionalist movement, which prizes the
Latin language, Roman and Gothic vestments, incense, and elabo-

rate rubrics, in place of the casual informality and easy secularity of the normal postconciliar vernacular liturgy. Not infrequently the new quest for tradition is allied with a revived ethnic consciousness. The most thriving Protestant churches are conservative and sectarian groups unashamed of their apartness, and some elements of Judaism exhibit a similar tendency toward tribalism. Martin Marty, in the course of an excellent survey of these developments, speaks of "the trauma experienced by all forms of the ecumenical movement in an era of renewed particularism and the separate searches for identity or assertions of tradition."[19]

If ecumenism is to recover its previous élan, it needs to be interpreted in a new way that does not pose a direct threat to the religious identity of those groups who take part in it. We need a vision less abstract and utopian, more in touch with the realities of the ecumenical process. Such a vision, I believe, is already surfacing in various quarters but still lacks the capacity to articulate itself clearly. In relation to the actual religious situation, ecumenism, I would propose, might appropriately take as its proximate goal the achievement of a heterogeneous community of witnessing dialogue.

This proposal presupposes that there are two basic types of community—the homogeneous and the heterogeneous. Classical ecumenism neglected this duality; it rested on the unspoken premise that community is necessarily homogeneous. Ecumenists seemed to take for granted that one could not have truly communal relationships except with persons who shared one's own religious beliefs, behavioral standards, and styles of worship.

It is very important, I agree, to have associations with persons who believe and feel as we do and who respond to the same religious symbols. We normally need the support of fellow believers who constitute our own close family in the sense that we and they inhabit one and the same spiritual home. In religious, as in secular, life we sometimes need the intimacy of a spiritual family. Such families exist on many levels—the flesh-and-blood family as a worshiping community, the so-called "base community" described in the Medellín documents as "the first and fundamental ecclesiastical nucleus,"[20] the local parish, the diocese, and, at the highest level, the worldwide family of those who live within a given Christian tradition. The worldwide communion, being inevitably less homogeneous than the base community, might be described as the religious counterpart of an extended family or a family of families.

Classical ecumenism, it seems to me, did not sufficiently respect the concern of particular groups of Christians to preserve their own distinctive identity and to protect their own traditions. The so-called Lund principle, accepted by several World Council meetings, asserted "that Christians ought always to seek to do together everything which conscience did not compel them to do separately."[21] Whence comes this ecumenical obligation? Following another well-known principle—that of subsidiarity[22]—I should prefer to say that any congenial group ought to be encouraged to do by itself what it can effectively do alone. This, of course, would not preclude others from being invited, when appropriate, to share in the activities of a group to which they do not belong. But there is a legitimate distinction between the member and the guest.

For heterogeneous communities, the model might be friendship rather than the family, though admittedly in some families there is striking inner diversity, while in some friendships there is marked similarity. Families, however, if they live much by themselves, tend to adopt common ways of thinking and acting. They run the risk of becoming too set in their ways, and for this reason need the stimulation of contact with outsiders. The friend who visits the family is expected to bring the challenge of new experiences, new ideas, and new points of view. It is not necessary that friends should always agree. On the contrary, some of our best friends are those with whom we vehemently differ. The deeper the friendship, the more capable it is of sustaining disagreements that, without love, could be divisive.

The greatest value of the ecumenical movement, as we have known it thus far, is that, perhaps quite unintentionally, it introduced into the religious sphere the benefits of heterogeneous community. The various churches, confessions, and denominations were suffering from excessive inbreeding, relating to one another, if at all, on a hostile basis. Ecumenism was therefore experienced as a breath of fresh air; it led to a thrilling revitalization of all the communities concerned. They discovered to their great benefit that it is possible to have real and precious friendships with groups of Christians whose ideas they could not share.

The distinctive value of a heterogeneous community is precisely the element of tension or of challenge. The supposition is that the parties do not see things the same way; that they must exert themselves to understand one another's point of view. Where this effort is made, it proves extremely rewarding. We begin to discover certain limitations and imbalances in our own previous views and to appreciate how the Christian mystery might appear to those who see it through other eyes. At the same time we have the satisfaction of being able to explain our own position to those who did not previously understand it.

I speak, therefore, of a "community of witnessing dialogue." *Dialogue* takes place insofar as friends with different points of view cordially exchange their insights, speaking and listening respectfully to one another. The dialogue is one *witness* if the several parties are deeply committed to their own outlook. In ecumenism, I take it, we are not content to hold a casual conversation about trivial matters, but we seek an earnest confrontation about things that really matter. Some of the most fruitful ecumenical discussion in my experience involves serious disagreements. We sometimes feel that the other communion has less to offer than our own. We may even feel that some of its doctrines and practices are distortions of the gospel. If so, we have every right to say so. In charity we must try to help the others correct and enrich their grasp of revelation. But we must not do so without being prepared to admit that there may be a beam in our own eye, preventing us from perceiving what some other church possesses. For dialogue by its very nature demands openness.

Ecumenical dialogue teaches us to steer a middle path between polemicism and indifferentism. The polemicist sees the other groups simply as adversaries. He is determined to win the upper hand. The indifferentist, by contrast, is content with a simple agreement to disagree. His policy is one of live and let live. For the true ecumenist, committed to witnessing dialogue, the truth is important and is to be achieved by a frank and open exchange of differing points of view.

The kind of ecumenism I am advocating implies a recognition of interdependence. In the past, churches, confessions, and sects have been too monopolistic. In the present state of Christian consciousness, especially in a country such as ours, no one religious organization is in a position to say: we and we alone are the true Church, the Body of Christ, the people of God. Each group has to abandon its claim to total self-sufficiency, although all are at times tempted to retreat into the narrow confines of their own private world. We must be on guard against confessionalism, sectarianism, or an exaggerated denominationalism. We are obliged to reach out to others, both for their sakes and for our own. If we were content to live immured in our own particularity, this would indeed be a scandal, contrary to the will of Christ. The spirit of the gospel forbids us to treat any other Christian community simply as a stranger or an enemy.

In the dialogue of ecumenical witness, we should not be too eager for easy victory. Much would be lost by an unprincipled compromise or capitulation on either side. The presumption of the dialogue is that every Christian tradition contains insights of potential value for the rest. Even when we cannot accept the views and practices of the other groups, we can be glad that differences exist. It often happens that while our own religious group is cultivating a certain line of thought or action, others may be exploring alternatives and thus building up a spiritual treasury on which we ourselves may later have to draw. By extensive borrowing, the Roman Catholic Church at Vatican II acknowledged its indebtedness to the theology of the word that had been built up by the Protestant churches and to the spiritual and liturgical patrimony that had been preserved in the Orthodox and other churches of the East.

As a Roman Catholic I gladly acknowledge that the existence of multiple autonomous traditions has been, providentially, a means of preserving pluralism at a time when there might have been too little tolerance for differences in any one organizational church. It is good that the Orthodox have insisted as they have on the sacredness of their holy traditions and their liturgy. It is good that Lutherans have insisted on a robust biblical faith, Calvinists on ecclesiastical discipline, Methodists on personal holiness, and Baptists on religious freedom. These and other distinctive emphases are precious values that must not be allowed to perish for the sake of Christian unity. It would be most unfortunate if the ecumenical imperative meant that the separate Christian traditions had nothing better to do than to die. At least until such a time as each church is in a position to accept the legitimate concerns of all the others, it is important that they retain their autonomous existence. In that way their distinctive heritage may someday be placed intact at the disposal of a larger community of faith and life.

As the process of witnessing dialogue goes on, it seems probable that one result may be a greater homogeneity among the participating churches. Thanks to the discussion, a common language is forged, unilateral emphases are corrected, and insights are exchanged. It becomes easier for the groups to recognize one another's doctrines, sacraments, members, and ministries. By gradual degrees, therefore, the communities tend to become less heterogeneous than they were; they move toward what I have described as the family-type relationship.

This very development might seem to imperil the values of heterogeneity, and thus to undermine what I have described as the prime value of ecumenism. This danger, however, is more theoretical than real. The conditions of the modern world discourage homogenization. Especially in the cultural and religious sphere, the present trend, as previously noted, is toward greater particularism. Any widely inclusive body of Christians will have to make provision for inner diversities within its own ranks. Let me illustrate this with reference to Roman Catholicism.

In spite of the efforts of certain ecclesiastical authorities to impose a monolithic uniformity, the Catholic Church has happily preserved a wide spectrum of internal differences. There are sharp dissimilarities between the Catholicism of the Eastern and Western rites. The different rites do not even recite the creed at Mass in the same form —for the affirmation that the Holy Spirit proceeds from the Father as well as from the Son is peculiar to the Western churches. Although Catholics of the East recognize the primacy of the bishop of Rome, they are not subject to the same discipline as the Western churches; they have a patriarchal style of government, and are exempt from the authority of the Roman Congregations pertaining to the pope as Patriarch of the West. The Eastern Catholic churches have their own liturgical ceremonies in accordance with their own traditions. All these differences in credal formulations, governmental forms, and liturgy do not amount to a division in the Church.

Even in the West, Catholicism exhibits marked diversities. It makes room for many theological schools and spiritual families. The religious orders represent distinct orientations within Catholicism, reflecting the particular genius of Benedict of Nursia, Bernard of Clairvaux, Francis of Assisi, Ignatius of Loyola, Teresa of Avila—to name but a few. The great founders and reformers of religious orders have left their mark upon whole traditions of theology, worship, spirituality, and community living.

In our own day still another religious style seems to be emerging in Roman Catholicism. The charismatic renewal is profoundly affecting the prayer and lifestyle of great numbers of the faithful. It remains to be seen exactly what modifications of Neo-Pentecostalism will be required in order for it to be fully at home in the Catholic Church, and what impact the new Spirit-guided communities will have upon Catholicism. The fact that the charismatic movement has come into the Catholic Church from sectarian Protestantism illustrates how ecumenical exposure can assist the Catholic Church to revitalize itself.

In the past, ecumenism has been regarded by many as a threat because contact with other churches might weaken the uniformity that the Church was seeking to maintain within itself. Today, however, there is an increasing agreement that, as John Macquarrie puts it, "the only worthwhile unity will be one which gathers up all the enriching diversity of the varying Christian traditions."[23] Many would be willing to say with Jan Kerkhofs:

1. Instead of striving after uniformity the Church should constantly try to evoke and stimulate man's creativity, to encourage and maintain diversity in communion and communion in diversity. As in the relationship between married partners, or between generations or cultures, both these factors are equally vital, and to overrate one at the expense of the other can only lead to imbalance, injustice and heresy.

2. It follows that, as the Church is today growing out of the cocoon of a static culture, described by the word "christendom" in history, it will have to guide Christians towards an acceptance of this diversity as a basic and constitutive value of man, as an individual and in groups, but at the same time it has to encourage new ways of fostering communion, of understanding the Stranger, and all those strangers whom He represents.[24]

If a pluralistic community of this kind is in fact a goal of the Church, it is easy to see how ecumenism, far from posing a threat, can be a singularly valuable resource. It can help the churches to introduce into their own ranks a more creative diversity.

In the past the ecumenical movement has tended to idealize a rather monolithic type of unity. Speaking of the Report on Unity issued by the New Delhi Assembly of the World Council of Churches (1961), Emmanuel Lanne comments:

> The particularisms of the different traditions, typological pluralism, would not seem to have found in the Report on Unity any appreciation of their positive significance. I do not refer here to a discovery of the significance which schisms and divisions might have in God's plan. That is another problem. But all the same it seems to me well worth noting that the only allusions found to the different forms of ecclesial life, to the different traditions which the Churches represent, are concerned more or less directly with the sinful aspect of these differences.[25]

Even as recently as the Salamanca Consultation (1973), the Faith and Order statements on unity seem to take a predominantly negative attitude toward the historical traditions of various Christian communities insofar as these are distinctive. This renders the objective of "organic union" as portrayed in these documents, in my judgment, unsatisfactory.

As an alternative concept of unity, Macquarrie proposes what he calls the "uniate model"—i.e., the relationship between the Roman Catholic Church of the West and the so-called "uniate" churches of the East. In this model, he points out, there is "no attempt to set up a unitary or uniform church, either by absorbing one body into the other or by trying to work out some sort of hybrid."[26] Macquarrie finds it very significant that these uniate churches do not exist only in particular geographical areas (Eastern Europe or the Middle East) but also alongside the regular Roman Catholic churches of the Western rite—thus suggesting the possibility that Anglican or Protestant churches might be received into some kind of uniate status without becoming Romanized.

While I do not substantially disagree with Macquarrie's proposal,

I would wonder whether uniatism, as the term is generally understood, is the best model. The term generally means the submission
of one church to the doctrinal and ecclesiological principles of another, in return for the permission to retain its own liturgical and
canonical practices. Thus the Ukranian church, under Polish rule,
joined Rome by the Union of Brest (Litovsk) in 1595 with the
promise that its liturgical rites and its discipline would be respected.
This type of procedure, Lanne points out, leads to an unfortunate
"dissociation between liturgical rite and discipline on the one hand,
and theological, doctrinal, confessional typology on the other."[27]
Lanne makes out a strong case for the possibility of several doctrinal
typologies within a single ecclesial allegiance.

Following Lanne's general line of thought, Cardinal Jan Willebrands, president of the Vatican Secretariat for Promoting Christian
Unity, has accepted the idea of typological diversity within a single
ecclesial allegiance. The idea of distinct *typoi* is admirably summarized by Willebrands in the following sentence:

> Where there is a long coherent tradition, commanding men's love
> and loyalty, creating and sustaining a harmonious and organic
> whole of complementary elements, each of which supports and
> strengthens the other, you have the reality of a *typos*.[28]

By the "complementary elements" mentioned in this definition, he
then explains, he has in mind such matters as a characteristic theological method, a characteristic liturgical expression, a characteristic
spiritual and devotional tradition, and a characteristic canonical discipline.

The notion of *typos*, which Willebrands here uses, is closely
linked with what in the preceding chapter on membership I referred
to as the "organic" model of the Church. For this reason the notion
seems more applicable to the ancient churches of the East and to
the Orthodox than to the Protestant churches of the West. Willebrands himself extends the notion to include the Anglican communion, but one might wonder in what measure his description of *typos*
would be verified by the Protestant Episcopal Church in the United
States.

I have no difficulty, then, in accepting the *typos* model of union
for the relationships between Rome and the Eastern churches, and

even perhaps for certain Western churches such as the Church of England and the Scandinavian Lutheran churches. More problematic is the question whether this model of union is applicable to the kind of denominations that make up the bulk of American Christianity today. Even though these denominations may represent vital spiritual traditions, it does not follow that they could appropriately exist as distinct "churches" within a larger Christian communion. Certain denominations, it would seem, were forced into existence almost against their will, and still retain their desire to be something like movements within a more inclusive Church. Where this desire exists, it should be respected.

With these exceptions, I should be prepared to acknowledge that some of the denominational entities in Western Christianity are rather analogous to *typoi*, as described by Cardinal Willebrands, and that his line of approach is therefore appropriate. Unlike the confessions and sects of previous centuries, these denominations freely recognize that God's revelation is too rich to be encompassed by any one church with a uniform body of doctrines, traditions, and rules of conduct. Thus there is value in having a plurality of ecclesial realizations, suited to the respective temperaments, historical experiences, and current concerns of different groups of Christians.

Denominations of this latter category are understandably reluctant to be absorbed into anything that might appear as a single, larger denomination. They wish to keep alive the distinctive spirit and traditions for which they stand. But they should not for that reason dwell in isolation. They are called, I believe, to practice an ecumenism of witnessing dialogue and to form corporate friendships with traditions other than their own. As the various denominations, through dialogue, overcome their present limitations and imbalances, they can move toward greater co-operation, mutual recognition, and mutual acceptance. Eventually the path may be clear for them, without disruptive changes, to become nuclear families— *typoi*, if you like—within a larger and more inclusive communion. A universal communion among all Christians as a single family of believers is an ideal which, no doubt, will never be realized within history, but one which nevertheless, by its attractive power, inspires worthy initiatives and guides ecumenical practice as a regulative norm.

In the vision of ecumenism I have sought to sketch in this chapter, the separated denominations and traditions have some other vocation than simply to die. Notwithstanding their unfortunate competitiveness in the past and present, they have served a useful purpose in discovering and keeping open Christian options that would otherwise have been ignored or closed off. If they employ their particular gifts or charismata not simply for their own corporate advantage but in the service of the wider community of faith, these splintered Christian groups may point the way toward a rich and pluriform unity—a unity in which the many churches on earth may echo, as well as human voices can, the polyphony of the angelic hosts who endlessly sing the praises of the Lord.

APPENDIX I

An Appeal for Theological Affirmation

*"An Appeal for Theological Affirmation"—the "Hartford Appeal,"
as it came to be known—was issued in January 1975 by an ecumenical group of eighteen theologians convened by Richard John
Neuhaus and Peter L. Berger and meeting in Hartford, Connecticut.*

The renewal of Christian witness and mission requires constant examination of the assumptions shaping the Church's life. Today an apparent
loss of a sense of the transcendent is undermining the Church's ability
to address with clarity and courage the urgent tasks to which God calls
it in the world. This loss is manifest in a number of pervasive themes.
Many are superficially attractive, but upon closer examination we find
these themes false and debilitating to the Church's life and work. Among
such themes are:

Theme 1:   *Modern thought is superior to all past forms of understanding
reality, and is therefore normative for Christian faith and life.*
    In repudiating this theme we are protesting the captivity to the pre-
vailing thought structures not only of the twentieth century but of any
historical period. We favor using any helpful means of understanding,
ancient or modern, and insist that the Christian proclamation must be
related to the idiom of the culture. At the same time, we affirm the need
for Christian thought to confront and be confronted by other world
views, all of which are necessarily provisional.

Theme 2:   *Religious statements are totally independent of reasonable
discourse.*
    The capitulation to the alleged primacy of modern thought takes two
forms: one is the subordination of religious statements to the canons of
scientific rationality; the other, equating reason with scientific rationality,
would remove religious statements from the realm of reasonable discourse
altogether. A religion of pure subjectivity and nonrationality results in

treating faith statements as being, at best, statements about the believer. We repudiate both forms of capitulation.

Theme 3:   *Religious language refers to human experience and nothing else, God being humanity's noblest creation.*
Religion is also a set of symbols and even of human projections. We repudiate the assumption that it is nothing but that. What is here at stake is nothing less than the reality of God: *We did not invent God; God invented us.*

Theme 4:   *Jesus can only be understood in terms of contemporary models of humanity.*
This theme suggests a reversal of "the imitation of Christ"; that is, the image of Jesus is made to reflect cultural and countercultural notions of human excellence. We do not deny that all aspects of humanity are illumined by Jesus. Indeed, it is necessary to the universality of the Christ that he be perceived in relation to the particularities of the believers' world. We do repudiate the captivity to such metaphors, which are necessarily inadequate, relative, transitory, and frequently idolatrous. Jesus, together with the Scriptures and the whole of the Christian tradition, cannot be arbitrarily interpreted without reference to the history of which they are part. The danger is in the attempt to exploit the tradition without taking the tradition seriously.

Theme 5:   *All religions are equally valid; the choice among them is not a matter of conviction about truth but only of personal preference or life style.*
We affirm our common humanity. We affirm the importance of exploring and confronting all manifestations of the religious quest and of learning from the riches of other religions. But we repudiate this theme because it flattens diversities and ignores contradictions. In doing so, it not only obscures the meaning of Christian faith, but also fails to respect the integrity of other faiths. Truth matters; therefore differences among religions are deeply significant.

Theme 6:   *To realize one's potential and to be true to oneself is the whole meaning of salvation.*
Salvation contains a promise of human fulfillment, but to identify salvation with human fulfillment can trivialize the promise. We affirm that salvation cannot be found apart from God.

Theme 7: *Since what is human is good, evil can adequately be under-stood as failure to realize potential.*

This theme invites false understanding of the ambivalence of human existence and underestimates the pervasiveness of sin. Paradoxically, by minimizing the enormity of evil, it undermines serious and sustained attacks on particular social or individual evils.

Theme 8: *The sole purpose of worship is to promote individual self-realization and human community.*

Worship promotes individual and communal values, but it is above all a response to the reality of God and arises out of the fundamental need and desire to know, love, and adore God. We worship God because God is to be worshiped.

Theme 9: *Institutions and historical traditions are oppressive and inimical to our being truly human; liberation from them is required for authentic existence and authentic religion.*

Institutions and traditions are often oppressive. For this reason they must be subjected to relentless criticism. But human community inescapably requires institutions and traditions. Without them life would degenerate into chaos and new forms of bondage. The modern pursuit of liberation from all social and historical restraints is finally dehumanizing.

Theme 10: *The world must set the agenda for the Church. Social, political, and economic programs to improve the quality of life are ultimately normative for the Church's mission in the world.*

This theme cuts across the political and ideological spectrum. Its form remains the same, no matter whether the content is defined as upholding the values of the American way of life, promoting socialism, or raising human consciousness. The Church must denounce oppressors, help liberate the oppressed, and seek to heal human misery. Sometimes the Church's mission coincides with the world's programs. But the norms for the Church's activity derive from its own perception of God's will for the world.

Theme 11: *An emphasis on God's transcendence is at least a hindrance to, and perhaps incompatible with, Christian social concern and action.*

This supposition leads some to denigrate God's transcendence. Others, holding to a false transcendence, withdraw into religious privatism or individualism and neglect the personal and communal responsibility of Christians for the earthly city. From a biblical perspective, it is precisely because of confidence in God's reign over all aspects of life that Christians must participate fully in the struggle against oppressive and dehumanizing structures and their manifestations in racism, war, and economic exploitation.

Theme 12: *The struggle for a better humanity will bring about the Kingdom of God.*

The struggle for a better humanity is essential to Christian faith and can be informed and inspired by the biblical promise of the Kingdom of God. But imperfect human beings cannot create a perfect society. The Kingdom of God surpasses any conceivable utopia. God has his own designs which confront ours, surprising us with judgment and redemption.

Theme 13: *The question of hope beyond death is irrelevant or at best marginal to the Christian understanding of human fulfillment.*

This is the final capitulation to modern thought. If death is the last word, then Christianity has nothing to say to the final questions of life. We believe that God raised Jesus from the dead and are ". . . convinced that there is nothing in death or life, in the realm of spirits or superhuman powers, in the world as it is or in the world as it shall be, in the forces of the universe, in heights or depths—nothing in all creation that can separate us from the love of God in Christ Jesus our Lord" (Romans 8:38 f.).

Signers of the Appeal:

Dr. Peter L. Berger
Department of Sociology
Rutgers University

Dr. Elizabeth Ann Bettenhausen
Lutheran Church in America
Department for Church and
  Society

The Rev. William Sloane
  Coffin, Jr.
Chaplain, Yale University

Father Avery Dulles, S.J.
Department of Theology
The Catholic University of
  America

Dr. Neal Fisher
United Methodist Church
Board of Global Ministries

Dr. George W. Forell
School of Religion
The University of Iowa

Dr. James N. Gettemy President
The Hartford Seminary Foundation

*Dr. Stanley Hauerwas
Department of Theology
University of Notre Dame

*Father Thomas Hopko
St. Vladimir's Orthodox
  Theological Seminary

Dr. George A. Lindbeck
The Divinity School
Yale University

Dr. Ileana Marculescu
Visiting Professor of Philosophy
  and Religion
Union Theological Seminary

Dr. Ralph McInerny
Department of Philosophy
University of Notre Dame

*The Right Rev. E. Kilmer Myers
Bishop of The Diocese of
  California
The Protestant Episcopal Church

Dr. Richard J. Mouw
Department of Philosophy
Calvin College

Pastor Richard John Neuhaus
Church of St. John the Evangelist
Brooklyn, N.Y.

*Dr. Randolph W. Nugent, Jr.
United Methodist Church
Board of Global Ministries

Dr. Carl J. Peter
Department of Systematic
  Theology
The Catholic University of
  America

Father Alexander Schmemann
St. Vladimir's Orthodox
  Theological Seminary

Father Gerard Sloyan
Department of Religion
Temple University

Dr. Lewis B. Smedes
Department of Theology
Fuller Theological Seminary

Father George H. Tavard
Methodist Theological School in
  Ohio

*Father Bruce Vawter, C.M.
Department of Theology
DePaul University

*The Venerable John D. Weaver
Director of Future Planning
Diocese of California
The Protestant Episcopal Church

Dr. Robert Wilken
Department of History
University of Notre Dame

* Signers who were involved in the preparation for the Hartford meeting but were not able to participate in the meeting itself.

APPENDIX II

Toward the Mutual Recognition of Members
An Affirmation

A resolution from the Twelfth Plenary of the Consultation on Church Union, Cincinnati, November 4–8, 1974

I. AN AFFIRMATION

As a witness to the faith that animates our participation in the Consultation on Church Union, we, the . . . . Church, confess that all who are baptized into Christ are members of His universal Church and belong to and share in His ministry through the People of the One God, Father, Son, and Holy Spirit.

At this time, when we are living our way toward church union, we affirm that membership in a particular church is membership in the whole People of God. As a participating church in the Consultation we intend to work toward removing any impediments in our life which prevent us from receiving into full membership all members so recognized.

In the divided state of our churches the word "membership" is used to refer to enrollment in a particular church. Affirming our oneness in baptism does not abolish membership in a particular church and substitute a common membership in all particular churches, nor does it mean plural simultaneous membership in several, nor does it refer merely to the practice of transferring membership from one particular church to another.

Therefore, we covenant with the other participating churches in the Consultation on Church Union to do everything possible to hasten the day when, together with other churches to whom through the Spirit's leading we may yet be joined, we all shall be one in a visible fellowship truly catholic, truly evangelical, and truly reformed.

II. AN INQUIRY ABOUT THE IMPLICATIONS
OF THIS AFFIRMATION

The Consultation on Church Union believes that the commitment to seek mutual recognition of membership can be a new and creative ecumenical step if each affirming church undertakes an inquiry into the implications of the affirmation, and shares its findings with the other churches in the Consultation. To help open this inquiry, the Consultation asks the following questions:

1. Does not mutual recognition of membership imply recognition that the baptism of each church, whatever its mode or time of life, is an expression of and witness to our one baptism into the body of the one Lord?

2. Does not mutual recognition of membership imply a new appreciation of the importance of confirming, nurturing and instructing each member in the understanding and practice of a church membership which is recogizable to all as new life in Christ?

3. Does not mutual recognition of membership imply recognition that at each celebration of His eucharistic supper, our Lord's invitation and hospitality are extended to all who, baptized and repentant, draw near with faith?

4. Does not mutual recognition of membership imply the acknowledgment that each member is called to ministry, and has been endowed by the Spirit of Christ with gifts for that ministry which the whole Church requires for the building up of the body of believers and for their total ministry in the world?

5. Does not mutual recognition of membership imply an obligation to explore the new possibilities for mutual recognition of the ordained and licensed ministries of both men and women?

6. Does not mutual recognition of membership imply that our practices of congregational and denominational membership need re-examination? Does it not imply that membership in one communion is valid and acceptable in another communion? Does it not also imply a repudiation of the practice of one church intentionally increasing its membership at the expense of another?

7. Does not mutual recognition of membership imply the importance of developing a richer ethnic, cultural and other diversity in our congregations and traditions?

8. Does not mutual recognition of membership imply a deeper commitment than we have yet made to racial and social justice in all our churches and communities, and to joint ministry to overcome racism, sexism and other injustices?

9. Does not mutual recognition of membership imply a readiness on the part of each member to accept responsibility for the discipline of the church in which his or her membership is exercised, and likewise a readiness on the part of each church to develop its understanding and

practice of discipline so as to prepare for the day when the churches can share a common understanding of discipline?

III. RECOMMENDATIONS FOR ACTION

A. *Participating Church Actions*

1. We recommend that "Toward the Mutual Recognition of Members: An Affirmation" be referred to each participating church in the Consultation with the request that it be affirmed by its competent body as a commitment of that church with and to the other participating churches in the Consultation on Church Union.

2. We recommend that each affirming church be asked to undertake a serious inquiry into the implications of its own affirmation, and to share its findings with the other churches in the Consultation.

B. *The Consultation's Supporting Action*

1. We recommend that the Consultation undertake a common inquiry concerning the implications of mutual recognition of members, which aims both to stimulate and to bring together the fruits of the several inquiries by the declaring churches.

2. We recommend that the Consultation actively and steadily seek to interest other churches in affirming this mutual recognition of members.

Notes

CHAPTER I

1. Paul VI, Apostolic Exhortation, "On Evangelization in the Modern World," § 2 (Washington, D.C.: USCC, 1976), p. 6.

2. *Lumen gentium,* § 1, in W. M. Abbott, ed., *The Documents of Vatican II* (New York: America Press, 1966), pp. 14–15.

3. A. Dulles, *Models of the Church* (Garden City: Doubleday, 1974).

4. Latin American Episcopal Council, *The Church in the Present-day Transformation of Latin America in the Light of the Council,* vol. 2, *Conclusions* (Washington, D.C.: USCC, 1968), p. 226.

5. Tomás G. Bissonnette, "Comunidades Eclesiales de Base: Some Contemporary Grass Roots Attempts to Build Ecclesial Koinonia," *The Jurist,* 36, nos. 1–2 (1976), 24.

6. Karl Rahner, *The Shape of the Church to Come* (New York: Seabury, 1974), p. 108.

7. It should be evident that I am here using the term in a different sense than Andrew M. Greeley in his *The Communal Catholic* (New York: Seabury, 1976), but the phenomena to which Greeley calls attention are not unrelated to the more church-centered movements discussed in this chapter.

8. Jim Wallis and Robert Sabath, "The Spirit in the Church," *Post American,* (Feb. 1975), pp. 4–5, as quoted by Robert T. Sears, "Trinitarian Love as Ground of the Church," *Theological Studies,* 37 (1976), 656–57. Father Sears's entire article should be read in connection with the present chapter.

9. "Justice in the World," text in J. Gremillion, ed., *The Gospel of Peace and Justice* (Maryknoll, N.Y.: Orbis, 1976), p. 514.

10. For a clear and persuasive defense of this new category see Peter J. Henriot, "The Concept of Social Sin," *Catholic Mind,* 71, no. 1276 (Oct. 1973), 38–53.

11. For an example see Richard P. McBrien's early work *Do We Need the Church?* (New York: Harper and Row, 1969).

12. D. Bonhoeffer, *Letters and Papers from Prison,* enlarged ed. (New York: Macmillan, 1972), p. 382.

13. R. Adolfs, *The Grave of God: Has the Church a Future?* (London: Burns and Oates, 1967).

14. *Gaudium et spes,* § 43, in Abbott, p. 244.

15. "Justice in the World," § 37, text in Gremillion, p. 521.

16. "Political Responsibility: Reflections on an Election Year," in *Origins,* 5, no. 36 (Feb. 26, 1976), 568.

17. A. Dulles, "Dilemmas Facing the Church in the World," *Origins,* 4, no. 35 (Feb. 20, 1975), 549–50.

18. Paul VI, "On Evangelization," § 14, p. 12.

19. *Lumen gentium,* § 48, in Abbott, p. 79.

CHAPTER II

1. *Lumen gentium*, § 5, W. M. Abbott, ed., *The Documents of Vatican II* (New York: America Press, 1966), p. 18.

2. See the discussion of Luther's and Calvin's views on reform in Yves Congar, *Vraie et fausse Réforme dans l'Eglise* (Paris: Cerf, 1950), pp. 365–67.

3. J. Milton, *Areopagitica* (1644). Cf. G. B. Ladner, *The Idea of Reform: Its Impact on Christian Thought and Action in the Age of the Fathers* (Cambridge, Mass.: Harvard University Press, 1959), p. 34.

4. *Unitatis redintegratio*, § 6, in Abbott, p. 350.

5. Quoted by John W. O'Malley, "Reform, Historical Consciousness, and Vatican II's Aggiornamento," *Theological Studies*, 32 (1971), 575.

6. *Lumen gentium*, § 8, in Abbott, p. 24.

7. See Robert L. Wilken, *The Myth of Christian Beginnings* (Garden City: Doubleday, 1971), chap. 5, pp. 104–18.

8. For a careful statement of the extent to which Newman himself relied on organic analogies and favored what later came to be known as "homogeneous evolution," see Nicholas Lash, *Newman on Development* (Shepherdstown, W.Va.: Patmos Press, 1975), pp. 64–75.

9. O'Malley speaks in this connection of "reform by transformation or even by revolution" ("Reform, Historical Consciousness, and Vatican II's Aggiornamento," p. 595). Yves Congar asserts that our epoch of radical change and cultural transformation "calls for a revision of 'traditional' forms which goes beyond the level of adaptation or *aggiornamento*, and which would instead be a new creation. It is no longer sufficient to maintain, even by adapting it, what has already been; it is necessary to reconstruct it" ("Renewal of the Spirit and Reform of the Institution," in A. Müller and N. Greinacher, eds., *Ongoing Reform in the Church*, Concilium vol. 73 [New York: Herder and Herder, 1972], p. 47). For the reasons explained above, I hesitate to speak of revolution or reconstruction as reform; I prefer to speak of "creative interaction" to indicate both the element of novelty and the element of continuity with the Church's past.

R. P. McBrien in *The Remaking of the Church* (New York: Harper and Row, 1973), pp. 74–81, 168, relying on organizational theory, espouses a concept of reform by "self-determination." In spite of the difference of terminology, his general position is not, I think, in conflict with my own, since he is clearly favoring interaction between the Church and its changing environment.

10. This is the view of Karl Rahner in "Reflections on the Concept of 'Ius Divinum' in Catholic Thought," in his *Theological Investigations*, 5 (Baltimore: Helicon, 1966), 219–43. Carl Peter, "Dimensions of *Jus Divinum*," (Theological Studies, 34 [1973], 227–50), accepts basically the Rahnerian position, but gives greater emphasis to the distinction between the abiding essence and the historically changing forms of that which is divinely instituted. In this way his position comes close to what I call the third theory of reform.

11. See *Gaudium et spes*, § 44, in Abbott, p. 246.

12. K. Rahner, *The Shape of the Church to Come* (New York: Seabury, 1974), p. 38.

13. Peter Hebblethwaite, *The Runaway Church* (New York: Seabury, 1975), p. 237; cf. McBrien, *The Remaking of the Church*, p. xiii; also McBrien, "The Need for Changes of Church Structures from Within," *Liberty and Justice for All: St. Paul–Minneapolis Hearing, June 12–14, 1975* (Washington, D.C.: NCCB, 1976), p. 92.

14. Walter J. Ong, "Catholic Theology Now," *Theology Digest*, 23, no. 4 (Winter 1975), 341.

15. McBrien, *The Remaking of the Church*, p. 121.

16. See A. Dulles, "The Meaning of Freedom in the Church," *The Bulletin* (Lutheran Theological Seminary, Gettysburg, Pa.), 57, no. 1 (Feb. 1977), 18–37.

CHAPTER III

1. Gerald O'Collins, *The Case Against Dogma* (New York: Paulist, 1975).

2. This chapter represents a fresh approach but is, I think, consistent with my earlier work *The Survival of Dogma* (Garden City: Doubleday, 1971; Image Books, 1973).

3. Thomas Aquinas, *Summa theologiae*, 2–2ae, q. 1, art. 7 (Parma ed., vol. 3, p. 6).

4. Ibid., art. 8 (Parma ed., vol. 3, pp. 7–8).

5. Ibid., art. 9, esp. ad 2 (Parma ed., vol. 3, pp. 8–9).

6. Ibid., 1a, q. 32, art. 4 (Parma ed., vol. 1, p. 134); 2–2ae, q. 11, art. 2, ad 3 (Parma ed., vol. 3, pp. 47–48).

7. Ibid., 1a, q. 36, art. 2, ad 2 (Parma ed., vol. 1, p. 148); cf. *De potentia*, q. 10, art. 5 (Parma ed., vol. 8, pp. 214–18).

8. *Summa theologiae*, 2–2ae, q.1, art. 10 (Parma ed., vol. 3, p. 9); cf. *De potentia*, q. 10, art. 4, ad 13 (Parma ed., vol. 8, pp. 212–13).

9. R. L. Wilken, *The Myth of Christian Beginnings* (Garden City: Doubleday, 1971). See above, chap. II, note 7.

10. Vincent of Lérins, *Commonitorium*, § 2, in Migne, *Patrologia latina* 50, col. 640.

11. See for instance the "Comprehensive Summary, Rule and Norm" set forth in the Lutheran *Book of Concord* (ed. T. G. Tappert [Philadelphia: Fortress Press, 1959]), pp. 464–65, 503, 506.

12. Council of Trent, sess. IV (Apr. 8, 1546), text in H. Denzinger and A. Schönmetzer, eds., *Enchiridion symbolorum*, 32nd ed. (Freiburg im Breisgau: Herder, 1963), § 1501. (This anthology will subsequently be cited as DS.)

13. Quoted by Jan Walgrave, *Unfolding Revelation* (Philadelphia: Westminster, 1972), pp. 130–31.

14. J.-B. Bossuet, "Première instruction pastorale sur les promesses de l'Eglise," *Oeuvres complètes* (Paris, 1862–66), vol. 17, pp. 111–12. See Walgrave, *Un-*

folding *Revelation*, p. 132, and Owen Chadwick, *From Bossuet to Newman* (Cambridge University Press, 1957), p. 17.

15. On Möhler's theory of development see Walgrave, *Unfolding Revelation*, pp. 286–90, and H. Hammans, *Die neueren katholischen Erklärungen der Dogmenentwicklung* (Essen: Ludgerus-Verlag, 1965), pp. 29–33.

16. On Newman's theory of development see Walgrave, *Unfolding Revelation*, pp. 293–314; Chadwick, *From Bossuet to Newman*, pp. 139–95; Nicholas Lash, *Newman on Development* (Shepherdstown, W.Va.: Patmos Press, 1975).

17. Walgrave remarks that both Bossuet and Newman could support their positions by appealing to certain statements of Vincent of Lérins (*Unfolding Revelation*, p. 89).

18. See *Humani generis* (1950), DS 3886. Pius XII, echoing an 1870 pronouncement of Pius IX, here declares that it is the "noblest office of theology" (*nobilissimum theologiae munus*) to show in what way the doctrine defined by the Church is contained in the sources "in that very sense in which it was defined."

19. The explanations I here call "logical" and "organic" correspond approximately to those which Hammans calls respectively "intellectualistic" and "theological" and those which Walgrave calls respectively "logical" and "theological."

20. On the "logical" explanation see Chadwick, *From Bossuet to Newman*, chap. 2, pp. 21–48; Hammans, *Die neueren katholischen Erklärungen*, sec. IV, pp. 119–73; Walgrave, *Unfolding Revelation*, chap. 7, pp. 137–78.

21. See, for instance, K. Rahner, "The Development of Dogma," *Theological Investigations*, 1 (Baltimore: Helicon, 1961), 39–77; E. Schillebeeckx, "The Development of the Apostolic Faith into the Dogma of the Church," *Revelation and Theology*, 1 (New York: Sheed and Ward, 1967), 57–83.

22. G. A. Lindbeck, "Doctrinal Development and Protestant Theology," in E. Schillebeeckx, ed., *Man as Man and Believer*, Concilium vol. 21 (New York: Paulist Press, 1967), pp. 138–39.

23. Ibid., p. 139.

24. Cf. *Gaudium et spes*, § 44, in W. M. Abbott, ed., *The Documents of Vatican II* (New York: America Press, 1966), p. 246; quoted above, chap. II, (see note 11).

25. Constitution on the Catholic Faith (*Dei Filius*), chap. 4 (DS 3016).

26. *Lumen gentium*, § 8, in Abbott, p. 24.

27. *Mysterium ecclesiae*, § 5, Eng. trans., "Declaration in Defense of the Catholic Doctrine on the Church," in *Catholic Mind*, 71 (Oct. 1973), 58–60.

28. K. Rahner, "Considerations on the Development of Dogma," *Theological Investigations*, 4 (Baltimore: Helicon, 1966), 3–35.

29. *Unitatis redintegratio*, § 11, in Abbott, p. 354.

30. U. Valeske, *Hierarchia veritatum* (Munich: Claudius, 1968): H. Mühlen, "Die Bedeutung der Differenz zwischen Zentraldogmen und Randdogmen für den ökumenishen Dialog" in Leuba and Stirnimann, eds., *Freiheit in der Begegnung* (Frankfurt: Knecht, 1969), pp. 191–227; P. O'Connell, "Hierarchy of Truths," in P. S. de Achútegui, ed., *The Dublin Papers on Ecumenism*

(Manila: Loyola School of Theology, 1972), pp. 83–117; Y. Congar, "On the 'Hierarchia Veritatum,'" in D. Neiman and M. Schatkin, eds., *The Heritage of the Early Church: Essays in Honor of the Very Reverend Georges Vasilievich Florovsky* (Rome: Pontifical Oriental Institute, 1973), pp. 409–20.

31. Cf. DS 902 (against P. J. Olieu); DS 1440–41 (against P. Pomponazzi); and DS 2828 (against A. Günther).

32. On the ecumenical aspects of this question, see A. Dulles, "A Proposal to Lift Anathemas," *Origins*, 4, no. 27 (Dec. 26, 1974), 417–21; *Catholic Mind*, 74, no. 1293 (May 1975), 40–45.

33. *Dignitatis humanae*, § 7, in Abbott, p. 687.

34. See Rahner, "Reflections on the Problems Involved in Devising a Short Formula of the Faith," *Theological Investigations*, 11 (New York: Seabury, 1974), p. 231.

35. For a good sampling see vol. 2 of Roman Bleistein, *Kurzformel des Glaubens* (Würzburg: Echter Verlag, 1971). Further selections may be found in *Expository Times*, 83 (1971–72), 345; 84 (1972–73), 24, 151, 191, 214; 85 (1973–74), 343.

36. Text in *The Book of Confessions of the United Presbyterian Church in the U.S.A.* (Philadelphia: Office of the General Assembly, 1967).

37. Text in J. H. Leith, ed., *Creeds of the Churches* (Richmond: John Knox Press, rev. ed., 1973), pp. 590–91.

38. Text in *Expository Times*, 83 (1971–72), 345.

39. See the "Affirmations of Hope" presented in *Uniting in Hope: Commission on Faith and Order, Accra, 1974*, FO Paper No. 72 (Geneva: World Council of Churches, 1975), pp. 48–80. See also the further collection assembled under the title "Giving an Account of Our Hope in These Testing Times," *Study Encounter*, vol. 12, nos. 1–2 (1976).

40. Rahner's "short formula" appears in various versions. The first of these was published in *Geist und Leben*, 38 (1965), 374–79. In modified form, it appeared in K. Rahner, ed., *The Pastoral Approach to Atheism*, Concilium vol. 23 (New York: Paulist Press, 1967), pp. 70–82, and was reprinted in his *Theological Investigations*, 9 (New York: Seabury, 1972), 117–26. In *Theological Investigations*, vol. 11, pp. 230–44, Rahner proposes a briefer formula, presented in three forms, the "theological," the "sociological," and the "futurologist." Rahner's short formulas have been analyzed by Alexander Stock, *Kurzformeln des Glaubens* (Einsiedeln: Benziger, 1971).

41. Reprinted in Bleistein, *Kurzformel des Glaubens*, vol. 2, p. 100.

42. Printed in English translation in *Uniting in Hope*, p. 55.

43. H. Küng, *Christ sein* (Munich: Piper, 1974), p. 594; Eng. trans., *On Being a Christian* (Garden City: Doubleday, 1976), p. 602. A similar formula was presented in Küng's paper for the Brussels Concilium Congress in 1970, "Was ist die christliche Botschaft?" *Die Zukunft der Kirche* (1971), reprinted in Bleistein, *Kurzformel des Glaubens*, vol. 2, p. 102.

44. M. Hellwig, *The Christian Creeds* (Dayton: Pflaum, 1973), p. 96.

45. For commentary on these short formulas see Bleistein, *Kurzformel des Glaubens*, vol. 1; H. Keller, "Bekenntnisbildung in der Gegenwart," in G. Ruh-

bach and others, *Bekenntnis in Bewegung* (Göttingen: Vanderhoeck und Ruprecht, 1969), pp. 162–213; G. Baum, "A New Creed," in *The Ecumenist*, 6, no. 5 (July–Aug. 1968), 164–67 (a critique of the preliminary draft of the United Church of Canada creed referred to in note 38 above); W. Beinert, "Do Short Formulas Dilute the Faith?" *Theology Digest*, 22 (1974), 256; K. Lehmann, *Gegenwart des Glaubens* (Mainz: Matthias-Grünewald, 1974), pp. 109–99 (with excellent bibliography); J. Ratzinger, "Noch einmal: "Kurzformeln des Glaubens,'" *Communio*, 2 (1973), 258–64; P.-A. Liégé, "Un 'abrégé de la foi,'" *Catéchèse*, 12 (1972), 407–17.

46. A similar idea appears in *Gaudium et spes*, § 22, in Abbott, p. 220.

47. Baum, "A New Creed," p. 164.

48. The various functions of the primitive homologia are set forth in V. H. Neufeld, *The Earliest Christian Confessions* (Grand Rapids: Eerdmans, 1963).

49. For a view equating Barmen with dogma see Bernhard Lohse, *A Short History of Christian Doctrine* (Philadelphia: Fortress Press, 1966), pp. 14, 215–17, 235–36. Somewhat more reserved are the comments of Karl Barth in his *Church Dogmatics*, 2, pt. 1 (New York: Scribner's, 1957), pp. 172–78, and those of Arthur C. Cochrane in his *The Church's Confession Under Hitler* (Philadelphia: Westminster Press, 1962), pp. 212–13.

50. G. Baum, *Faith and Doctrine* (New York: Newman Press, 1969), pp. 107–8.

Chapter IV

1. Text in *Acta Apostolicae Sedis*, 58 (1966), 659–61. See the discussion by Karl Rahner in "Theology and the Church's Teaching Authority After the Council," in his *Theological Investigations*, 9 (New York: Seabury, 1972), pp. 83–100.

2. Langdon Gilkey, *Naming the Whirlwind* (New York: Bobbs-Merrill, 1969), p. 34.

3. P. Berger, "For a World with Windows," in Berger and R. J. Neuhaus, eds., *Against the World for the World* (New York: Seabury, 1976), p. 10.

4. Ibid., p. 11.

5. L. Gilkey, *Catholicism Confronts Modernity* (New York: Seabury, 1975), p. 40.

6. Ibid., p. 59.

7. Ibid., p. 64.

8. Ibid., p. 69.

9. D. Tracy, *Blessed Rage for Order* (New York: Seabury, 1975), p. 8. I have discussed this important work at some length in my review article "Method in Fundamental Theology," *Theological Studies*, 37 (1976), 304–16. For a fuller discussion of Tracy's relationships with Ogden and Gilkey, see P. L. Berger, "Secular Theology and the Supernatural," *Theological Studies*, 38 (1977), 39–56.

10. Tracy, *Blessed Rage for Order*, p. 9.

11. Ibid., p. 10.

12. Berger, "For a World with Windows," p. 13.

13. Quoted in Chapter III above (see note 50).

14. Quoted in Chap. III above (see note 47).

15. K. Rahner, "On Heresy," in his *Inquiries* (New York: Herder and Herder, 1964), pp. 403–63, esp. pp. 437–63.

16. Ibid., p. 460.

17. Emil Brunner's list of axioms, followed by lists of axioms from Great Britain, America, Germany, and France, may be found in *The Church's Witness to God's Design*, vol. 2 of the Amsterdam series, *Man's Disorder and God's Design* (London: SCM Press, 1948), pp. 80–84.

18. Ibid., p. 82.

19. J. Hitchcock, *The Decline and Fall of Radical Catholicism* (Garden City: Doubleday Image Books, 1972), pp. 187–89.

20. W. A. Visser't Hooft, "Evangelism in the Neo-Pagan Situation," *International Review of Mission*, 63 (1974), 81–86.

21. Text in Appendix I of this book.

22. G. Lindbeck, "A Battle for Theology," in Berger and Neuhaus, *Against the World for the World*, p. 25.

23. G. Tavard, "Locating the Divine," *Worldview*, 18, no. 6 (June 1975), p. 45.

24. Berger, "For a World with Windows," p. 13.

25. L. Dewart, *The Future of Belief* (New York: Herder and Herder, 1966), p. 51.

26. The positions of Braithwaite and Hare are well summarized, with references to their works, in Tracy's *Blessed Rage for Order*, pp. 100–1, 120–21. See also Frederick Ferré, *Language, Logic, and God* (New York: Harper Torchbooks, 1969), chap. 10, pp. 121–35.

27. P. van Buren, *The Secular Meaning of the Gospel* (New York: Macmillan paperback ed., 1966), pp. 99–101.

28. On van Buren's *The Edges of Language* (New York: Macmillan, 1972), see the comments of Richard J. Mouw, "New Alignments," in Berger and Neuhaus, *Against the World for the World*, p. 122.

29. G. Baum, *Religion and Alienation* (New York: Paulist Press, 1975), p. 252.

30. G. Baum, *New Horizon: Theological Essays* (New York: Paulist Press, 1972), p. 56.

31. Ibid., p. 56–57.

32. W. Pannenberg, "Breaking Ground for Renewed Faith," *Worldview*, 18, no. 6 (June 1975), 37–38.

33. G. Forell, "Reason, Relevance, and a Radical Gospel," in Berger and Neuhaus, *Against the World for the World*, p. 70.

34. M. Martin, *Jesus Now* (New York: Popular Library, 1973), p. 16. For a similar survey see the section "Which Christ?" in Hans Küng, *On Being a Christian* (Garden City: Doubleday, 1976), pp. 126–44.

35. See Albert Schweitzer, *The Psychiatric Study of Jesus: Exposition and Criticism* (Boston: Beacon Press, 1948; paperback ed., 1958).

36. P. Schoonenberg, *The Christ* (New York: Herder and Herder, 1971), pp. 100–1. Cf. Bernard Bro, "Man and the Sacraments," in E. Schillebeeckx, ed., *The Sacraments in General*, Concilium vol. 31 (Glen Rock, N.J.: Paulist Press, 1968), pp. 33–50.

37. Tavard, "Locating the Divine," p. 46.

38. For a fuller treatment of this point see my article "Contemporary Approaches to Christology," *The Living Light*, 13, no. 1 (Spring 1976), 119–44, esp. pp. 143–44.

39. Tracy, *Blessed Rage for Order*, p. 232, note 73.

40. Ibid., pp. 214–18.

41. In Moran's own words: "I think it would be preposterous to say that 'all religions are equally valid' (unless it were held that they are equally and absolutely invalid)" (G. Moran, "On Not Asking the Right Questions," *Worldview*, 18, no. 5 [May 1975], 25).

42. J. C. Bennett, "Silence on Issues of High Priority," *Worldview*, 18, no. 5 (May 1975), 23.

43. G. Moran, *The Present Revelation* (New York: Herder and Herder, 1972), p. 178.

44. G. Johnston, "Should the Church Still Talk About Salvation?" *International Review of Mission*, 61, no. 241 (1972), 46; he quotes G. H. Todrank, *The Secular Search for a New Christ* (Philadelphia: Westminster, 1969), pp. 34–36.

45. Johnston, "Should The Church Still Talk About Salvation?" p. 48.

46. Ibid., p. 59.

47. See note 9 above.

48. S. M. Ogden, *The Reality of God* (New York: Harper and Row, 1966), pp. 229–30; Ogden, "The Meaning of Christian Hope," *Union Seminary Quarterly Review*, 30, nos. 2–4 (Winter–Summer 1975), 153–74.

49. G. Baum, *Man Becoming* (New York: Herder and Herder, 1970), p. 228.

50. Pannenberg, "Breaking Ground for Renewed Faith," p. 38.

51. J. Wren-Lewis, "What Are Clergy For?" *The Listener*, 71, no. 1824 (Mar. 12, 1964), 418–19. This and several other articles are summarized with ample quotations in Philip Rieff, *The Triumph of the Therapeutic* (New York: Harper and Row, 1966), pp. 251–52.

52. See note 7 above.

53. Rieff, *The Triumph of the Therapeutic*, p. 253.

54. R. Ruether, "Schism of Consciousness," *Commonweal*, 88 (1968), 326–31.

55. R. Ruether, "A New Church?" *Commonweal*, 90 (1969), 64.

56. Gregory Baum is therefore wide of the mark when he accuses the Hartford Appeal of a "curious, untraditional separation of transcendence and immanence" ("On the Human Locus of the Divine," *Worldview*, 18, no. 5 [May 1975], 26–27). Equally unfounded is the charge of Rudolf Siebert that the Hartford Appeal "separates absolutely the Creator from his creation" and "tears apart human emancipation and divine transcendence" ("Christian Revolution: Liberation and Transcendence," *The Ecumenist*, 14, no. 6 [Sept.–Oct. 1976], 86).

57. W. J. Hollenweger, ed., *The Church for Others* (Geneva: World Council of Churches, 1968), p. 20 (italics supplied).

58. W. J. Hollenweger, "Agenda: The World," in "The World Provides the Agenda" (Papers from the Birmingham Consultation), *Concept,* 11 (Geneva: WCC, 1966), 20.

59. N. Goodall, ed., *The Uppsala Report* (Geneva: WCC, 1968), p. 32.

60. Bennett, "Silence on Issues of High Priority," p. 24.

61. Pannenberg, "Breaking Ground for Renewed Faith," p. 38.

62. R. J. Neuhaus, "Calling a Halt to Retreat," in Berger and Neuhaus, *Against the World for the World,* p. 156.

63. Ibid.

64. M. Marty, review of *Against the World for the World, Washington Post,* Aug. 1, 1976, section H, p. 10.

65. See Thomas Luckmann, *The Invisible Religion* (New York: Macmillan, 1967), esp. chap. 6.

66. H. Cox, "No Christological Center," *Worldview,* 18, no. 5 (May 1975), 22.

67. Quoted by Francine du Plessix Gray, "To March or Not to March," *The New York Times Magazine,* June 27, 1976, p. 34.

68. Cox, "No Christological Center," p. 22.

69. Quoted by Carl J. Peter, "A Creative Alienation," in Berger and Neuhaus, *Against the World for the World,* p. 83.

70. Tavard, "Locating the Divine," p. 46.

71. Peter, "A Creative Alienation," p. 85.

72. Cf. Rahner, "On Heresy," p. 447.

73. Paul VI, "On Evangelization in the Modern World," § 2 (Washington, D.C.: USCC, 1976), p. 21.

CHAPTER V

1. I. Kant, "What Is Enlightenment?" in C. J. Friedrich, ed., *Kant's Moral and Political Writings* (New York: Modern Library, 1949), pp. 132–39.

2. See A. Dulles, *The Survival of Dogma* (Garden City: Doubleday, 1971; Image Books, 1973), esp. chap. 2 and 3.

3. William Chillingworth gave this principle its sharpest formulation: "The BIBLE, I say, the BIBLE only, is the Religion of Protestants" (*The Religion of Protestants, A Safe Way to Salvation,* published 1638). The so-called "material principle" of the Reformation, "Scripture alone," is ably criticized by Wolfhart Pannenberg in his essay "The Crisis of the Scripture Principle," *Basic Questions in Theology,* 1 (Philadelphia: Fortress, 1970), 1–14. But Pannenberg, here and elsewhere, tends to exalt the role of reason to the detriment of authority. His positions are best understood as a reaction against the excesses of the "theology of the word" in some sections of contemporary European Protestantism.

4. For a critique, see K. Rahner, "The Teaching Office of the Church in the Present-day Crisis of Authority," *Theological Investigations,* 12 (New York: Seabury, 1974), 3–30.

5. See Alois Müller, ed., *Democratization of the Church*, Concilium vol. 63 (New York: Herder and Herder, 1971). A nuanced presentation of the problem is given by Patrick Granfield in his *Ecclesial Cybernetics: A Study of Democracy in the Church* (New York: Macmillan, 1973). While holding that the Catholic Church neither is nor should be a democracy (p. 186), Granfield contends that it is in need of "cybernetic reform through democratization" (p. 211). As a correction to the hierocratic model, this cybernetic model makes an important contribution.

6. *Lumen gentium*, § 12, in W. M. Abbott, ed., *The Documents of Vatican II* (New York: America Press, 1966), p. 29.

7. For a fuller statement of my position on this point see Dulles, *The Survival of Dogma*, chap. 5.

8. Y. Congar, "Norms of Christian Allegiance and Identity in the History of the Church," in E. Schillebeeckx, ed., *Truth and Certainty*, Concilium vol. 83 (New York: Herder and Herder, 1973), pp. 24–25.

9. *Dei Verbum*, § 10, in Abbott, p. 118.

10. See J. L. McKenzie, *Authority in the Church* (New York: Sheed and Ward, 1966), chap. 5.

11. A brief but very helpful study of the New Testament *episkopoi* may be found in R. E. Brown, *Priest and Bishop: Biblical Reflections* (New York: Paulist Press, 1970), esp. pp. 34–40.

12. See the paper drawn up by the International Theological Commission, "Apostolic Succession: A Clarification," *Origins*, 4, no. 13 (Sept. 19, 1974), 193–200.

13. Text in John Dedek, *Contemporary Medical Ethics* (New York: Sheed and Ward, 1975), p. 208.

14. Irenaeus, *Adversus haereses* 4.26.2, in *Patrologia Graeca* 7:1053; Eng. trans. in *The Ante-Nicene Fathers* (New York: Scribner's, 1899), vol. 1, p. 497.

15. Y. Congar, *Tradition and Traditions* (New York: Macmillan, 1967), p. 177. Congar is here following the view of K. Müller and D. van den Eynde. For an alternative interpretation see Louis Ligier, "Le *charisma veritatis certum* des évèques," in *L'Homme devant Dieu: Mélanges offerts au Père Henri de Lubac* (Paris: Aubier, 1963), vol. 1, pp. 247–68; also Norbert Brox, "*Charisma veritatis certum*," *Zeitschrift für Kirchengeschichte*, 75 (1964), 327–31.

16. On teaching authority in the Church of the apostolic age, see McKenzie, *Authority in the Church*, chaps. 5 and 6.

17. Myles M. Bourke, "Collegial Decision-making in the New Testament," in J. A. Coriden, ed., *Who Decides for the Church?* (Hartford: Canon Law Society of America, 1971), p. 13.

18. Thomas Aquinas, *In 4 Sent.*, Dist. 19, q. 2, a. 2, qua. 2, ad 4 (Parma ed., vol. 7, p. 852).

19. Thomas Aquinas, *Quodlibet* 3, qu. 4, art. 1 (Parma ed., vol. 9, p. 490).

20. See also Thomas Aquinas, *Contra Impugnantes Dei cultum et religionem*, chap. 2 (Parma ed., vol. 15, p. 7).

21. M.-D. Chenu, " 'Authentica' et 'magistralia.' Deux lieux théologiques aux

XII–XIII siècles," *Divus Thomas* (Piacenza), 28 (1925), 257–85. Cf. Chenu, *La théologie au douzième siècle*, 2nd ed. (Paris: Vrin, 1966), pp. 351–65.

22. Y. Congar, "Bref Histoire des Formes du 'Magistère' et ses relations avec les docteurs," *Rev. des sciences phil. et theol.*, 60 (1976), 104.

23. For some brief historical indications with further references see Dulles, *The Survival of Dogma*, chap. 6.

24. Collegial association of the members of the hierarchical magisterium and individual theologians is called for by the International Theological Commission in the fourth of its *Theses on the Relationship Between the Ecclesiastical Magisterium and Theology* (Washington, D.C.: USCC, 1977), p. 3. An excellent discussion of current relationships may be found in A. L. Descamps, "Théologie et magistère," *Ephemerides theologicae lovanienses*, 52, no. 1 (June 1976), 82–133. In discussing the relations between bishops and theologians, one should not lose sight of what has been said earlier in this chapter about the authority of the whole body of the faithful. It goes without saying that both pastors and theologians should seek to maintain close contact with the laity, upon whom rests the chief burden of living out the faith in the circumstances of today's world.

25. I thus differ from those who hold that the Christian theologian need not write from the perspective of Christian belief and that the Christian texts should not function as norms for theology. David Tracy, in his *Blessed Rage for Order* (New York: Seabury Press, 1975), argues that the theologian's commitment should be to the "faith of secularity" which is shared in common by the secularist and the modern Christian (p. 8), and that the fundamental loyalty of the theologian should be to "that morality of scientific knowledge which he shares with his colleagues, the philosophers, historians, and social scientists" (p. 7). Tracy accordingly contends that the traditional Christian beliefs may not serve as warrants for theological arguments (ibid.). Richard P. McBrien, in his review, rightly points out that Tracy's position apparently rests on a positivistic conception of "the Christian fact" and that it "seems to erase the difference between theology and philosophy" (*Commonweal*, 103, no. 25 [Dec. 3, 1976], 797–98). For a discussion of possible differences between Tracy and myself I refer again to my review article, "Method in Fundamental Theology," *Theological Studies*, 37 (1976), 304–16.

26. A brief catena of quotations from typical manualists and other "approved authors" of the period between the two Vatican Councils may be found in H. J. McSorley, "Some Ecclesiological Reflections on *Humanae vitae*," *Bijdragen*, 30 (1969), 3–8. For a fuller discussion of the same theme see J. A. Komonchak, "Ordinary Papal Magisterium and Religious Assent," in C. E. Curran, ed., *Contraception: Authority and Dissent* (New York: Herder and Herder, 1969), pp. 101–26.

27. See "Some Ecclesiological Reflections on *Humanae vitae*," McSorley, p. 3; Komonchak, "Ordinary Papal Magisterium and Religious Assent," pp. 104–5.

28. For some prudent reservations with regard to this last assertion, see L. J. O'Donovan, "Was Vatican II Evolutionary?" *Theological Studies*, 36 (1975), 493–502.

29. R. A. McCormick, "The Magisterium: A New Model," *America*, 122, no.

25 (June 27, 1970), 675. See also McCormick's fuller discussions of the magisterium and dissent in *Theological Studies*, 29 (1968), 714–18; 30 (1969), 644–68; and 38 (1977), 84–100; and in *Proceedings of the Catholic Theological Society of America*, 24 (1969), 239–54.

30. *Lumen gentium*, § 8, in Abbott, p. 24.

31. M. Polanyi, *The Tacit Dimension* (Garden City: Doubleday Anchor Books, 1967), pp. 53–92.

32. *Gaudium et spes*, § 62, in Abbott, p. 270.

CHAPTER VI

1. Karl-Heinz Ohlig, *Why We Need the Pope* (St. Meinrad, Ind.: Abbey Press, 1975), p. ix.

2. For an excellent summary see ibid., pp. 71–87. A detailed treatment of the theological background may be found in H. J. Pottmeyer, *Unfehlbarkeit und Souveränität* (Mainz: Matthias Grünewald, 1975). See also G. H. Williams, "*Omnium christianorum pastor et doctor*: Vatican I et l'Angleterre victorienne," *Nouvelle revue théologique*, 96 (Feb.–Apr. 1974), 113–46, 337–65; V. Conzemius, "Why Was the Primacy of the Pope Defined in 1870?" in G. Baum and A. M. Greeley, eds., *The Church as Institution*, Concilium vol. 91 (New York: Seabury, 1974), pp. 75–83; D. Warwick, "The Centralization of Ecclesiastical Authority: An Organizational Perspective," ibid., pp. 109–18.

3. J. H. Newman, *Apologia pro vita sua* (New York: Longmans, Green, 1905), p. 205. The entire passage from which this quotation is taken provides a splendid illustration of the mentality I am here seeking to describe.

4. C. Davis, "Questions for the Papacy Today," in H. Küng, ed., *Papal Ministry in the Church*, Concilium vol. 64 (New York: Herder and Herder, 1971), p. 12.

5. G. Thils, *La primauté pontificale. La doctrine de Vatican I. Les voies d'une révision* (Gembloux: Duculot, 1972). See also his article "The Theology of the Primacy: Towards a Revision," *One in Christ*, 10, no. 1 (1974), 13–30.

6. "Declaration in Defense of the Catholic Doctrine on the Church," *Catholic Mind*, 71 (Oct. 1973), 54–64, esp. § 5, pp. 58–60; cited above, chap. III, note 27. The principles of § 5 stand on their own merits even though some commentators have pointed out that other sections of *Mysterium ecclesiae* do not utilize these principles to the best advantage.

7. See A. C. Piepkorn, "*Ius Divinum* and *Adiaphoron* in Relation to Structural Problems in the Church: The Position of the Lutheran Symbolical Books," in P. C. Empie and T. A. Murphy, eds., *Papal Primacy and the Universal Church*, Lutherans and Catholics in Dialogue vol. 5 (Minneapolis: Augsburg, 1974), pp. 119–27; G. A. Lindbeck, "Papal Primacy and *Ius Divinum*: A Lutheran View," ibid., pp. 193–208; C. J. Peter, "Dimensions of *Jus Divinum* in Roman Catholic Theology," *Theological Studies*, 34 (1973), 227–50. See chap. II, note 10, above.

8. R. Pesch, "The Position and Significance of Peter in the Church of the

New Testament," in Küng, *Papal Ministry in the Church*, pp. 21–35; R. E. Brown, K. P. Donfried, and J. Reumann, eds., *Peter in the New Testament* (Minneapolis: Augsburg, and New York: Paulist Press, 1973).

9. See J. F. McCue, "Roman Primacy in the First Three Centuries," in Küng, *Papal Ministry in the Church*, pp. 36–44; McCue, "The Roman Primacy in the Patristic Era: The Beginnings Through Nicea," in Empie and Murphy, *Papal Primacy and the Universal Church*, pp. 44–72.

10. "The Gospel and the Church" (Report of the Joint Lutheran–Roman Catholic Study Commission), *Lutheran World*, 19 (1972), 259–73, par. 31; "Differing Attitudes Toward the Papacy" (Report of the U.S. Lutheran–Roman Catholic Dialogue), *Origins*, 3, no. 38 (Mar. 14, 1974), §§ 30, 42, and 50.

11. In this chapter this key term will be used in a sense slightly broader than in "Differing Attitudes Toward Papal Primacy," § 4.

12. I. Salaverri, *De ecclesia* in *Sacrae theologiae summa* (Madrid: Biblioteca de Autores cristianos, 1952), §§ 441–42, p. 634.

13. J. D. Mansi, ed., *Sacrorum Conciliorum nova et amplissima collectio*, 52 (Arnhem and Leipzig: Welter, 1927), col. 720.

14. Constitution on the Church, *Pastor aeternus*, in H. Denzinger and A. Schönmetzer, eds., *Enchiridion symbolorum*, 32nd ed. (Freiburg im Breisgau: Herder, 1963; hereafter cited as DS), § 3055.

15. DS 3059–64; cf. Salaverri, *De ecclesia*, p. 638.

16. For a presentation and updating of the Batiffol position see H. Marot, "Unité de l'Eglise et diversité géographique aux premiers siècles," in *L'Episcopat et l'Eglise universelle* (Paris: Cerf, 1962), pp. 565–66.

17. Mansi, *Sacrorum Conciliorum collectio*, vol. 52, col. 683B.

18. *Collectio Lacensis*, 7 (Freiburg, 1890), pp. 350–51.

19. C. Ernst, "The Primacy of Peter: Theology and Ideology," *New Blackfriars*, 50 (1969), 347–55, 399–404.

20. Ibid., p. 403.

21. Pierre Duprey, "Brief Reflections on the Title 'Primus Inter Pares,'" *One in Christ*, 10, no. 1 (1974), 7–12.

22. *Lumen gentium*, § 13, in W. M. Abbott, ed., *The Documents of Vatican II* (New York: America Press, 1966), p. 32.

23. DS 3074.

24. Cf. the Gallican Four Articles of 1682, DS 2284.

25. DS 3074.

26. The recent discussion is thoroughly reviewed in John T. Ford, "Infallibility: Who Won the Debate?" *Proceedings of the Catholic Theological Society of America*, 31st Annual Convention, vol. 31 (Bronx, N.Y.: Manhattan College, 1976), pp. 179–92.

27. Cited above, note 6.

28. *Lumen gentium*, §§ 12 and 25, in Abbott, pp. 29–30.

29. *Lumen gentium*, § 25, in Abbott, p. 49. Vatican II is here practically quoting Gasser's famous *relatio* on papal infallibility at Vatican I (Mansi, *Sacrorum Conciliorum collectio*, vol. 52, cols. 1213–14). For the interpretation

see T. A. Caffrey, "Consensus and Infallibility: The Mind of Vatican I," *Down-side Review*, 88 (1970), 107–31.

30. *Schema constitutionis de ecclesia* (Vatican City: Typis Polyglottis, 1964), p. 98.

31. Such was the view stated by Bishop Gasser in his *relatio*; see Mansi, *Sacrorum Conciliorum collectio*, vol. 52, col. 1214.

32. See H. McSorley, "Some Forgotten Truths About the Petrine Ministry," *Journal of Ecumenical Studies*, 11, no. 2 (Spring 1974), 208–37, esp. p. 225.

33. Speech to the Secretariat for Promoting Christian Unity, Rome, April 29, 1967, reported in *National Catholic Reporter*, May 10, 1967, p. 10; also in *Documentation catholique*, May 21, 1967, col. 870.

34. For illustrative quotations see A. Dulles, "The Papacy: Bond or Barrier?" *Catholic Mind*, 72, no. 1285 (Sept. 1974), 45–59; also, more recently, the articles in the collection cited in note 35 below.

35. Empie and Murphy, *Papal Primacy and the Universal Church*, p. 22.

36. P. J. McCord, ed., *A Pope for All Christians?* (New York: Paulist Press, 1976).

37. Michael A. Fahey, book review of *A Pope for All Christians?*, in *America*, 134, no. 22 (June 5, 1976), 501.

38. *The Uppsala Report* (Geneva: World Council of Churches, 1968), p. 17.

39. See the report "Patterns of Relationships Between the Roman Catholic Church and the World Council of Churches," *Catholic Mind*, 70, no. 1268 (Dec. 1972), 22–54.

40. Ohlig, *Why We Need the Pope*, pp. 142–43.

41. See A. Spencer, "The Future of the Episcopal and Papal Roles," *IDOC International*, May 9, 1970, pp. 63–64; also Paul Misner, "Papal Primacy in a Pluriform Polity," *Journal of Ecumenical Studies*, 11, no. 2 (Spring 1974), pp. 239–61, esp. pp. 254–55.

42. A. M. Greeley, "Advantages and Drawbacks of a Center of Communications in the Church: Sociological Point of View," in Küng, *Papal Ministry in the Church*, pp. 101–14; quotation from p. 101.

CHAPTER VII

1. George Gallup, Jr., "Evangelizing the 80,000,000 Unchurched Americans," a report given at the Catholic University of America, Nov. 11, 1975. According to this report, out of a total adult Roman Catholic population of some 39 million, 27 per cent (or some 11 million Catholics) stated that they are not members of a church. Andrew M. Greeley is reported as holding that in the over-thirty age group of Catholics "a stable 'apostasy' rate of about seven percent between 1955 and 1965 . . . was up to approximately 14 percent by 1970 and 18 percent by 1974" (*The Catholic Messenger* [Davenport, Ia.], April 1, 1976, p. 7).

2. See Colman E. O'Neill, "St. Thomas on Membership in the Church," in

A. D. Lee, ed., *Vatican II: The Theological Dimension* (Washington, D.C.: Thomist Press, 1963) (*The Thomist*, vol. 27, Apr.-July-Oct. 1963), pp. 88–140.

3. E. Troeltsch, *The Social Teaching of the Christian Churches*, 1 (New York: Macmillan, 1931), 338.

4. R. Bellarmine, *De controversiis*, vol. 2, *De conciliis et ecclesia*, bk. 3, chap. 2 (Naples: Giuliano, 1875, vol. 2, p. 75). In fairness it must be added that this one sentence, accenting the visible and juridical elements, does not convey Bellarmine's full notion of the Church. See H. Mühlen, *Una mystica Persona* (Paderborn: Schöningh, 1968), pp. 3–8.

5. Troeltsch, *The Social Teaching of the Christian Churches*, vol. 2, p. 522.

6. J. A. Hardon, *A Comparative Study of Bellarmine's Doctrine of the Relation of Sincere Non-Catholics to the Catholic Church*, dissertation excerpt (Rome: Gregorian University, 1951), p. 46.

7. See Charles Journet, *L'Eglise du Verbe Incarné*, vol. 2 (Paris: Desclée de Brouwer, 1951), pp. 841–50; also A. Gommenginger, "Bedeutet die Exkommunikation Verlust der Kirchengemeinschaft?" *Zeitschrift für katholische Theologie*, 73 (1951), 1–71.

8. Pius XII, *Mystici corporis*, 3rd ed. (New York: America Press, 1957), § 29, p. 18; H. Denzinger and A. Schönmetzer, eds., *Enchiridion symbolorum*, 32nd ed. (Freiburg im Breisgau: Herder, 1963), § 3802.

9. *Codex iuris canonici*, can. 87. See discussion in T. Sartory, *The Ecumenical Movement and the Unity of the Church* (Westminster, Md.: Newman, 1963), pp. 144–50.

10. A. Bea, *The Unity of Christians* (New York: Herder and Herder, 1963), pp. 19–37.

11. *Lumen gentium*, § 8, in W. M. Abbott, ed., *The Documents of Vatican II* (New York: America Press, 1966) pp. 22–23. See commentary by A. Grillmeier in H. Vorgrimler, ed., *Commentary on the Documents of Vatican II*, vol. 1 (New York: Herder and Herder, 1967), pp. 146–52; also J. Feiner, in ibid., vol. 2, p. 69.

12. *Lumen gentium*, § 11, in Abbott, p. 28; *Unitatis redintegratio*, § 3, in Abbott, p. 345; ibid. § 22, pp. 363–64.

13. *Lumen gentium*, § 14, in Abbott, p. 33.

14. This is the prevalent theory in the so-called denominations, on which see, for example, D. A. Martin, "The Denomination," *British Journal of Sociology*, 13 (1962), 5.

15. See A. M. Greeley, *The Denominational Society: A Sociological Approach to Religion in America* (Glenview, Ill.: Scott, Foresman and Co., 1972).

16. I have shown this more fully in my *Church Membership as a Catholic and Ecumenical Problem*, 1974 Père Marquette Lecture (Milwaukee: Marquette Univ. Theology Dept., 1974), pp. 34–47.

17. *Lumen gentium*, § 14, in Abbott, pp. 32–34; *Ad gentes*, § 7, in Abbott, p. 593.

18. See H. Carrier, *The Sociology of Religious Belonging* (New York: Herder

and Herder, 1965), pp. 52–58; and especially J. H. Fichter, *Social Relations in the Urban Parish* (University of Chicago Press, 1954), pp. 9–22.

19. On the notion of Church as sacrament see my *Models of the Church*, chap. 4; also F. Klostermann, *Gemeinde—Kirche der Zukunft*, 1 (Freiburg: Herder, 1974), 72–78.

20. On the Church as communion see the special issue of *The Jurist*, vol. 36, nos. 1–2 (1976). Michael A. Fahey clarifies the basic theological notions in his lead article, "Ecclesial Community as Communion," pp. 4–23.

21. *Unitatis redintegratio*, § 3, in Abbott, p. 345.

22. See R. C. Dodds, "The Meaning of Membership," *The Christian Century*, 85 (July–Dec. 1968), 1135–40; D. Horton, *Toward an Undivided Church* (New York: Association Press, 1967), pp. 58–61; R. Schutz, *Violent for Peace* (Philadelphia: Westminster, 1970), p. 77. Still more recently, A. C. Outler, in his "Ecumenism for Third-generation Ecumenists" (*Mid-Stream*, 14, no. 4 [Oct. 1975], 525–40), has argued eloquently for what he calls the "new principle of mingled memberships."

23. Text in *Mid-Stream*, 14, no. 2 (April 1975), 335–37; reproduced in this book as Appendix II.

24. *Unitatis redintegratio*, § 22, in Abbott, p. 364.

25. J. Eagan, "COCU and Baptism: A New and Creative Ecumenical Step," *Mid-Stream*, 15, no. 3 (July 1976), 233–45; quotation from pp. 238–39.

Chapter VIII

1. See, for instance, Thomas Aquinas, *Summa theologiae* 3a, q. 73, art. 2, *sed c* (Parma ed., vol. 4, p. 334); 3a, q. 83, art. 4, ad 3 (Parma ed., vol. 4, p. 398).

2. *Faith and Order: Louvain 1971*, FO Paper No. 59 (Geneva: World Council of Churches, 1971), p. 223.

3. A. Flannery, ed., *Vatican II: The Conciliar and Post Conciliar Documents* (Northport, N.Y.: Costello, 1975), p. 557.

4. "Orthodox Ecumenical Guidelines," in *Guidelines for Orthodox Christians in Ecumenical Relations* (published by the Standing Conference of Canonical Orthodox Bishops in America, [1974]), pp. 17–18.

5. *Unitatis redintegratio*, § 8, in W. M. Abbott, ed., *The Documents of Vatican II* (New York: America Press, 1966), pp. 352–53.

6. Ibid., § 18, in Abbott, pp. 360–61.

7. *Orientalium Ecclesiarum*, §§ 26–29, in Abbott, pp. 383–85.

8. *Ecumenical Directory: Part One*, § 55, in Flannery, p. 499.

9. "Instruction on Admitting Other Christians to Eucharistic Communion," in Flannery, pp. 554–58.

10. "Note Interpreting the 'Instruction on Admitting Other Christians to Eucharistic Communion,'" in Flannery, pp. 560–63.

11. The points in this paragraph are made at greater length by George A. Lindbeck and myself in our contributions to the special issue on the Eucharist published by the *Journal of Ecumenical Studies*, 13, no. 2 (Spring 1976), 241–57.

12. *Unitatis redintegratio,* § 22, in Abbott, p. 364.

13. *Ecumenical Directory: Part One,* §§ 55 and 59, in Flannery, pp. 499–500.

14. "Note Interpreting the 'Instruction on Admitting Other Christians to Eucharistic Communion,'" § 9, in Flannery, p. 562.

15. "Apostolic Succession: A Clarification," *Origins,* 4, no. 13 (Sept. 19, 1974), 200.

16. "L'Hospitalité eucharistique pour les foyers mixtes," *Documentation catholique,* 70, no. 1626 (Feb. 18, 1973), 161–70; Eng. trans. in *One in Christ,* 9 (1973), 371–87.

17. Ibid., p. 164 (cf. Eng. trans., p. 378).

18. Ibid.

19. The statement of Bishop Schmitt is quoted in "Reports and Documentation," *Lutheran World,* 22 (1975), 151.

20. "Note du comité épiscopal français pour l'unité des chrétiens concernant le document du Groupe des Dombes: 'Vers une même foi eucharistique?'" *Documentation catholique,* 72, no. 1669 (1975), 126–29.

21. "Vers l'unité de la communion eucharistique: Instruction pastorale du Synode suisse concernant l'hospitalité eucharistique," *Documentation catholique,* 72, no. 1677 (1975), 529–31.

22. "An Agreed Statement on Eucharistic Doctrine," in *Modern Eucharistic Agreement* (London: SPCK, 1973), § 5, p. 27.

23. For some examples of discrepancies and continued disagreements among Anglicans and Roman Catholics after Windsor, see A. Dulles, "Eucharistic Consensus?" *Commonweal,* 96, no. 19 (Aug. 25, 1972), 447–50.

24. Council of Trent, sess. XXII, can. 1, in H. Denzinger and A. Schönmetzer, eds., *Enchiridion symbolorum,* 32nd ed. (Freiburg im Breisgau: Herder, 1963; hereafter cited as *DS*), § 1753.

25. See Vatican II's Constitution on the Liturgy, *Sacrosanctum concilium,* § 7, in Abbott, pp. 140–41. See also Paul VI, *Mysterium fidei* (Glen Rock, N.J.: Paulist Press, 1966), §§ 35–38, pp. 40–42.

26. M. Thurian, *The One Bread* (New York: Sheed and Ward, 1969), pp. 36–44; see also his *The Eucharistic Memorial,* part II (Richmond, Va.: John Knox Press, 1961), pp. 108–24.

27. Council of Trent, sess. XIII, cap. 4 (*DS* 1642) and can. 2 (*DS* 1652).

28. *Mysterium fidei,* §§ 46–55, pp. 45–48.

29. "An Agreed Statement on Eucharistic Doctrine," in *Modern Eucharistic Agreement,* note 2, p. 31.

30. "Note Interpreting the 'Instruction on Admitting Other Christians to Eucharistic Communion,'" § 6, in Flannery, p. 561.

Chapter IX

1. *Unitatis redintegratio,* § 6 in W. M. Abbott, ed., *The Documents of Vatican II* (New York: America Press, 1966), p. 351.

2. Text in L. Vischer, ed., *A Documentary History of the Faith and Order Movement 1927–1963* (St. Louis: Bethany, 1963), pp. 136–37; cf. the text

from the New Delhi Report of the Third Assembly of the World Council of Churches (1961), ibid., p. 145.

3. *Unitatis redintegratio*, § 4, in Abbott, p. 348.

4. Ibid., § 9, in Abbott, p. 353.

5. Ibid., § 14, in Abbott, p. 358; § 18, in Abbott, p. 361.

6. Ibid., §§ 19–23, in Abbott, pp. 361–65.

7. For a survey see N. Ehrenström and G. Gassmann, *Confessions in Dialogue*, 3rd ed., rev. (Geneva: World Council of Churches, 1975).

8. *One Baptism, One Eucharist and Mutually Recognized Ministry: Three Agreed Statements*, FO Paper No. 73 (Geneva: World Council of Churches, 1975).

9. *Unitatis redintegratio*, § 12, in Abbott, p. 354.

10. Text in D. M. Paton, ed., *Breaking Barriers: Nairobi 1975* (Grand Rapids: Eerdmans, 1976), pp. 317–18.

11. *The Uppsala Report* (Geneva: World Council of Churches, 1968), § 17, p. 17.

12. Ibid.; cf. *Faith and Order: Louvain 1971*, FO Paper No. 59 (Geneva: World Council of Churches, 1971), pp. 225–29.

13. A. Samuel, "What Are United Churches?" *Mid-Stream*, 14, no. 4 (Oct. 1975), pp. 500–1.

14. "The Unity of the Church: Next Steps," *What Kind of Unity?* FO Paper No. 69 (Geneva: World Council of Churches, 1974), p. 121.

15. See on this point G. Baum, "Unity or Renewal?" *The Ecumenist*, 13, no. 1 (Nov.–Dec. 1974), 5–9.

16. Paton, *Breaking Barriers*, p. 60.

17. J. Macquarrie, *Christian Unity and Christian Diversity* (Philadelphia: Westminster, 1975), pp. 25–26.

18. Ibid., p. 17.

19. M. E. Marty, "*E Pluribus Unum*: The Religious Dimension Today," *Catholic Mind*, 74, no. 1295 (Sept. 1975), 14.

20. Latin American Episcopal Conference, *The Church in the Present-day Transformation of Latin America in the Light of the Council*, vol. 2, *Conclusions* (Washington, D.C.: USCC, 1968), p. 226.

21. From the New Delhi Report; text in Vischer, *Documentary History*, p. 151; cf. ibid., pp. 86 and 104 for other enunciations of the same principles.

22. First set forth in Piux XI's *Quadragesimo anno* (*Acta Apostolicae Sedis*, 23 [1931], 203), this principle was quoted and reaffirmed by John XXIII in *Master et magistra*, § 53, text in J. Gremillion, ed., *The Gospel of Peace and Justice* (Maryknoll, N. Y.: Orbis, 1976), p. 154.

23. Macquarrie, *Christian Unity*, p. 9.

24. "Pluralism, Polarization and Communication in the Church: Some Theological Aspects," *Pro Mundi Vita*, 45 (1973), 5, quoted in A. M. Greeley, *The Communal Catholic* (New York: Seabury, 1976), p. 158.

25. E. Lanne, "Pluralism and Unity," *One in Christ*, 4, no. 3 (1970),

448–49. Lanne somewhat tempers this criticism of the New Delhi report in his footnote, p. 449.

26. Macquarrie, *Christian Unity*, p. 43.

27. Lanne, "Pluralism and Unity," p. 444.

28. "Cardinal Willebrands' Address in Cambridge, England," *Documents on Anglican/Roman Catholic Relations* (Washington, D.C.: USCC, 1972), p. 39.

Index